The Sign Of The End Revealed
(Originally Titled Matthew 23-24-25)
By Ron McRay
Copyrighted © 1st Edition January 2008
2nd Edition April 2015

Printed in the United States of America

Ron McRay
204 Joy Street, Henrietta, Texas 76365
nonelbc@gmail.com

Thank you for purchasing
"The Sign Of The End Revealed"

I would like to give you a special gift

My gift to you is a free audio version of my book
"Are There Three Heavens… Or More?"

Please use the link on the last page to Download Your Bonus Book

This book is just one of my books in the series:

Things That Your Preacher Forgot To Tell You!

Use it to enhance your Bible study

Listen on your way to work or while walking or working in the yard

I hope you enjoy this valuable addition

Bonus#2

Want to learn more about Matthew 24-25? Sign up for my weekly Bible study. www.EschatologyReview.com/Matt24-signup This study will go into more depth and will be verse by verse study. This free study will be emailed to you once per week. Join here now!

Ron McRay

Table of Contents

ABOUT THE AUTHOR

"There were giants in the earth in those days" [**Gen. 6:4**].

Have you ever met a Giant? I don't mean a10 foot tall, 600 hundred pound giant; I never met one of those either. I am talking about one of those once-in-a life time people who stand head and shoulders above the average person in understanding things that many never even consider. For example, "*string theory*" or "*quantum mechanics*" or perhaps" *the Holy Bible*?"

When I came to the United States from Ireland, I thought that this would be the place to learn advanced Bible study. Through a chance meeting with Dr. Jerry Wayne Bernard, I made the acquaintance of Dr. Ron McRay, a giant in the field of eschatology. Our meeting was chance, in that Dr. McRay was researching the Old Testament and he wanted to read something that I had written. With that encounter began a fast friendship that has lasted over the years. We have traded studies on various subjects and shared long conversations deep into the night.

Dr. McRay was a full time pastor from 1954 until 1990. He then took on the work of conducting and participating in seminars throughout the country and continued that until just immediate to the passing of his wife in March, 2008. A little over seven years ago, he began a publication that was titled "Eschatology Review," and edited it for three years, at which time he gave it to a very careful Bible student to edit. About the same time, he began, in earnest, researching, writing and publishing his extensive findings. He is indeed a unique researcher of Bible topics. The reader may not always agree with him, but one thing is certain, he will challenge one's thinking. The reader is encouraged to read what he has written because one will learn to think critically and out of "*the box*."

As Roux said, "*Two sorts of writers possess genius: those who think and those who cause others to think.*" Dr. McRay has the unique ability to do both. His education is unusual with a **Ph.D**. in Theology and a Doctorate of Letters, **Litt.D.** for his substantive written work in the field of "*End time studies,*" such as, "The Last Days," and "Behold I Am Making All Things New," as well as "Through The Water, Through The Fire." To top that off, he also has a Doctorate in Philology, **D. Phil.** (linguistics), which makes us both together a paradox.

Dr. McRay will do one of two things for you in his writing. 1) He will drive you to the "Book" just to see if what he says could possibly be true. 2) Challenge you to study your Bible as if you can never get enough of the wondrous and exciting truths that are hidden there in plain sight. He will provide a Bible study that you never thought possible and in turn you will grow in grace, knowledge and wisdom as you begin to understand a wee bit of the mind of God.

I heartily recommend that you read and study with this "*giant*" that you may grow.

Dr Denis O'Callaghan Ph.D., Th.D., D.D.

Director of Scripture Institute
www.drcallahan.bravemusings.com
http://parsontoperson.blogspot.com

FOREWORD

This is <u>**VOLUME NUMBER NINE**</u> of a series of books that I have written under the general heading of ...

<u>**THINGS THAT YOUR PREACHER FORGOT TO TELL YOU**</u>.

I want to be humble when I say this, but most of the things that you will find in these books are not in print anywhere else. I will bring to light things that very few have even begun to think about in searching the Bible.

There are things in the Bible that are not surface materials. As we pay closer attention to the reading and wording of all of the Bible, we will begin to see things that have been ...

<u>**HIDDEN IN PLAIN SIGHT**</u>.

They are not to be "*uncovered*," because they are not covered. The only reason why we have not seen them is that we have not given as much attention to all of the verses and their contexts.

It is traditionally taught that there is only one Heaven. Is that correct?

This book takes a very serious look at that tradition and with the help of other passages of Scripture, opens up other areas of thought that the reader will find simply amazing.

If you, the reader, are interested in digging deeper into the truths of the Bible, then this book is for you.
Enjoy yourself! But, you must ...

<u>Think for yourself!</u>

This book is to be read in the order in which it is written. Each chapter is a building block for the next.

NOTICE

This study requires no mental fitness program …

_if_

everyone gets enough exercise _jumping_ to conclusions,

flying off of the handle, _running_ down other brethren,

knifing friends in the back, _dodging_ responsibility and

pushing opinions.

Verses will be high-lighted using this feature MATTHEW 24:1

All chapters will be a verse by verse study

PREFACE

I shall begin this book with this paragraph. When I was a child, and Easter time came along, my parents took white chicken eggs and colored them all sorts of colors, even polka-dot ones. I had a major problem to begin with, which was to figure out how a rabbit could lay a polka-dot chicken egg. I finally gave up trying to solve that problem. At the proper time, they went out and "*hid*" the eggs and it was our (I had three brothers and one sister) time to go "*find*" the "*hidden eggs.*" Little did I realize then that the eggs were **hidden in plain sight**, so that we would find all of them, but they were in "*unexpected places.*" I understood more when I "*hid*" eggs for my two daughters to "*find.*" I made sure that they could see them, being right out in the open, but they had to be in a certain spot to see them. Their real search, unknown to them, was **the spot** in which to stand to see the eggs that were in plain sight, rather than try to see the eggs from just anywhere that they were standing. So, they had to run around and around, all over the place in order to "*find*" all of the eggs, even though they had been in "*plain sight*" all of the time.

That is the way that truth is in the Bible. It is in plain sight, but we have to run around and around, from book to book, from "*old testament*" to "*new testament*" to look at many different and varied verses in order to understand what real truth is. If we do not follow that procedure, we will not "*find all of the eggs,*" i.e. we will not uncover the real truth on any subject.

INTRODUCTION

"And it came to pass, when Jesus had finished all these sayings, he said unto his disciples" [Matthew 26:1].

First, we will find out that chapters and verses never came along until the sixteenth century, and this passage above really belongs to Matthew 25:47 because from Matthew 24:1 everything was told by Jesus to **ONLY four apostles**. Let that sink in even before we begin reading the book. Now read the beginning verse in 24:1 and read the ending verse in 25:47. **READ BOTH NOW FROM YOUR BIBLE** BEFORE YOU READ ANOTHER LINE! ------------**READ IT NOW!**

When the apostles came to Jesus and asked him the two questions of *"when"* and *"what"* (a two-part question) in Matthew 24:3, the remainder of Matthew 24 and all of chapter 25 was his answer to those questions. It ends in Matthew 26:1 and the entire discourse of Jesus would not be complete without it.

The clause, *"When Jesus had finished all these sayings,"* shows conclusively that all of Matthew 24 and all of Matthew 25 belong together. There is never a verse anywhere in those two chapters that shows that he interrupted his response and started on a different subject.

Since Mark 13 and Luke 21 are parallel to this study by Matthew, and there are a few things in each of them that help explain some things that are not explicitly set forth by Matthew, I believe that it will be well for us to at least hit the highlights of the additional information that we can gleam from those two books as we go through Matthew 23-24-25.

Many preachers in the 21st century are teaching that the doctrine that is taught in these three chapters of Matthew is a prophecy of things that are happening right now in 2015 A.D.. A few will vary slightly, allowing for them to happen in the near or unknown future. There are a few who will teach that the things herein were only for the benefit of the first century believers. Which one or more is it with you?

For "*church*," most times it is ekklesia (*called out*).

The <u>King James Version</u> will be used.

"*New Testament*" is unscriptural – should be **new covenant**.

Your courteous feedback is appreciated, whether in agreement or not.

If you profit from this book, please ask your friends to purchase one. Details of other books and DVD's are at the end of this book.

I hope that the contents of this book will stretch your minds and that you will gain much profit from them. Enjoy your study!

Ron McRay

Chapter One

MATTHEW 23

It is almost impossible to study this chapter by itself. First of all, it is necessary to understand that the chapter and verses were inserted into the biblical text in the sixteenth century A.D., about 500 years ago. Here is a quotation from Wikipedia.

> *"In the New Testament, the verse divisions were first added by Robert Estienne in his 1551 edition of the Greek New Testament. In 1557, the first English New Testament with verse divisions were used in a translation by William Whittingham (c. 1524-1579). These divisions have been used by nearly all English Bibles since then. Unlike the Hebrew of the Old Testament, the structure of the Greek language makes it highly susceptible to being broken up syntactically into inappropriate and even sense-contrary divisions. Inexact apportionment of Greek into verses therefore could easily obscure the intent, relation, emphasis and force of the words themselves, and thus elicited the most strenuous objections of theologians. The retention of Robert Estienne's verse divisions essentially without alteration is a tribute not only to the inherent utility of his contribution to Bible study, but also to his excellent knowledge of the scriptures and grasp of the fine points of the ancient Greek language. The first Bible in English to use both chapters and verses was the Geneva Bible in 1560, coming soon after Estienne's introduction of New Testament verse numbers, and quickly rising to acceptance as a standard way to notate them."*

The chapters and verses were not there when all of the letters were written in the first century A.D..

When one examines the text of these three chapters of Matthew, he will find very quickly that it is only a segment of what Jesus taught his disciples. One should begin reading with the first verse of chapter 23 and continue to the first verse of chapter 26. Matthew 24 is in the middle of the context of dealing with the attitudes of the first century people and **their** end times. I will not do a study here as a verse by verse study in chapter 23, but rather taking topics from it throughout those three chapters and dealing with them.

The Blindness Of Certain Israelites

It is at this point that we should be reminded of Jesus' quoting Isaiah saying that God told him to preach to the rebellious Israelites and **make them blind** [Isaiah 6:10]. Jesus said that Isaiah's prophecy was fulfilled in his teaching to the Judeans of the first century A.D. [Matthew 13:14]. Here are the passages in Matthew 23 that show that they were indeed **blind** when Jesus was speaking to them.

*"Woe unto you, ye **blind** guides, which say, Whosoever shall swear by the temple, it is nothing; but whosoever shall swear by the gold of the temple, he is a debtor"* [v-16].

*"Ye fools and **blind**: for whether is greater, the gold, or the temple that sanctifieth the gold"* [v-17]?

*"Ye fools and **blind**: for whether is greater, the gift, or the altar that sanctifieth the gift"* [v-19]?

*"Ye **blind** guides, which strain at a gnat, and swallow a camel"* [v-24].

*"Thou **blind** Pharisee, cleanse first that which is within the cup and platter, that the outside of them may be clean also"* [V-26].

It is evident to the student of the Bible that Jesus made those remarks to the scribes and Pharisees of the 1st century A.D. while he was biologically alive. In their blindness, they were hypocrites. There is much **prophecy** in those chapters.

They Were Hypocrites

Here are the verses in the chapters that show that the 1st century Judeans were hypocrites.

> *"Woe unto you, scribes and Pharisees, hypocrites! For ye shut up the kingdom of heaven against men: for ye neither go in yourselves, neither suffer ye them that are entering to go in* [v-13].

> *"Woe unto you scribes and Pharisees, hypocrites! For ye devour widow's houses, and for a pretense make long prayer: therefore ye shall receive the greater damnation* [v-14].

> *"Woe unto you, scribes and Pharisees, hypocrites! for ye compass sea and land to make one proselyte, and when he is made, ye make him twofold more the child of hell than yourselves"* [v-15].

> *"Woe unto you, scribe and Pharisees, hypocrites! for ye pay tithe of mint and anise and cumin, and have omitted the weightier matters of the law, judgment, mercy, and faith: these ought ye to have done, and not to leave the other undone"* [v-23].

> *"Woe unto you, scribes and Pharisees, hypocrites! for ye make clean the outside of the cup and of the platter, but within they are full of extortion and excess"* [v-27].

> *"Woe unto you, scribes and Pharisees, hypocrites! because ye build the tombs of the prophets, and garnish the sepulchers of the righteous ..."* [v-29].

The scribes were the ones that took pen and ink and copied the then known scriptures. The Pharisees were the strictest (legalist) sect of the Judahite religion. Of all people living in the 1st century A.D., those were the two groups that should have known what God desired and should have been the ones who did it. They knew what was right. They taught what was right, but they did **not do** what they taught or wrote. Here is the scripture that proves that they were hypocrites – a person who *"play acted"* as if he was righteous when he was inwardly corrupt.

*"… The scribes and the Pharisees sit in Moses' seat: All therefore whatsoever they bid you observe, that observe and do; but do not ye after their works; **for they say, and do not**"* [vv-2-3].

How Were They Hypocrites?

There are many verses in Matthew 23 that show the different things that the scribes and Pharisees did that made them hypocrites.

"For they bind heavy burdens and grievous to be borne, and lay them on men's shoulders; but they themselves will not move them with one of their fingers" [v-4].

"But all their works they do for to be seen of men; they make broad their phylacteries, and enlarge the borders of their garments" [v-5].

"And love the uppermost rooms at feasts, and the chief seats in the synagogues" [v-6].

"And greetings in the markets, and to be called of men, Rabbi, Rabbi" [v-7].

"… For ye shut up the kingdom of heaven against men: for ye neither go in yourselves, neither suffer ye them that are entering to go in" [v-13].

"… for ye devour widow's houses, and for a pretense make long prayer: therefore ye shall receive the greater damnation" [v-14].

"… for ye compass sea and land to make one proselyte, and when he is made, ye make him twofold more the child of hell than yourselves" [v-15].

"… which say, Whosoever shall swear by the temple, it is nothing; but whosoever shall swear by the gold of the temple he is a debtor" [v-16].

"... and, Whosoever shall swear by the altar, it is nothing; but whosoever sweareth by the gift that is upon it, he is guilty" [v-18].

"... for ye pay tithes of mint and anise and cumin, and have omitted the weightier matters of the law, judgment, mercy and faith: these ought ye to have done, and not to leave the other undone" [v-23].

"... for ye make clean the outside of the cup and of the platter, but within they are full of extortion and excess" [v-25].

"... for ye are like unto whited sepulchers, which indeed appear beautiful outward, but are within full of dead men's bones, and of all uncleanness. Even so ye also outwardly appear righteous unto men, but within ye are full of hypocrisy and iniquity" [vv.-27-28].

"... because ye build the tombs of the prophets, and garnish the sepulchers of the righteous, and say, If we had been in the days of our fathers, we would not have been partakers with them in the blood of the prophets" [vv.-29-30].

Have times changed that much over 2,000 years? Since I have been *"preaching"* for sixty years, and having been around the *"clergy"* for longer than that, I have seen it all. While there are exceptions to the following statement, I have found it to be generally true. The greater majority of the leadership in all churches can be traced by **following the money trail, the power trail, or the pride trail.** We truly do not have many *"servants,"* **do we**? Tell me what you think about the following three cases.

When I was a very young preacher, I became acquainted with the preacher of the same persuasion as was I, in the next town, and also the one in the next succeeding town, and I had a recent experience. In the first town, there was a younger preacher, who had a wife, a daughter of three years old and a young, in arms, baby boy. What did he do? He ran off with a lady in his church and deserted his family. Was that a good influence on a young preacher such as I?

The second preacher was older, I would say about 55 years old. One day, he asked me, …

> *"Ron, you being a young preacher, just starting out, and I, being a much older preacher, would you like some advice?"*

I replied that any good advice would be very welcome. What was his reply?

> *"The church that hired you expects you to work and they are paying you to do that. Let me tell you what I do. I get up every morning, shower, shave, eat and dress. Then I drive my car down to the square at the court house and park it and walk back home, leaving the impression with the church that I am out trying to convert someone. I spend the day at home and go back and get my car at 5 pm."*

Third one was a preacher with whom I had become acquainted. He was about thirty-five years old. I began writing books in 1989 and I have right now about 30 books, most on AMAZON.COM. This pastor visited in my home at times and one time I told him about one of my new books and asked him if he would like one. My stipulation was that I would give it to him **if he would read it!** Yes, he would like it but it may take a couple of months to read it. After six months, he was in my home and I asked him if he read it. Long story – he **LIED** about it, he never read it, supposed that I was wrong in the first couple of pages and put it in the trash. How many preachers do you think will lie, especially in their position? In my experience - most of them. **Watch out for the preachers**! In fact, just fire them. There is no authority in the Bible for located hired pastors anyway. Give your money to someone who needs some food on the table. I did not get paid for my book either!

Hypocrites? Did they give the appearance of *"whited sepulchers"* while being inside *"full of all uncleanness?"* You be the judge. How many like that have you seen? **WATCH**!

Why Did Jesus Tell Them The Above?

The reason begins with Jesus' statement:

> *"Woe unto you, scribes and Pharisees, hypocrites! Because ye build the tombs of the prophets, and garnish the sepulchers of the righteous, and say, If we had been in the days of our fathers, we would not have been partakers with them in the blood of the prophets. Wherefore ye be witnesses unto yourselves, that ye are the children of them which killed the prophets. Fill ye up then the measure of your fathers"* [vv. 29-32].

Jesus then instructed those hypocritical Judeans that of the prophets and wise men and scribes, they would *"of them ye shall kill and crucify; and some of them shall ye scourge in your synagogues and persecute them from city to city"* [v-34]. Is it not interesting that they **crucified** Jesus, they **killed** James, they scourged other apostles and others they **persecuted** from city to city? The question then is **why**?

> *"... that upon **you** may come **all** the righteous blood shed upon the earth, from the blood of righteous Abel unto the blood of Zacharias son of Barachias, whom **ye** slew between the temple and the altar"* [v-35].

That the Abel mentioned here was the brother of Cain (whom Cain murdered) is without question among Bible scholars. But who was Zacharias? Most of the scholars refer to 2 Chronicles 24:20-22 in the case of the Zacharias who was murdered, but there is some speculation here as the *"son of Barachias"* is not the name mentioned here. However, it is possible that he was indeed the one of which Jesus spoke, since many people had two names, e.g. Peter was called Cephas, etc.. The prophet Zechariah is called the son of Berekiah in Zechariah 1:1, but it is unlikely that this was the one of which it is spoken. But the main point is yet to come.

Jesus said that he would send prophets, wise men and scribes and that the current generation then alive would kill some of them, and that action would be that which v-32 was speaking …

"Fill __ye__ up then the measure of __your__ fathers. __Ye__ are serpents, __ye__ generation of vipers, how can __ye__ escape the damnation of hell?"

Why did they have to do that? In order that ...

"... upon __you__ may come all the righteous blood ..." [v-35].

Who were the **you** of whom Jesus was speaking? To the honest truth seeker, they could be only one group: The Judeans who were rebellious, blind and hypocritical – the **very ones to whom Jesus was speaking at the very end of his biological life** only a few hours before his trial and crucifixion.

Since we will be discussing the English word **generation**, it is needful to understand that the Greek language has different words with different meanings as to the way that we translate the word. For example, in Matthew 23:33, the word **generation** comes from the Greek word **genema**, which is defined as an **offspring**, in this case a **descendant** of the Judeans who had lived before the current Judeans to whom Jesus was speaking. But in v-36 of this same chapter, the English word **generation** comes from another Greek word, **genea**, which is defined as **a generation, by implication, an age (the period or the persons)**. While in both verses, the translators chose the same English word, in the original, the Holy Spirit chose two different Greek words, which meant two separate and distinct things. Simply stated, **a descendent is not an age** because two different Greek words are used. When Jesus stated ...

"Verily I say unto you, All these things shall come upon __this generation__" [v-36],

... he was **not** saying that all of those things would come upon a race, group or offspring of some group. He was saying that all of those bad things would happen **to that current age of people who were living and listening to Jesus speak** those words. They all happened nearly 2,000 years ago. There is nothing here for our generation or future generations. God destroyed Jerusalem in that **age**, at the close of that 40 year generation between 66 A.D. – 70 A.D. – that **age** – that **people**, <u>not a race of people!</u>

My grandfather was a Bible reader, but with little help in reading in those early days. Grandfather spent the night with the Jesse James boys as a youngster. That will give you some reading ability of that generation. You know what? My grandfather read the Bible and was persuaded that the coming of the lord was in that very century – but he died without such taking place. My dad has been dead for thirty-four years and he was a master machinist during his lifetime. And he read his Bible religiously, especially for his generation. And do you know what? He was persuaded that the "*second* coming" was in his generation. He made the same mistake that his father made. He died as did his father without that **second coming**. In fact, there are no words in the entire Bible that says "*second coming!*" Now you will just have to check me out on that – will you not? That is not to say that I am smarter than either of my ancestors, but I did have opportunities in schooling that were not afforded to them. But for 35 years, I made the same mistakes.

Being an American who began studying the subject of eschatology in the 1950's, meant that I was living in a hotbed of eschatological activity, having made telephone calls to two other students on the subject by 1989 (but not having met them). By 1989, I had met others but people had not written much material on the subject. By 1990, it appears that you could only find four books on the subject (one by me). Thousands have learned the truth since then, due to the first few seminars that the three or four of us conducted. This appeared to be an area of monumental discoveries that greatly impacted the study of the Bible to thousands of people. But you know what? Jesus did not come in his day and he did not appear in the days of my father. And do you want to know something else? He is not going to come in our generation either. Do you want to know about the time that my grand-children will grow up? He will not make his **second appearance** 90 years into our future either. Do you know why? Because Jesus made his "*second appearance*" in the 70's A.D., the only one that he will ever make. But the church preachers have so influenced most people that he is looking for Christ to appear **soon** that they will never understand why he has not appeared **while on their death bed**! A real shame!

Jerusalem, Jerusalem

"O Jerusalem, Jerusalem, thou that killest the prophets, and stonest them which are sent unto thee, how often would I have gathered thy children together, even as a hen gathereth her chickens under her wings and ye would not" [v-37].

Jerusalem was a city – a city of many people – the center of the worship of God by His people. However, in a few verses in the *"new testament,"* the name of the city was used metaphorically, i.e., of **the people** of the city. Also, the name of the city was used metaphorically of the **Mosaic system**, which was about to be fulfilled. Let us look at some of those verses.

V-37 (above) is such a verse. It was **the people** of Jerusalem who killed the prophets. In fact, the people who were alive to whom Jesus was speaking were not the only ones who actually killed the prophets, it included their ancestors who murdered them. It was former rebellious Israelites who had killed them, but the ones to whom Jesus was speaking were their offspring and had they been living way back then, they would have killed the prophets. That is what Jesus knew and said of that current **generation** of the 1st century A.D..

"When Herod the king had heard these things (about Jesus being born king of the Jews), *he was troubled, and all Jerusalem with him"* [Matthew 2:3].

It was not the bricks, stones and dirt of the city that was troubled, it was **the people**. The term **Jerusalem** was used for the people of the **religious** system.

"But Jesus turning unto them said, Daughters of Jerusalem, weep not for me, but weep for yourselves, and for your children" [Luke 23:28].

Of course, we know that the literal city did not have children. So, the word **Jerusalem** is used metaphorically for the Mosaic law system, which would also be a metaphor. The usage here is as it was used in Matthew 23:37. Please refresh your memory from its use above.

> "*Saying, did we not straitly command you that ye should not teach in this name? and behold, ye have filled* **Jerusalem** *with your doctrine, and intend to bring this man's blood upon us*" [Acts 5:28].

It was not the stones in the buildings that was the city, it was **the people** of the city. We must learn when it is used metaphorically and when it was used literally.

It is obvious that it was not the stones and dust that was filled with the teaching concerning Jesus – it was the people.

> "*For this Agar is mount Sinai in Arabia, and answereth to Jerusalem which* **now is**, *and is in bondage with her children. But Jerusalem which is above is free, which is the mother of us all*" [Galatians 4:25-26].

We have two Jerusalems in these verses – one earthly and one heavenly. The saints would not be able to be in the heavenly city until we see the earthly city fulfilled. The old, natural city of Jerusalem was a metaphor for the old covenant system with its rituals and laws. Paul was not talking about the literal city with stones, wood and ground. In the second part, the apostle was speaking of another Jerusalem, again a metaphor. This was a **new** Jerusalem. It was a "*city which had foundations, whose builder and maker is God*" [Hebrews 11:10]. It was a metaphor for the people of the new covenant, which made the people free as sons of the Almighty.

"But ye are come unto mount Sion, and unto the city of the living God, the heavenly Jerusalem, and to an innumerable company of angels" [Hebrews 12:22].

This Jerusalem is the *"Jerusalem which is above"* of Galatians 4:26. It is here called **heavenly** Jerusalem, denoting that it was not the earthly city called Jerusalem that was destroyed in 66 A.D. – 70 A.D. by the Romans. That **heavenly** city is referred to in the book of Revelation as follows …

"Him that overcometh will I make a pillar in the temple of my God, and he shall go no more out: and I will write upon him the name of my God, and the name of the city of my God, which is new Jerusalem, which cometh down out of heaven from my God: and I will write upon him my new name" [Revelation 3:12].

"And I John saw the holy city, new Jerusalem, coming down from God out of heaven, prepared as a bride adorned for her husband" [Revelation 21:2].

"And he carried me away in the spirit to a great and high mountain, and showed me that great city, the holy Jerusalem, descending out of heaven from God" [Revelation 21:10].

These verses follow the sense of the two preceding verses at which we have looked. This is a figurative use of the city of Jerusalem. It was not an earthly city. It was (1) heavenly, (2) new, (3) above and (4) holy. You may want to say that a contrast is made between the **earthly** Jerusalem to the **heavenly** Jerusalem. You also may want to observe that a contrast is made between the **lower – earthly** city and the city that was **above**. It is also observable that a contrast was being made between the **unholy** city that God destroyed, ending in 70 A.D., and the **holy** city into which the saints were allowed entrance. And then notice that the **old** city was contrasted with the **new** Jerusalem.

The writer of Hebrews said that the believers in the 1st century A.D. **had come to the foot** of the mountain, to the gateway to the heavenly

Jerusalem, but had not climbed the mountain, nor entered into that **eternal** city yet.

John, in those three verses from the book of Revelation, was permitted to see the immediate future. He saw the heavenly city come down to men. If you want something to seriously consider, then carefully think about this. When the **old** Jerusalem was destroyed, then, and only then could the believers have an entrance into the **new** Jerusalem. The old, earthly Jerusalem system was destroyed in 66 A.D. – 70 A.D.. When do you think that the saints *"would go marching in"* and were allowed to enter the new, heavenly Jerusalem?

Let us group a number of the concluding verses of Matthew 23 together and notice what Jesus said of the things in those verses.

> *"Fill **ye** up then the measure of **your** fathers"* [v-32].

> *"**Ye** serpents, **ye** generation of vipers, how can **ye** escape the damnation of hell"* [v-33].

> *"Wherefore, behold I send unto **you** prophets, and wise men, and scribes: and some of them **ye** shall kill and crucify; and some of them shall **ye** scourge in **your** synagogues, and persecute them from city to city"* [v-34].

> *"That upon **you** may come all the righteous blood shed upon the earth, from the blood of righteous Abel unto the blood of Zacharias son of Barachias, whom **ye** slew between the temple and the altar"* [v-35].

> *"O Jerusalem, Jerusalem, **thou** that killest the prophets, and stonest them which are sent unto **thee**, how often would I have gathered **thy** children together, even as a hen gathereth her chickens under her wings, and **ye** would not"* [v-37]!

> *"Behold, **your** house is left unto **you** desolate"* [v-38].

> *"For I say unto **you**, **ye** shall not see me henceforth, till **ye** shall say, Blessed is he that cometh in the name of the Lord"* [v-39].

The big question that is left is, *"When would those things happen?"* Jesus answered that in the context of Matthew 23 that we have been studying.

> *"Verily I say unto **you, all these things shall come upon this generation**"* [v-36].

Of the word **generation**, let me repeat what I have already said …

> *"Since we will be discussing the English word generation, it is needful to understand that the Greek language has different words with different meanings as to the way that we translate the word. For example, in Matthew 23:33, the word generation comes from the Greek word **genema**, which is defined as an offspring, in this case a **descendant** of the Judeans who had lived before the current Judeans to whom Jesus was speaking. But in v-36 of this same chapter, the English word generation comes from another Greek word, **genea**, which is defined as a **generation**, by implication, an **age** (the period or the persons).While in both verses, the translators chose the same English word, in the original; the Holy Spirit chose two different Greek words, which meant two separate and distinct things. Simply stated, **a descendent is not an age** because two different Greek words are used. When Jesus stated …*

> *"Verily I say unto you, All these things shall come upon **this** generation"* [v-36],

> *"… he was **not** saying that all of those things would come upon **a race**, group or offspring of some group. He was saying that all of those bad things would happen to that current **age** of people who were living and listening to Jesus speak those words. They all happened nearly 2,000 years ago. There is nothing here for our generation or future generations. God destroyed Jerusalem in that age, at the close of that 40 year generation between 66 A.D. – 70 A.D. – that age – that people, not a race of people!"*

Let it not be misunderstood. Jesus was not talking about our generation in the 21st century. He was speaking to the people who were biologically alive when he was speaking to them. It was the people who lived when Jesus was a little over thirty years of age. Notice that when speaking to those 1st century Judeans, that he used the word **you** (not centuries later). Now take the time to go back and read all of the above scriptures that I noted and placed their meaning and fulfillment in the first century A.D., not in our time or any future time.

That will obviously raise a lot of questions in your minds. Good! Think for yourself. Begin to figure out what God really meant in the writings of the book that we call the Bible. We have now seen the foundation of Matthew 24. Jesus laid it out in Matthew 23.We know **who** God was going to destroy (and when). We shall find out more about that destruction and the people who were going to be destroyed as we begin studying Matthew 24.

We have looked carefully at the foundation of Matthew 24. Those were the things that Jesus said concerning the unbelieving, unfaithful, hypocritical, 1st century A.D. Judeans in chapter 23. They were the ones who were to be destroyed. All of the woes of which Jesus spoke were to come upon them (not us, some 2,000 years later). Jesus was more emphatic with that thought in chapter 24, which I shall now begin to discuss. Jesus got right into the subject of the discussion of the **Jewish** system by referring to it as the destruction of Jerusalem. The destruction of their system was to be evidenced (seen – perceived) by the literal destruction of the physical city of Jerusalem by the Romans, including their temple, in their war with the Judeans from 66 A.D. to 70 A.D.. He continued his discourse of chapter 23 immediately with chapter 24, which I now begin.

Chapter Two

MATTHEW 24

> *"And Jesus went out, and departed from the temple: and his disciples came to him for to shew him the buildings of the temple, And Jesus said unto them, See ye not all these things? Verily I say unto you, There shall not be left here one stone upon another, that shall not be thrown down"* [Matthew 24:1-2].

To show that the destruction of the Herodian temple was no accident, the word **thrown** was specifically chosen by Jesus. The word means **violently**. Notice how the same thought is used by John …

> *"And a mighty angel took up a stone like a great millstone, and cast it into the sea, saying, Thus with **violence** shall that great city be **thrown** down, and shall be found no more at all"* [Revelation 18:21].

Having said in the preceding chapter that all of those things that were mentioned would come upon that current living generation of Judeans, Jesus continued his warnings of that destruction by telling of the destruction of the temple and the temple buildings – a complete destruction.

What does that really mean? Well, as one studies from the *"old testament,"* he or she can learn that there had to be an annual sacrifice by the high priest for the atonement of the sins of the people. In order to be an earthly high priest, one had to trace his lineage back to Aaron (the first high priest of Israel). When the Herodian temple was destroyed, all of the records were burned and therefore there **can never be** a biblical biological high priest again – forever! So, it was extremely important for those listening to Jesus speak, to know of the destruction of the temple and the old covenant system, for the annual atonement sacrifice by an authentic high priest could never happen again. It was by the **violence** of the Roman army (and other armies of joining nations) that the system was **thrown** down, and notice carefully the expression, it *"shall be found no more at all."* How come preachers ignore that sentence? Yes, Jesus said it very plainly but everyone seems to either by-pass it or just flatly ignores it. The city was demolished by 70 A.D. just like Jesus said and it will never be built again. That is right – the old Jewish temple will ***be found no more at all*** – period! It does not matter how much church members look for it over the years or how many preachers are looking for one -------- by 70 A.D. it was gone **forever**! That is what Jesus said, so why do we not believe it? After the destruction of that temple by the ten or eleven armies in 70 A.D., there was only one high priest remaining – the king of kings and the lord of lords – the eternal high priest – Jesus the only Messiah that Israel had. His priesthood is in heaven. He had made an offering **one time** for sin, and there was no need ever again for an offering every year for the sins of the people.

Things are not as they always appear on the surface. For example, did you know that mile for mile, Jacksonville, Florida is the largest city in the US? Well, you do now. Did you know that those things in these three chapters that were spoken by Jesus applied to those rebellious Israelites who lived almost 2,000 years ago? Well, you do now. What will you do with the facts? Since most people hold to preconceived ideas and very reluctantly let them go (if ever), it will be easier to believe that Jacksonville is larger than New York City than to consider that the temple, people and covenant were those of 2,000 years ago and not to us.

The foregoing might be new to you, but do not count it as something that should not be very seriously considered. Remember that in chapter 23, Jesus told who was to be destroyed and when it was to happen – in that existing generation to whom he was speaking. He continued to show how that was to be accomplished. If we put the two together, then we know that the temple was to be destroyed during that generation. With the Herodian temple, the old covenant was to be replaced with a new **spiritual temple** and a **new covenant**. What did Jesus' apostles think about what he had said?

It is important to know what Jesus' apostles thought about what he had said in chapter 23 and the first **two verses of Matthew 24.**

> *"And as he sat upon the mount of Olives, the disciples came unto him privately, saying, Tell us, **when** shall these things be? And **what** shall be the sign of thy coming, and of the end of the world"* [Matthew 24:3].

In order to arrive at the correct understanding, the understanding that Jesus' apostles understood in the 1st century A.D., it is necessary to look at many things in this one verse, for it gives the setting for the remainder of Jesus' answers, which included the remainder of chapters 24 – 25.

Jesus had taught the good and evil people in chapter 23, telling the evil ones that they would be destroyed by 70 A.D. when their temple was destroyed if they did not repent. He had left the temple, where he was doing the teaching to the Judeans (gentiles were not allowed in the temple), and had gone with his apostles privately. That which was revealed to the apostles was not revealed to the multitude of evil Judeans.

The apostles asked two questions, **when** and **what**. Some people think that there were three questions, but there were only two. The second question of **what** was the **sign** that they would know the time **when** those things were coming to pass.

The first question that the apostles asked was, "***When*** *shall the **time** come when all of the buildings of the temple would be thrown down, not one stone left on another?"*

The second question was a two-part question that was connected with the word **and**. The question was, "***What*** *shall be the **sign** of thy coming **and** of the end of the world?"*

The second question was a compound question that the apostles understood to apply to the **sign** of the time when the temple would fall. Now follow me closely.

Think for yourself.

> **They did not ask for two signs. The same sign that they were to receive was for both the <u>coming</u> of Jesus and of <u>the end of the world</u>. I repeat – only one sign for both – remember that as we continue to study!**

Regardless of what you think about any past coming or future coming of Jesus, the one under consideration by the apostles here in Matthew 24 was his coming **in judgment upon those Judean hypocrites** of chapter 23 when he destroyed the Herodian temple and their system of worship and their **old** covenant. The apostles recognized that the destruction of their temple was the thought that is scattered throughout these next two chapters and also throughout the entire *"new testament."* We will talk of some of them later. The next part deals at length with two things.

Verse 3 shows that Jesus had moved from the Herodian temple in Jerusalem, across the valley and up on the side of the Mount of Olives. That is why the preachers speak of the **Olivet Discourse**. There he sat down. In another verse, that we will look at later, four of his apostles came to him **privately**. They were Peter, Andrew, James and John. They understood very well from what Jesus had said, the temple and all of the buildings of the temple would be destroyed to the point where not one stone would be left upon another. They also knew from what he had said in chapter 23 that he was referring to a **time within that current generation** of people who were biologically alive. They understood who the **you** were in chapter 23 and they comprehended who the **you** were in Matthew 24:4 (them, the apostles – their generation). They were intently interested in knowing the exact time in **their generation** that those horrible things would happen, and they wanted to know the **sign** when Jesus **was about to come** and destroy those buildings and that it consequently would end their **world**.

(For a detailed study of the Greek word **mello**, which means **about to**, obtain my book that is titled "Things that were about to happen in the days of Jesus and his apostles," where I cover every verse in the *"new testament"* in which it occurs. Look at the back page of this book for ordering information or go to AMAZON.COM)

The apostles asked Jesus concerning his **coming** …

> *"And as he sat upon the mount of Olives, the disciples came unto him privately, saying, Tell us, when shall these things be? And what shall be the sign of thy **coming**, and of the end of the world"* [Matthew 24:3].

The Greek word for **coming** is the word **parousia**. Here is what it means.

> *The … context is speaking of the **coming** of Jesus. Many comings of Jesus are mentioned in the Bible. To which one was Peter referring? That can more plainly be seen when we understand that the word **coming** … was his **parousia.** Contrary to the way that it is many times translated and taught, the word **parousia** means **presence** and not "coming." The N.I.V. even puts the word "coming" in quotation marks, obviously meaning that there was something not quite right about its translation by the word "coming." The Greek word **parousia** occurs only twenty-two times in the entire "new testament."*
>
> *This might be the first time that you have been exposed to this Greek word. It is* not *the commonly used Greek word **erchomai** that is correctly translated by the word "coming." The **parousia** was to be **seen** by the 1st century A.D. generation … The word "parousia" does not refer to a coming of Jesus in bodily form, but rather the **perception** of Jesus' **presence** in the destruction of the natural Judean nation in 70 A.D. by the Romans … This book is not about the "parousia," but I did have to initiate some thoughts for you to study further.* [Shortly, the new book titled Parousia will be at AMAZON.COM]

So, we should understand that Jesus' **presence** would be **seen** in the Roman army that conquered the land, city, temple and the old covenant system between 66 A.D. – 70 A.D.. Let us compare this "*coming*" with the **coming** of God in the "*old testament*."

> "*The burden of Egypt. Behold the LORD **rideth** upon a swift **cloud**, and shall come into Egypt: and the idols of Egypt shall be moved at **His presence**, and the heart of Egypt shall melt in the midst of it*" [Isaiah 19:1].

Notice that the verse describes a coming of God **in judgment**. Notice also that He did **not** literally, biologically or physically come into Egypt. Now notice the following verse about Jesus' **parousia** and tell me if you are absolutely sure that it is referring to a bodily return on the clouds **or** if it was his **presence in judgment** upon Jerusalem – in the same **manner** that God came to Egypt.

> "*Which (angels) also said, Ye men of Galilee, why stand ye gazing up into heaven? This same Jesus , which is taken up from you into heaven, shall so **come** in **like manner** as ye have seen him go into heaven*" [Acts 1:11].

Two verses before, it was stated that Jesus ascended and a **cloud** received him out of their sight. Now here is a very, very big question. Before you answer it to yourself, **think for yourself!** Does this verse say **in like form** or **in like manner**?

Did Jesus come **riding on a cloud** on a white horse in the **manner** of God's **riding on a swift cloud** in the Book of Isaiah, or did the Bible speak of his coming in some bodily **form**? **Manner or form**? That is the question! Do we need to remind ourselves of Albert Einstein's admonition: "*We can't solve problems by using the same kind of thinking that we used when we created them?*"

Before we go to the next important word in this verse, let us consider the statement of Jesus that "*not one stone shall be left upon another that shall not be thrown down*" [Matthew 24:2]. Almost weekly, we see pictures on the television set of men at the *"wailing wall"* in Jerusalem. It is argued that because those stones are still standing, that Jesus did not tell the truth. However, careful study will reveal that very qualified men have examined everything in that area and have conclusively stated that the original temple did **not** stand in the area of the *"wailing wall,"* neither did it stand where the <u>Dome of the Rock</u> is now located. They state that the stones that we see on the television set belonged to the Roman fort, named Antonia. So, the *"wailing wall"* stones are not stones of the temple, neither are they stones of the other *"buildings of the temple."* Indeed, almost 2,000 years ago, the Romans burned the temple, which caused the gold to melt from the sacred things, running down into the foundations. Every stone was **thrown** down and the **ground** was ploughed and sifted to retrieve all of the gold. Absolutely! Jesus told the truth. Not one single stone of which he spoke remained on top of another **original** one.

Now let us look at another word that is very confusing because of the way that it is translated in the <u>King James Version</u>. That will be a study of the word **world** of which the apostles desired to know the time of its end. The Greek word from which the word **world** is translated in this verse is **aionos**. The definition of the Greek word is …

> *"Properly, **an age**; by extension, perpetuity; by implication, the world, **specially the Jewish age**."*

What the scholars said was that the Greek word means *"an age,"* **not the planet Earth** (world). It is amazing how many people (including preachers) think that this clause has reference to the end of the planet Earth (world), but just tell me what the Bible means that the earth abideth forever? In this verse, the word **world** is not a good translation of **aionos**. Consult the <u>New King James Version</u> (and other translations) and you will see the word *"world"* **deleted**, and in its place the correct translation, which is **age**.

So, again, what were the apostles asking? First, they wanted to know **when** the buildings of the temple would be thrown down. Secondly, they wanted to know **what** the (one) sign was of the parousia (presence) of Jesus in that destruction, coupled with the **end of the Mosaic age**. That is all that they asked, so in the following verses, we should see Jesus laying the foundation for the **time** of his **presence** (~~coming~~) in the destruction, which would be the **end of the Mosaic age** (which happened in 66 A.D. – 70 A.D.). The verse should read:

> *"And as he sat upon the mount of Olives, the disciples came unto him privately, saying, Tell us, when shall these things be (the judgment and destruction of the temple)? And what shall be the sign of thy **presence** (not coming), and the end of the **age** (not world)"* [Matthew 24:3]?

Eyewitness accounts of Roman actions concerning one stone not left upon another that was not thrown down.

I received the following comment from a friend of mine.

> *"Your comment in the first paragraph strikes me as hyper-literalism. Even if you throw down every last stone, you still would have quite a few piled on other stones, though perhaps not in their original positions. The Jews regard the wailing wall as the foundation of the Herodian temple. You are saying they are wrong? Where is your source for this? The Bible often uses hyperbole – cut off your hand, pluck out your eye, the sluggard buries his hand in the dish and will not bring it to his mouth etc.. Is this not an example of hyperbole in the words of Jesus? Not every stone has to be thrown down to make the point that the temple will be destroyed."*

Jesus did say that not **one** stone would be left on another that would not be thrown down. That is very plain and we need to say that he knew exactly what he was talking about. I will accept that as truth, not exaggeration. Jesus did **not** say that when they were thrown down that some may lay or not lay on top of other stones that had also been thrown down. I would probably say that they were but that would only be a probable guess. Secondly, the **wall** surrounding Jerusalem was not the topic of the question by the apostles, neither under consideration in the response by Jesus. The apostles came to show him *"the **buildings** of the temple,"* **not the walls that surrounded Jerusalem**, neither was he speaking of the **three Roman forts** that were constructed there – the three great towers that were **connected** with the outside walls of Jerusalem. Even if the **Roman** towers all stood standing, Jesus' prophesy will stand 100% complete.   The entire wall could have remained and it not conflict with the destruction of the **buildings of the temple**. The wall around Jerusalem, of which the *"wailing wall"* was part, was not part of the *"**buildings** of the temple."* The most reliable source is the *"Jewish"* historian, Josephus, who traveled with the Roman army and wrote of the catastrophe. Here is his quote.

"Now as soon as the army had no more to slay or to plunder, because there remained none to be the objects of their fury (for they would not have spared any, had there remained any other work to be done), [Titus] Caesar gave orders that they should now demolish the entire city and temple, but should leave as many of the towers standing as were of the greatest eminence; that is, Phasailus, and Hippicus, and Mariamne; and so much of the wall as enclosed the city on the west side. This wall was spared, in order to afford a camp for such as were to lie in garrison [in the Upper City], as were the towers [the three forts] also spared, in order to demonstrate to posterity what kind of city it was, and how well fortified, which the Roman valor had subdued; but for all the rest of the wall [surrounding Jerusalem], it was so thoroughly laid even with the ground by those who dug it up to the foundation, that there was left nothing to make those

that came by the madness of those that were for innovations, a city otherwise a great magnificence and of mighty fane among all mankind.

"And truly, the very view itself was a melancholy thing; for those places which are adorned with trees and pleasant gardens, were now become desolate country every way, and its trees were all cut down. Nor could any foreigner that had formerly seen Judaea and the most beautiful suburbs of the city, and now saw it as a desert, but lament and mourn sadly at so great a change. For the war had laid all signs of beauty quite waste. Nor had anyone who had known the place before, had come on a sudden to it now, would he have known it again. But though he [a foreigner] were at the city itself, yet would he have inquired for it.

"… The Romans set fire to the extreme parts of the city [the suburbs] and burnt them down, and entirely demolished [Jerusalem's] walls.

"When [Titus] entirely demolished the rest of the city, and overthrew its walls, he left [three] towers as monuments of his good fortune, which had proved [the destructive power of] his auxiliaries, and enabled him to take what could otherwise have been taken by him."

In my understanding, the *"wailing wall"* was not part of the foundation of the Herodian temple, regardless of what those living in that part of the country **today** think. As Jesus did in his parables, do you think that possibly he was using that literal language of stones, to show that not one single *"stone-headed Judean"* would not be uprooted or thrown down (*twice dead, plucked up by the roots"*)?

"And Jesus answered and said unto them, Take heed that no man deceive you. For many shall come in my name, saying, I am Christ; and shall deceive many" [Matthew 24:4-5].

Continue to notice throughout our study of Matthew 24 that Jesus was talking to his apostles, and the **time** reference was between 30 A.D. and 70 A.D.. If it were not possible for Peter, Andrew, James and John to be deceived, then Jesus was giving them that warning in vain. It was possible that those four apostles could be deceived. However, Jesus himself said that many would be deceived because there would be many that would come during that generation who would claim to be the Anointed of God. Jesus was laying the foundation for the answers that he would give his apostles concerning the time **when** the things would happen that he had told his apostles would happen, and the groundwork for his response to their question about **what** would be the sign of the end of the Mosaic age. First and foremost, they must listen to Jesus and no one else, even if they claimed to be the Messiah.

> *"And ye shall hear of wars and rumors of wars and rumours of wars: see that ye be not troubled: for all these things must come to pass, but the end is not yet. For nation shall not rise against nation and kingdom against kingdom: and there shall famines, and pestilences, and earthquakes, in divers places"* [Matthew 24:6-7].

Under Augusta Caesar, there was made a peace pack titled **Pax Ramano**, which forced peace on the people. That peaceful condition continued through the other Monarchs until the time of Nero when everything was to break out into war in all different quarters. The apostles were still living in that forced peaceful condition, but it was about to end, and Jesus warned them of the coming wars and rumors of wars that was about to commence. Technically, the verse has the word **shall** in it, which should be correctly translated as **about to** from the Greek word **mello**. That means that the apostles were **about to** hear of those wars and rumors of wars. But it was not quite the time for the end of the Mosaic age (even though it was to come in that generation).

It is probable that the apostles were expecting the destruction of the temple and the consequent end of the Mosaic age rather quickly, so Jesus told them that many things would happen before the end. During that time, before they should expect the end of the **age**, they (the apostles in the 1st century, not us in the 21st century) would hear of wars and rumors of wars, and they were told not to be troubled about those wars and rumors. When those things happened, it was not time for the end of the **age**. Neither were they the sign of which they had inquired of Jesus. They were simply things that would happen along the way and they could expect them to happen.

Also, nation would rise up against nation and kingdom against kingdom, but the end of the Mosaic age would not be immediate. Yes, history speaks of nations and kingdoms battling each other, however I believe (like Jesus' parables) there were spiritual applications to those statements. The kingdom of the natural Judean world would rise up against the kingdom of Jesus that was known as *"living stones, being built up a spiritual house"* [1 Peter 2:5]. From reading the book of Acts, we certainly know they were diverse from one another and there was a battle going on between them.

There would also be biological famines, pestilences and earthquakes. Are we also to consider that between the unbelieving Judeans and the believing saints who were eventually called Christians, one would find pestilences *(one definition is a noxious or malign doctrine, influence, etc.)* and a famine of the bread of life or an earthquake of tremendous proportions in the shaking up and change of the old covenant to the new covenant? Well, maybe I am stretching it a little – or maybe not. Is it not time for us to think for ourselves?

"All these are the beginning of sorrows" [Matthew 24:8].

Concerning the word translated **sorrows**, it is interesting that the Greek word **odin** means **birth pangs**, or **birth pains**, the pains that precede a birth. It is so translated in many translations. The word "sorrow" is not a very good modern word to use as a translation of the original word. Other translations render it as **birth pangs**.

It is here that Jesus' answer to the apostles becomes very interesting. There is probably something that I am overlooking as yet that describes the time of the "*conception*" but here we are concerned with the birth, because we have the **beginning** of the birth pangs. "*Pangs*" are defined as "*sudden sharp pains, mental anguish, especially concerning childbirth.*"

The first question is what was the beginning of those sharp, sudden pains or mental anguish to those apostles who were listening to Jesus? Was it the wars or rumors of wars of which they were to hear? Was it a kingdom rising to fight against another kingdom? Was it a nation rising to fight another nation? They were to hear of those things, but the end of the age was not quite yet (about almost another forty years when Jerusalem was destroyed). It does not seem that the things that were mentioned previous to this verse were the **beginning** "*of the sharp birth pangs or mental anguish.*"

The word **then** that begins the next verse gives us a clue to understanding this. The Greek word is described as not only a possible consecutive action, but also "*at the time that (of the past or future).*" **At the time that** the apostles (in what age were the apostles living?) who were listening to Jesus tell the apostles that they would be delivered up and killed, that would be a time of "*mental anguish*" and "*a sharp pain.*" That seems to be the **beginning** of the sharp pains, like a woman attempting to give birth to a child. Why would Jesus say to the people who were weeping for him (as he was being crucified) …

> "*But Jesus turning unto them said, Daughters of Jerusalem, weep not for me, but weep for yourselves, and for your children*" [Luke 23:28].

The next four verses should give you the answer.

*"For, behold, the days are coming, in the which they (**women**) shall say, Blessed are the barren, and the wombs that never bare, and the paps which never gave suck. Then shall they begin to say to the mountains, Fall on us (**children**); and to the hills, Cover us. For if they do these things in a green tree, what shall be done in the dry? And there were also two other, malefactors, led with him to be put to death."*

If there were to be *"sharp birth pangs"* that the apostles of Jesus were going to see while they were biologically alive, was there not going to be a birth very shortly? Or, had the birth already happened? Or was the birth two-thousand (2,000) years into the future, even in our time in the 21st century?

Jesus had stated that a person had to be **born from above** (again or anew) in order to see or enter into the kingdom of God?

"Except a man be born again, he cannot see the kingdom of God" [John 3:3].

"Except a man be born of water and of the Spirit, he cannot into the kingdom of God" [John 3:5].

Do you think that the *"new birth"* would occur **after** the birth pangs had begun?

Do you think that the *"birth pangs"* began **before** the apostles had heard of wars and rumors of wars and the battle between kingdoms and nations?

Do you think that the *"new birth"* happened then or shortly after Nicodemus' conversation with Jesus and when he told him of that **birth from above**?

While the believers, especially for the next forty years, were *"being born again"* [1 Peter 1:23], do you know of any passage that shows that the birth was **completed** by the time that natural Jerusalem fell in A.D. 70?

Is it possible that the **new birth** was completely accomplished into the spiritual kingdom of God when the old natural kingdom was destroyed in 70 A.D.?

It will probably be argued by some that the context of Matthew 24, only the Father knew the **day and hour**. I will deal more with that in particular when I get to v-36. In the meantime, it is necessary that we remind ourselves that Jesus was very emphatic in his statement that …

"All these are the beginning of sorrows" [Matthew 24:8].

So, regardless of any delay in our minds, such does not do away with the fact that the birth pangs had begun when the apostles began to be rounded up, persecuted and killed. That was the middle of the 1st century A.D. (about 2,000 years ago).

When my wife began having birth pangs with our youngest daughter, I took her immediately to the hospital (which was only about two blocks away). Within thirty minutes she was born. That was a very short time with very little delay between the time of the beginning of the birth pangs until the delivery and birth.

When my grand-daughter began having birth pangs, they were three months early. She had to have almost total bed rest in order to carry the baby full term (which she did, and my third great-grand-child was born). There was some delay between the beginning of the birth pangs and the final birth.

God has set a basic term limit, which we usually refer to as nine months. Of course, a birth might occur a little early or a little later from the date at which the doctor guesses, because in most cases the doctor cannot be sure, for he usually has no idea when the conception occurred. Be that as it may, I want to make a point. The baby will always be born somewhere in the proximity of the nine months – not wait a year or so, or a hundred years or so, or a couple of thousand years or so before it is born.

Jesus told his apostles **when** the birth pangs would begin, and the apostles could see the beginning when they individually began to be killed, exactly as Jesus had prophesied. Why in the world would we get the idea that the birth would be put off for some extended time – maybe a hundred years – maybe two thousand years – maybe still in our future? It is time for us to think for ourselves and be rational in our understanding. My wife **knew the time** of the expected birth, but did not know the day and hour. My granddaughter **knew the expected time** of the birth, but did not know the day and hour. **Jesus knew the time** of the expected birth, but did **not know** the day and hour.

God was the only one who knew the **day and hour**. In fact, He is the **only** one who knows the day and hour of each birth all over the world. If we are going to understand this verse, we need to know the difference between the **time** and the **day and hour** and quit mixing them up. They do not mean the same and we need to separate them as God did. It is winter here now. Do you know the **time** when we will get the first month when the thermometer will hit the 90 degree mark? Is the exact **day and hour** the same? Surely you know that they are not the same. If you cannot figure those things out, surely your words are so mixed up that your pictures are only worth 200 words.

The birth pangs began in the 1st century and the birth occurred in the 1st century. Jesus said so in this very chapter. I will deal more with that when we get to v-36.

"Then shall they deliver up to be afflicted, and shall kill you: and ye shall be hated of all nations for my names sake" [Matthew 24:9].

To which four people did he tell that? Peter, Andrew, James and John – correct? This is not for our age, 2,000 years later. Come on now – who were the recipients of this chapter? How many of you have been delivered, hated and killed? At the time of the beginning of the birth pangs, the apostles would be delivered up to be afflicted. They would also be killed because they would be hated by all of the **nations**. The reason for them being hated was because of Jesus. The birth pangs that had begun on the apostles in the middle of the 1st century would continue for a short time until the birth of the new creation in 70 A.D.. He had already told them …

"Remember the word that I said unto you, the servant is not greater than his lord. If they have persecuted me, they will also persecute you; if they have kept my saying, they will keep yours also" [John 15:20].

The primary **nations** to which Jesus was referring were the twelve tribes (nations) of Israel. It was to them that they were primarily sent. Of course, I do not think that it reaches too far to include any nation to which they might eventually have preached. The idolatry of those nations would place those nations in an adversarial position to the apostle's teaching.

This is probably as good a place as any to introduce you to a translation problem. The Greek word that is translated as **nations** is the word **ethnos**. That is the root word from which we get our word **ethnic**. The word *"nations"* is the correct meaning, but the problem is that the Greek word (ethnos) and Hebrew word (goyim) are not very easily translated into English in the many places in which they occur in the Bible. Many times, the words are translated by the word **gentiles**. That word is of Latin origin and does not readily translate either of the original words.

For example, try translating the word **ethnos** in this verse by the word *"gentiles"* and here is the way that it would look:

> *"Then shall they deliver you up to be afflicted, and shall kill you: and ye shall be hated of all **gentiles** for my names sake."*

That would leave out any hatred by the Judeans (commonly called *"Jews"*), as well as any hatred among the scattered Israelites. If *"all gentiles"* hated the apostles, how would they ever preach to them and cause them to be converted? Truly, the word **gentile** should not be in our English Bibles, but I do not know of another word or words (in English) that would work any better. That should give you about a year's worth of studying to do own those two words alone. At this point, I will not pursue the subject of the **goyim and ethnos** more at this time. I will return to it.

> *"And then shall many be offended, and shall betray one another, and shall hate one another"* [Matthew 24:10].

It is not as though there are not some who are offended in the 21st century or that some people betray others, or that there is hate today. But the point that Jesus was making to those four apostles was that **then** (at the time that those four apostles were suffering persecution and being murdered) was the time when the offences, betrayals and hate would arise. This is not speaking of 21st century time – it was for the 1st century believers.

> We must respect the time elements that Jesus placed on any event. Respecting God's time elements are the only way of understanding the Bible. This is one such time element.

Some very interesting observations are to be observed from a study of some of the words in this passage of scripture. For example, the Greek word from which the word **offended** comes is **skandalizo**. Compare our English word *"scandalize"* (only the *"k"* is changed to *"c"* and the *"o"* is changed to "*e*"). See how close they are in spelling. They are also that close in meaning. The root word means "*to entrap, to trip up (figuratively), stumble (transitively) or entice to sin, apostasy or displeasure.*" I think that a good case can be made for all of those definitions for the time when the apostles were being killed and persecuted in the 1st century A.D., how about you?

The Greek word **paradidomi** is translated as **betray**. The meaning is "*to surrender, i.e. yield up, intrust, transmit.*" In that time of peer pressure, the threat of being kicked out of the synagogue, tortured or even killed, people were spying on and betraying their friends. Sounds like our government today, does it not? In fact, all governments have always been the same and always will be. They were giving them up and entrusting them to people who would torture and murder them. To secure their own safety, they would reveal the names, places of abode or places of concealment of believers. Luke records that the believers would be betrayed by "*parents, and brethren, and kinsfolks, and friends*" [Luke 21:16].

> "*Were there no evidence that this **had** been done, it would scarcely be 'credible.' The ties which bind brothers and sisters, and parents and children together, are so strong that it could scarcely be believed that division of sentiment on religious subjects would cause them to forget these tender relations. Yet history assures us that this has been often done. If this be so, then how inexpressibly awful must be the malignity of the human heart by nature against religion! Nothing else but this dreadful opposition to God and His gospel ever has induced or ever can induce people to violate the most tender relations, and consign the best friends to torture, racks, and flames. It adds to the horrors of this, that those who were put to death in persecution were tormented in the most awful modes that human ingenuity could devise. They were crucified: were thrown into boiling oil; were burned at the stake; were roasted slowly over coals; were compelled to drink melted lead; were torn in pieces by beasts of*

pray; were covered with pitch and set on fire. Yet, dreadful as this prediction was, it was fulfilled; and, incredible as it seems, parents and children, husbands and wives, were found wicked enough to deliver up each other to these cruel modes of death on account of attachment to the gospel. Such is the opposition of the heart of man to the gospel! That hostility which will overcome the strong ties of natural affection, and which will be satisfied with nothing else to show its power, can be no slight opposition to the gospel of God" [from Barnes' Notes, Matthew 10:21].

If we had lived in the 1st century A.D. and were believers who saw our mentors, the apostles themselves being persecuted and murdered, what would we have done? Do not shrug that question off lightly; for in answering that privately to ourselves, it tells us of our own true character – good or bad. It might happen again in your lifetime. If it does, what will you do?

Then there is the third category. It is one that is defined by the Greek word **miseo** that is translated as **hate**. The definition of the word is *"from a primary hatred; to detest; especially to persecute."* Those were people, some in the very households of believers who would themselves persecute their loved ones because they were believers in their Messiah. Their lack of love was not the issue. Hatred! Hatred! Hatred! - was their problem! And it was their problem from about 50 A.D. to 70 A.D.. About 70 A.D. it ceased from being their problem – God destroyed both their temple, worship and them.

> *"And many false prophets shall rise, and shall deceive many"* [Matthew 24:11].

Again, when trying to understand this verse, it is necessary that we recall that Jesus was speaking to his apostles in the 1st century A.D. (not to us today).

In order to understand the main thrust of this verse, we must understand the meaning of the word **prophet**. The <u>King James Version</u> translates the word from different meaning Greek words, which basically means *"one who speaks by inspiration,"* whether concerning things past, present or future. Its meaning is not simply one who foretells the future, although that could be part of the message. Remember that Moses wrote of the present but also spoke of the beginning of the world, even when man did not exist, and spoke of future things as well. Keep in mind the meaning of *"one who was inspired of God"* as we look at the modifying word.

During the 1st century A.D., there would be **many** prophets. Such is usually not considered, but Jesus very plainly said so in this verse. What would those particular **many** prophets be?

Notice that I did not ask *"what would those many prophets be **doing**?"* That is not necessary, for what they should be doing is speaking by the inspiration of God, but they were not doing so. What were they doing? **Deceiving many!** Did what they told the people that caused them to be deceived make them **false** prophets? The following is a segment quotation of a chapter in my book that is titled <u>The Church</u> and sub-titled <u>It is not the ekklesia of the Bible</u>. Amazon.com – shortly.

What Is A False Teacher?

Is it not true that when we disagree with another, that there is a tendency to call the other person a false teacher?

> *"But **false prophets** also arose among the people, just as there will be **false teachers** among you, who will secretly introduce destructive heresies, even denying the Master who bought them, bringing **swift** destruction upon themselves"* [2 Peter 2:1].

Did you ever wonder how a person could be a false prophet if he could not prophesy? Was the gift of prophecy given to someone other than a prophet? If he could prophecy, did God give him that power, or did he get such from "*satan*?" What makes a false prophet or a false teacher?

There is much said about false teachers in our day, especially in view of the fact that the above passage is the only time that the expression **false teacher** occurs anywhere in the Bible. What is a pseudo-teacher? This term is usually used by preachers and pastors to **brand** other preachers who differ from them, all the while, I believe, not knowing what a false teacher is. The attitude today is, it is *"open season"* and everyone who disagrees with me is *"fair game"* and I can take *"pot shots"* at anyone I want and run back to the protection of my local church organization. May God have mercy on us for having such attitudes.

In the hard-line approach of most preachers, there are only two kinds of preachers – themselves and false teachers. They allow for no possibility of honestly mistaken preachers, or for a change of mind on biblical matters. When a person does make a change, was he then, or is he now, a false teacher? I know many honestly mistaken preachers.

In 2 Peter 2:1-3 does Peter say false teacher or false teaching? A **teacher** is the person. **Teaching** is what the person says. The Bible is not saying to avoid false teaching, but rather to avoid the **person** – because the **teacher** is false! Peter stated in the N.A.S.V. that false teachers were those who **secretly** introduced destructive heresies. They were sensual and engaged in shameful ways. They exploited believers with false words. In Jude 4 in the N.A.S.V., the writer said that those people did what they did **for pay**; they followed their own lusts, speaking **arrogantly** and flattering people for the sake of gaining advantage. Those were the ones who caused divisions. Neither Peter nor Jude described an honestly mistaken teacher who had honorable motives and declared what he sincerely believed to be the truth. One can tolerate a person like this. Can anyone at anytime read another's motives? Can anyone know his heart? They must be careful!

Further, the word false (an adjective) modifies or describes **the teacher himself** – as a **person**. It has nothing to do with **what** is taught. In fact, one can teach the truth and still be a **false** teacher. That is what Peter was when he taught that the Jews and gentiles were equal in Jesus, yet withdrew from the gentile believers when certain Jewish believer were present. **He** was wrong. **He** was false, even though what he taught was the truth.

A false teacher is one who **knowingly** teaches, whether truth or error, for the wrong reason. If the teacher loves preeminence, the chief seat, honor and praise of men, to be called Rabbi, Preacher, the Pulpit Minister, Reverend, Pastor, or our Minister, he is covered with pride and is a false teacher, minister, preacher, etc. These men do good or bad as it serves their purposes. This includes the compromiser; one who knuckles under to pressure to save or secure his job, retirement, housing, or reputation. He can ignore a lot of sin or be biblically inconsistent – or be silent! if he has something to lose; if he wants to save his hide, pride, and/or pocketbook.

A *"false prophet"* was a **false person** who happened to be a prophet. Such hypocritical persons with fair speeches made merchandise of people's lives during that trying time from the middle of the 1st century till 70 A.D..

"And because iniquity shall abound, the love of many shall wax cold" [Matthew 24:12].

The original Greek word **anomia** is translated by the word **iniquity**. The definition is more inclusive than expressed. It is defined as *"illegality, i.e. violation of law or (in the genitive case) wickedness."*

The word **abound** would be better translated for us in the 21st century as *"increase or multiply."* Again, let us not forget that Jesus was speaking of people in the 1st century A.D.. Wickedness was already present, otherwise it could not abound. It was to multiply and get really bad, which it did before the Roman onslaught on Jerusalem in 66 A.D. and which culminated in its destruction in 70 A.D. with over a million Jews killed or starved to death and from 60,000 to 100,000 carried captive and scattered all over the then known Roman world.

In context, the word *"iniquity"* here seems to include the brutality of the Judeans and Romans in their persecutions; the betraying of believers by those who professed to be such; and the insidious errors of false prophets and others. The effect of all of this would be that the passion of emotions of many believers would be lessened. The word **wax** means to **become**. It is an out-dated Saxon word and not used now in this sense except in the Bible. The fear of death and the deluding influence of false believers, would lessen the zeal of many timid and weak professors of faith in God; perhaps, also, of many genuine but weak believers.

The <u>King James Version</u> only says *"the love of many,"* but the original says *"the love of **the** many."* With the addition of the article *"the,"* it is emphasized that the majority of those who had a love for God would allow that love to diminish – many to the point of being deceived and consequently destroyed in the three and one-half year war with the Romans from 66 A.D. to 70 A.D..

Even during those difficult, trying and testing times of the 1st century A.D. for the believers, they were to maintain their love for God and Jesus. Most did not and consequently *"fell away."* For us in the 21st century, the words *"wax cold"* would better be translated by **chill**. But there was another problem with the believers who were losing their love and faith – the **middle of the roaders** – you have heard of them, no doubt.

To and of the so-called church of the Laodiceans of the 1st century A.D., Jesus said …

"I know thy works, that thou art neither cold nor hot: I would thou wert cold or hot. So then because thou art lukewarm, and neither cold nor hot, I will spue thee out of my mouth" [Revelation 3:15-16].

So, the middle of the roaders, lack of love believers in that city of Asia would be rejected by God and Jesus along with the rejection of Jerusalem.

Is there any lesson for us today? Certainly! Do not let trials and false, hypocritical people cause us to love God less – in fact, place more love in Him and be more confident that He will work out His purpose in our lives.

"But he that shall endure unto the end, the same shall be saved" [Matthew24:13].

I will begin a study of this verse by noting the first word, **but**. In English, this word is a coordinating conjunction and connects things of equal rank, although they may be the same or the exact opposite. In this case, what was before the word "*but*" and what follows are opposites.

In the preceding verse, we saw false men, even **false** prophets. We saw all sorts of deception and belief of that deception. We saw very many who were deceived. We saw the love that the believers had for God, dwindle and become less and less. At one time their love and zeal had been "*hot*" and then we see that it had "*chilled*" and became **cold** (lukewarm). Any and all sorts of reasons might have been the causes of such. Those believers between 30 A.D. and 70 A.D. who had fallen away were destroyed along with those who had never believed. They were like the "*dog is turned to its own vomit again; and the sow that was washed to her wallowing in the mire*" [2 Peter 2:22].

However, in this verse, hope was still held out by Jesus that some of the believers would remain faithful to the end, despite their persecution and even their death. He did observe that it would require endurance.

The original word that is translated as **endurance** is used figuratively and means *"to remain, to undergo, i.e. to bear trials, to have fortitude, to persevere."* Those believers who wanted to be saved must have remained faithful even if being betrayed; they must have been able to bear the trials even in their being persecuted; they must have been able to persevere even if it meant their death. Their salvation depended upon their fortitude in being able to remain faithful to God through all of those trials (which they would and indeed did go through).

There are two words in this verse that have given the commentators of this world many problems. The first one is **the end** – the end of what? Was it the end of their biological lives? Was it the end of the Mosaic system at the fall of Jerusalem and the temple in 70 A.D.? Maybe it is a combination of all of those things. But one thing that we have learned for sure is that Jesus was speaking to his apostles about **their end time** almost 2,000 years ago, and any interpretation that we put on the **end** in this verse must agree with what they understood for themselves in the 1st century A.D.. Jesus expanded more on *"the end"* in this discourse that he was making on the Mount of Olives to his apostles very shortly before he was murdered. We will study more on this subject a little later in our study of this chapter.

The second word that has given problems, even to scholars, is the word **saved** – saved from what? Do not pass over that question lightly. In fact, read it at least ten times and think about it very seriously each time – **saved from what**? The definition of the Greek word **sozo** is *"to save, i.e. **deliver or protect**."* Is there more than one answer? Perhaps, saved from persecution? – or protected from someone? Or saved/delivered/protected from something else? – or saved from all of these, maybe more? A study of Matthew 24 is not a study of salvation. An entire book needs to be written about that subject.

But understand this one thing in the context of what Jesus said here to his apostles in the first century A.D. – if they endured to the end, they would be saved or delivered or protected – **from something** in or from the very generation in which they were biologically living.

Matthew 24 is a prophecy from God through the Messiah. Did He fulfill His prophecy in the time that He himself had set? We need to consider that very carefully, for it is generally taught today in the 21st century that He did **not** fulfil it as He said. Very sad!

> *"And this gospel of the kingdom shall be preached in all the world for a witness unto all nations; and then shall the end come"* [Matthew 24:14].

Remember that Jesus was speaking to his apostles about 30-33 A.D. (not to us in the 21st century). We must understand this verse as Peter and John understood what Jesus was saying. Then and only then can we get any application for us to use thousands of years later.

I think that the first word that we should consider is the word **this**. The original word simply means *"that thing."* What **thing** specifically was it to which Jesus was referring? Well, we only have to go back to the preceding verse to find out. Here is the *"thing,"* that good news that was to be preached.

> *"But he that shall endure unto the end, the same shall be saved"* [Matthew 24:13].

Amidst all of the persecutions, afflictions and tribulations that the apostles and 1st century believers were to undergo, the **good news** was that if they *"endured to the end, they would be saved."* For a review, see the previous comments on 3-13.

The word *"gospel"* only means *"good news or glad tidings."* The context always must determine what the *"good news"* was and to what and to whom it referred. It does not always mean the *"good news"* of the death, burial and resurrection and witnessing of Jesus. The original root word is the same word that we have translated as *"evangelist"* or as *"evangelism."* An **evangelist** was one who preached to the **lost** people, **not** taught the believers.

I shall discuss the word **preached**. It is defined by Strong's Greek study as **"*kerusso* (kay-roos-so); *of uncertain affinity; to herald (as a public crier)*, *especially divine truth (the gospel)."* This word is not used in the Bible as it is normally used today. When a *"preacher"* stands before a *"church assembly"* of believers, he is giving instructions to believers, not unbelievers. The word in the Bible for instructing believers is *"teaching – **not** preaching."* The *"gospel or good news"* listed above was *"heralded"* to the entire *"world"* of unbelievers for a witness. This was preached to all of the unbelievers – to every creature of the world. To simplify it, teaching was to believers – preaching was to unbelievers. We need to understand the difference.

The good news or gospel concerning salvation to those who endured to the end, concerned the *"kingdom"* of God. The original word is **basileias**, which properly and primarily means *"royalty, i.e. rule."* It is in a secondary sense used concretely used as *"a realm."* The question here is …

> *"Is the gospel of the **rule** of God or is the gospel of the **realm** of people under the rule of God?"*

That gospel of the kingdom was to be preached *"in all the world."* There are different original words that are translated as *"world"* in the Bible. The Greek word here means wherever the Romans ruled – **the entire Roman Empire** – the **world** of the Romans. It did not have anything to do with places like China or the American Indian (if America had people inhabiting it at that time). Was it preached to *"every creature"* of the Roman Empire during the 1st century A.D.? Let the apostle Paul answer the question …

> *"If ye continue in the faith grounded and settled, and be not moved away from the hope of the gospel, which ye have heard, and which **was preached to every creature** which is under heaven; whereof I Paul am made a minister"* [Colossians 1:23].

Was that gospel preached *"in all the world"* during the days that the apostle Paul lived? Let him answer that question …

> *"Which is come unto you, as it is **in all the world**: and bringeth forth fruit, as it doth also in you, since the day ye heard of it, and knew the grace of God in truth"* [Colossians 1:6].

Why are preachers today saying that it has never been preached to every creature and therefore the end mentioned here cannot come until it is – therefore we should get busy and evangelize every person on planet Earth?

As the apostle Paul said twice in Colossians 1:6,23, the gospel or good news of God **was** preached in all of the Roman Empire during the 1st century A.D.. Besides the benefit to those who heard and received, another benefit was that its being preached to the complete Roman **world** was that it was a *"witness"* of the good benefits to other nations. The Greek word from which the word **witness** comes is **marturion**, which is defined as *"something evidential, i.e. evidence given."* Notice how close our English word *"martyr"* is. Steven is said to have been the first martyr, i.e., the first one to die as a witness to the truth of God. So the nations that were not part of the Roman Empire would have **evidence** of the kingdom of God, and when it would be preached to them, they should receive the preaching and submit to being good and righteous before God who ruled over them.

The root word from which the word **nation** is translated is **ethnos**. It is translated in the <u>King James Version</u> by the words *"people, nations, gentiles and heathen."* We are accustomed to using the English word *"ethnic."* The word is defined as *"a race, i.e. **a tribe, specially a foreign, non-Jewish one**."* I cannot get into all of the aspects at this point, but consider that in the 8th century B.C., ten tribes of the Israelites (plus some from Judah, Benjamin and Levi) were carried away captive by Assyria. The tribes (ethnos) were scattered into different cities and countries. They are usually erroneously referred to as the *"lost tribes."* However, they were not lost. Because of their idolatrous rebellion to God, they ceased to be called *"the people"* of God and were scattered among the *"goyim"* (nations). The Hebrew word *"goyim"* is equivalent to *"ethnos"* in Greek.

The people of those tribes became *"innumerable as the sand by the sea shore,"* and as *"innumerable as the stars of heaven."* They intermarried with the *"nations"* and essentially became those *"goyim"* among whom they were scattered. God prohibited them from returning to Judea and Jerusalem. However, He did say that the time will come when He would again bring them into a land where their enemies could not touch them. And with careful study, we all know that the Israelites had the gospel preached to them, and they were gathered into the **place** that Jesus said, *"I am going to prepare a **place** for you"* where their enemies could not conquer them (the kingdom which is spiritual and unseen).

In order to understand this verse (indeed, the whole Bible), it is necessary to understand that when God called all of the Israelites out of Egypt, He gave them a covenant. Fast-forwarding through time, Solomon, the son of David became king and he allowed his foreign wives to lead him into idolatry. Because of his sinfulness, God *"rent"* ten of the tribes away from Solomon's son. They are always referred to in scriptures as the Israelites. It was only the tribe of Judah (inclusive of some from Benjamin and Levi) who were called *"Jews,"* and that only when they were taken captive into Babylon, many decades after the Israelites were taken captive by the Assyrians and ceased to be in a covenant relationship with God. The *"Jews"* were told to return to Jerusalem and rebuild the temple. They continued in a covenant relationship with God. They were rebellious also, so God destroyed them by the Romans in 66 A.D. – 70 A.D.. He gathered the Israelites (along with the remnant believing Judeans) into His kingdom in the first century A.D. thereby ceasing His covenant relationship with the house of Judah and making a **new covenant with the WHOLE house of Israel**.

Later, I will get more detailed about this subject, for if one does not understand these things from what we call the *"new testament,"* he will never be able to understand this verse, nor any of the fulfillments of the prophecies of the Bible. It is that critical.

Just one short observation here and I shall move on to the last clause in v-14. Jesus *"came to his own and his own received him not."* That was the **Judahites**. Jesus' purpose in coming in the flesh was to save *"the lost sheep of the house of Israel"* (not the house of Judah).

Jesus said, *"and then shall the end come."* The word *"then"* shows a sequential thing. The *"end"* could not occur before those other things had occurred. It should be carefully observed that whenever the word *"end"* occurs in the Bible that it does not mean the same thing in every place that it occurs. What *"end"* is in view here? The definition of the Greek word from which we get the word *"end"* is defined by Strong's as …

> *"Telos (tel-os); from a primary tello (to set out for a definite point or goal); properly, the point aimed at as a limit, i.e. (by implication) the conclusion of an act or state (termination)."*

Remember that we must stay within the context of a word in order to determine its meaning. The context here is Jesus speaking to four of his apostles – Peter, Andrew, James and John. He was on the Mount of Olives, shortly after he had left the Herodian temple for the last time and shortly before his arrest, mock trial and crucifixion. His apostles had asked him two questions and he was answering one of them. The question and response under consideration here was "***when*** *shall these things be (happen)*" [v-3]. The "*things*" of which they were asking were the tearing down of all of the buildings of the temple. Notice very carefully that the apostles asked "*when?*" and Jesus was telling them things that they could expect before the "*end*" of the tearing down of all of the temple buildings that were connected with the temple in Jerusalem.

The key to understanding the time element of **when** the **end** was to occur of which Jesus answered their query, is to be found in such statements as "***Ye*** *shall hear of wars and rumors of wars*" [v-6], and "*Then they shall deliver **you** up to be afflicted and shall kill **you**,*" and "***Ye*** *shall be hated of all nations for my name's sake*" [v-9], and jumping ahead one verse, "*When therefore **ye** shall see the abomination of desolation spoken of by Daniel the prophet*" [v-15]. The "*ye*" and "*you*" of these contextual verses were the apostles of Jesus, while they were still alive, in the 1st century A.D..

One cannot read those contextual verses and "*honestly*" say that the "*end*" that was under consideration was none other than the end of the old covenant (the Mosaic covenant) in the 1st century A.D.. The only Israelites that were at that time still in a covenantal relationship with God was the house of Judah (for the house of Israel had ceased to be God's people in the 8th century B.C. when they were taken captive by the Assyrians and God divorced them). Of the buildings of the Herodian temple in Jerusalem, God was going to cause that not one stone would be left standing upon another. Jesus told the apostles that at least some of them would see at least part of it. Jesus' answer was more than the destruction of the physical stone buildings of the temple. It was the "*end*" of the marriage covenant that God had with the house of Judah. When the Romans destroyed all of the buildings in 66 A.D. to 70 A.D., the "*end*" of God's covenantal relationship with the house of Judah occurred and as a nation they ceased to exist. A new covenant was to take its place with a renewed people as He gathered them together from the *"four corners of the earth"* from whence He had scattered them under the Assyrians eight centuries before [Jeremiah 31:31]. I shall discuss more of this as we move through our study. In the meantime, if you have questions or disagreements, go back and study very carefully all of the prophets of the *"old testament,"* for they tell exactly all the things that Jesus was foretelling in these verses. One cannot understand the *"new testament"* without a proper understanding of the *"old testament."* **It is utterly impossible!**

> It should be abundantly clear that the *"__end__"* of which Jesus was speaking occurred in the 1st century A.D. and is not an *"end"* that will occur in our time or to a future generation.

> *"When __ye__ therefore shall see the abomination of desolation, spoken of by Daniel the prophet, stand in the holy place, (whoso readeth, let him understand:)"* [Matthew 24:15].

This particular verse has given writers more problems than most of the verses of the Bible. There are as many various interpretations, or should I say *"opinions"* as to the meaning of this verse as there are people who write about it. I think that it is necessary to look at this verse in reverse order to understand it. Recall that Jesus was speaking to his apostles. **He was not writing anything.** So, the expression, *"whoso __readeth__, let him understand,"* was written by Matthew. Jesus wrote nothing of which we have record except writing in the sand twice, and it has long since blown away. When the phrase *"whoso readeth (or heareth), let him understand"* is used in the Bible, it called attention to the fact that a person had to look very deeply and search out the real meaning – as the real meaning was not expressed superficially in what was said or written. So, we will look deeper in order to see what the real meaning was to the believers to whom Matthew wrote in the 1st century A.D..

Notice that the abomination of desolation stood in the holy place, not the Most Holy Place. To make an offering on the altar that was different from that which was commanded of God would be an idolatrous act. Where was the location of the altar in the tabernacle or temple?

> *"And he put the altar of burnt offering by the door of the tabernacle of the tent of the congregation, and offered upon it the burnt offering and the meat offering; as the LORD commanded Moses"* [Exodus 40:29].

There was a king, spoken of in Daniel 11, named Antiochus Epiphanes IV. He was the fourth ruler who was mentioned for the purposes of Daniel's writings. He was a very vile man, having **apostatized** from the ways of the three before him. He did many things that his predecessor kings did not do. I shall note some of them later. He was the one of whom Daniel wrote as doing something in the temple that caused the desolation of the temple. God did not tolerate unclean sacrifices. Antiochus did just that in the holy place. It was an abomination. God deserted the temple at that point. The phrase concerning Daniel's writing could well be translated as *"The idol of the desolator"* or *"The idol that causeth desolation."*

The **immediate** adulteration of the holy place was caused by Antiochus Epiphanes IV. His abomination of the temple was but a *"type"* of one that was to come in the 1st century A.D.. Jesus told his apostles that **they** would see the *"antitype,"* like the one of which Daniel spoke. Daniel was not speaking directly of the abomination of the Herodian temple in 66-70 A.D. and the destruction of the Judahites.

I will do something now that I usually refrain from doing. I will quote a long number of verses that deal with Antiochus Epiphanes IV (although his name is not mentioned). In the verse before we begin our quotation, Daniel spoke of the king who preceded Antiochus, whose name was Selenens. He only lived for twelve years and was killed, *"neither in anger, nor in battle,"* but was poisoned by a woman. Antiochus IV took his place.

"And in his estate shall stand up a vile person, to whom they shall not give the honor of the kingdom: but he shall come in peaceably, and obtain the kingdom by flatteries. 22 And with the arms of a flood shall they be overflown from before him, and shall be broken; yea, also the prince of the covenant. 23 And after the league made with him he shall work deceitfully: for he shall come up, and shall become strong with a small people. 24 He shall enter peaceably even upon the fattest places of the province; and he shall do that which his fathers have not done, nor his fathers' fathers; he shall scatter among them the prey, and spoil, and riches; yea, and he shall forecast his devices against the strong holds, even for a time. 25 And he shall stir up his power and his courage against the king of the south with a great army; and the king of the south shall be stirred up to battle with a very great and mighty army; but he shall not stand: for they shall forecast devices against him. 26 Yea, they that feed of the portion of his meat shall destroy him, and his army shall overflow: and many shall fall down slain. 27 And both these kings' hearts shall be to do mischief, and they shall speak lies at one table; but it shall not prosper: for yet the end shall be at the time appointed. 28 Then shall he return into his land with great riches; and his heart shall be against the holy covenant; and he shall do exploits, and return to his own land. 29 At the time appointed he shall return, and come toward the south; but it shall not be as the former, or as the latter. 30 For the ships of Chittim shall come against him: therefore he shall be grieved, and return, and have indignation against the holy covenant: so shall he do; he shall even return, and have intelligence with them that forsake the holy covenant. 31 And arms shall stand on his part, and they shall pollute the sanctuary of strength, and shall take away the daily sacrifice, and they shall place the abomination that maketh desolate. 32 And such as do wickedly against the covenant shall he corrupt by flatteries: but the people that do know their God shall be strong, and do exploits. 33 And they that understand among the people shall instruct many: yet they shall fall by the

sword, and by flame, by captivity, and by spoil, many days. 34 Now when they shall fall, they shall be holpen with a little help: but many shall cleave to them with flatteries. 35 And some of them of understanding shall fall, to try them, and to purge, and to make them white, even to the time of the end: because it is yet for a time appointed. 36 And the king shall do according to his will; and he shall exalt himself, and magnify himself above every God, and shall speak marvelous things against the Gods, and shall prosper till the indignation be accomplished: for that that is determined shall be done. 37 Neither shall he regard the God of his fathers, nor the desire of women, nor regard any God: for he shall magnify himself above all. 38 But in his estate shall he honour the God of forces: and a God whom his fathers knew not shall he honour with gold, and silver, and with precious stones, and pleasant things. 39 Thus shall he do in the most strong holds with a strange God, whom he shall acknowledge and increase with glory: and he shall cause them to rule over many, and shall divide the land for gain. 40 And at the time of the end shall the king of the south push at him: and the king of the north shall come against him like a whirlwind, with chariots, and with horsemen, and with many ships; and he shall enter into the countries, and shall overflow and pass over. 41 He shall enter also into the glorious land, and many countries shall be overthrown: but these shall escape out of his hand, even Edom, and Moab, and the chief of the children of Ammon. 42 He shall stretch forth his hand also upon the countries: and the land of Egypt shall not escape. 43 But he shall have power over the treasures of gold and of silver, and over all the precious things of Egypt: and the Libyans and the Ethiopians shall be at his steps. 44 But tidings out of the east and out of the north shall trouble him: therefore he shall go forth with great fury to destroy and utterly to make away many. 45 And he shall plant the tabernacles of his palace between the seas in the glorious holy mountain; yet he shall come to his end, and none shall help him. [Daniel 11:21-44].

That was the man who offered an unclean pig upon the altar in the temple where God met with humankind, who also spread swine's blood throughout the temple. Thereby, the temple became unclean and God left it – it became desolate. Apparently that was the *"abomination that made desolate"* that became a *"type"* of what was to come as the *"antitype"* in the 1st century A.D..

Note that what is stated is not that an unclean animal was offered on the altar in the last half of the 1st century A.D., but that there was someone who "***stood***" in the holy place that was not supposed to be there.

The following is a quote from a yet unpublished work that is copyrighted by Francis A. Beffert. It is printed here by his permission. If you would like to use it, you need to obtain his permission. His email address is bet.fab@frontier.com .

> *"To properly see the picture that Jesus was presenting, we must consider the accounts of Matthew and Luke as one. Some see the 'abomination of desolation" as being identified by Luke as "Jerusalem surrounded by armies;" however, this is not the case. If the Roman legions surrounding the city was the 'abomination of desolation,' how were the faithful expected to flee a city that had become surrounded by an enemy force, as mandated by the following verses? Is not the purpose of surrounding a city during a siege to prevent those who are inside from escaping? The record of Josephus supports this objection, as he records the fate of those who attempted to flee the city. He stated that a deserter from the city was found to have swallowed gold before escaping the city; as a result, all those who came out of the city were disemboweled in search of such treasure. Josephus states that 2,000 such people were killed in a single night (<u>Josephus</u>: Wars, 5.13.4).*

*"While the 'abomination of desolation' and 'Jerusalem being surrounded by armies' are closely associated, they are not one and the same. The phrase, 'abomination of desolation' is a Hebrew idiom that means 'the abomination that maketh desolate' or 'the abomination that bringeth desolation' – indicating cause and effect. What Matthew was stating is that the temple would be subjected to an abomination – a foul or detestable thing – and that the 'detestable thing' would bring, or be responsible for, its desolation (destruction). While Luke's account clearly states that the desolation would come at the hands of the armies that surround the city, this is not the 'detestable thing.' The 'detestable thing' was that which caused the desolation to take place, just as Daniel stated that the destruction would come on the wings of abomination (9:27) – the destruction was brought on by the abomination. Many scholars refer to Josephus' record of the destruction of the city and point to the Roman desecration of the temple **after** the city fell at the 'abomination/detestable thing.' However, this cannot be the 'detestable thing,' as the detestable thing must precede the desolation. The cause must precede the consequence.*

"We find the answer portrayed in the record of Josephus. The Jewish rebels that controlled the city of Jerusalem consisted of three factions – the Zealots under Eleazar, the band of John of Gischala, and the band of Simon, son of Giora. These three factions warred with one another for control of the city. Eleazor and his Zealots finally entrenched themselves in the temple and turned it into a battleground. This defilement of the temple took place prior to Titus surrounding the city.

"After a desert march from Egypt, Titus arrived at Caesarea where he organized his forces. Meanwhile civil strife in Jerusalem had reached a new climax when another faction was bred within a faction, like some raving beast, preying on its own flesh. Eleazar, who had caused the Zealots to withdraw into the

sacred precincts, could not stand submission to John (of Gischala), a tyrant younger than himself. And so he seceded with a considerable number of Zealots, seizing the inner court of the temple. They were well supplied, but with fewer numbers than John's, and they confined themselves to their retreat, where they could easily repel his attacks. Although he lost heavily, John, in his rage, made continual assaults on them, and the temple was defiled with the slaughter.

"Then there was Simon, son of Giora, who was master of the upper and larger part of the lower city. He attacked John with greater vigor, seeing that John was also assailed by Eleazar from above. But John had the same advantage over Simon that Eleazar had over John. From this superior height he easily repelled attacks from below with hand weapons, reserving his machines for hurling projectiles against the part above him.

"The missiles shot by catapults, stone throwers, and 'quick fires' flew all over the temple, killing priests and worshippers at the very alter itself. For despite war, the sacrifices went on, and those who had journeyed from all over the world to worship there, sprinkled the altar with their own blood.

"The three warring camps regularly rushed out and burned each other's food supplies. Thus the area around the temple became a mass of ruins, and great stores of grain, which would have supplied the besieged for years, were destroyed, and the city would fall to self-imposed famine. Terrorized by the bloody contentions of the three factions, many prayed that the Romans might come and deliver them from the internal strife. Day after day the factions fought, each party devising new ways to destroy the other" (<u>Josephus</u>, *The Essential Writings; 1988; pg. 329-330).*

"But for John, when he could no longer plunder the people, he betook himself to sacrilege, and melted down many of the sacred utensils, which had been given to the temple; and also many of the vessels which were necessary for such as ministered about holy things ... he emptied the vessels of that sacred wine and oil which the priests kept to be poured on the burnt offerings, and which lay in the inner court of the temple, and distributed among the multitude, who, in their anointing themselves and drinking, used (each of them) about an hin of them; and here I cannot but speak my mind, and what the concern I am under dictates to me, and it is this: I suppose that had the Romans made any longer delay in coming against those villains, the city would either have been swallowed up by the ground opening up upon them, or been overflowed by water, or else been destroyed by such thunder as the country of Sodom perished by, for it had brought forth a generation of men much more atheistical than were those that had suffered such punishments; for by their madness it was that all the people came to be destroyed" (Josephus: Wars:5.13.6).

*"The wars and dissention of these factions is the "abomination that brings desolation,' and is the 'sign' of Jesus' **presence** in judgment upon those who pierced him and slew the prophets. This internal strife would desecrate the **temple and herald the end of the Jewish age**, which would be finalized by the Roman legions that would surround the city.*

"Josephus records that Titus, with Josephus as his emissary, encouraged the city to surrender, but those bands of rebels would have none of it. Josephus clearly stated that it was those brigands who insured the destruction of the city and its temple, as Titus desired no such end.

"Titus, anxious to preserve the city from destruction, sent Josephus to negotiate with the Jews in their native tongue" (Josephus: The Essential Writings; 1988; pg. 345).

"For there was a certain ancient oracle of those men, that the city should be taken and the sanctuary burnt, by right of war, when a sedition should invade the Jews and their own hands should pollute the temple of God. Now while these Zealots did not (quite) believe these things, they made themselves the instruments of their accomplishment" (<u>Josephus:</u> Wars; 4.6.2).

"... for I venture to affirm, that the sedition destroyed the city, and the Romans destroyed the seditions ... so that we may justly ascribe our misfortunes on our own people (<u>Josephus:</u> Wars; 5.6.1).

"To insure that the inhabitants of the city would fight to the death, the Jewish leaders employed false prophets to make proclamations, assuring them of God's deliverance.

"Now there was then a great number of false prophets suborned by the tyrants to impose on the people, who denounced this to them, that they should wait for deliverance from ; and this was in order to keep them from deserting, and that they might be buoyed up above fear and care by such hopes" (<u>Josephus</u>; Wars; 6.5.2).

"How one choses to view the details of this verse will not alter the circumstances or the end result. The event would take place in the lifetime of the apostles, as they are told that they would see it unfold. The event would result in the total destruction of the temple complex and the city by the armies of Rome. While the Roman legions would be the hammer of God, it was their own "detestable" actions that insured its end."

Continuing our study in v-15, seemingly we find that the word *"abomination"* referred especially to such **<u>idolatry only as was perpetrated by apostates</u>** from God.

*"And he did that which was evil in the sight of the LORD, **after the abominations of the heathen**, whom the LORD cast out before the children of Israel. For he built up again the high places which Hezekiah his father had destroyed: and he reared up altars for Baal and made a grove, as did Ahab king of Israel; and worshipped all the host of heaven, and served them. And he built altars in the house of the LORD, of which the LORD said, in Jerusalem will I put my name. And he built altars for all the host of heaven in the two courts of the house of the LORD. And he made his sons go through the fire, and observed times, and used enchantments, and dealt with familiar spirits and wizards; he wrought much wickedness in the sight of the LORD, to provoke him to anger. And he set a graven of the grove that he had made in the house, of which the Lord said to David, and to Solomon his son, in this house, and in Jerusalem, which I have chosen out of all tribes of Israel, will I put my name for ever"* [2 Kings 21:2-7].

*"And the high places that were before Jerusalem which were on the right hand of the mount of corruption, which Solomon the king of Israel had builded for Ashtoreth the **abomination** of the Zidonians, and for Chemosh the **abomination** of the Moabites, and for Milcom the **abomination** of the children of Ammon, did the king **defile**"* [2 Kings 23:13].

Josephus (B.J., 4:6, sec. 3) referred to the Judahites traditions that the temple would be destroyed *"if **domestic** hands should first pollute it."* The verses that could apply to Jesus' teaching in this verse about the *"abomination of desolation"* are the following verses.

*"And he shall confirm the covenant with many for one week; and in the midst of the week he shall cause the sacrifice and the oblation to cease, and for the **overspreading of abominations** he shall **make it desolate**, even until the consummation, and that determined shall be poured upon the desolate"* [Daniel 9:27].

*"And arms shall on his part, and they shall pollute the sanctuary of strength, and shall take away the daily sacrifice, and they shall place the **abomination that maketh desolate**"* [Daniel 11:31].

*"And from the time that the daily sacrifice shall be taken away, and the **abomination that maketh desolate** set up, there shall be a thousand two hundred and ninety days"* [Daniel 12:11].

The Lord alludes to those verses, which in Matthew 24:15 is *"the abomination of desolation,"* as the sign of Jerusalem's coming destruction. Daniel makes the ceasing of the sacrifice and obligation the preliminary to it. Jewish rabbis considered the prophecy fulfilled when the Judeans erected an idol altar, described as *"the abomination of desolation"* in 1 Maccabees 1:54; 6:7. This was necessarily followed by the profanation of the temple under the old covenant person, Antiochus Epiphanes. He built an idolatrous altar on the altar of burnt offering to Jupiter Olympius, and dedicated the temple to him, and offered swine's flesh.

The bringing of the idolatrous, Roman image crowned standards into the temple, where they were set over the East gate, and sacrificed to, upon the destruction of Jerusalem under the Roman Titus, 37 years after Jesus' prophecy in 70 A.D., **is not enough to meet the requirements of the term *"abomination,"* unless it were shown that the Judeans shared in the idolatry**. Perhaps the Zealots perpetrated some abomination that was to be the sign of the nation's ruin. They had taken possession of the temple, and having made a **secular** country fellow, Phannias, their high priest (who was not a descendant of Aaron), they made a mockery of the sacred rites of the law. Some such desecration within the city, *"in the holy place,"* coinciding with Cestius Gallus' encampment outside, was the sign foretold by Jesus. Noting it, the believers fled from the city to Pella and the caves of the mountains, and all escaped, we are told. There is no other fulfillment in our future – that event prior to 70 A.D. was the final and complete fulfillment. Jesus said that the disciples would live to see it. Are they still alive, being about 2,000 years old at this present time?

Some of the apostles of Jesus would see those Judean Zealots kill the legitimate high priest and put an imbecile in his place, one who was not a descendant of Aaron and could not offer the sacrifices that a legitimate high priest could and did offer. Therefore, God deserted the temple. It served no purpose for Him after that and He had the Romans destroy it along with the Judahites between 66 A.D. and 70 A.D..

"Then let them which be in Judaea flee into the mountains" [Matthew 24:16].

The land of Palestine that was inherited by the Israelites, consisted primarily of the northern providence that was named Galilee, the central province that was named Samaria, and the southern province that was called Judea.

The Israelites from Samaria had been removed by the Assyrians many centuries before Jesus took on biological form. Galilee still had people to whom Jesus himself had pronounced judgment upon them for refusing to believe in him. Judea had more of the original Israelites (Judahites, descendants of Jacob) than the other two provinces because after their captivity in Babylon for seventy years, they came back and rebuilt the temple. The people from that group are usually referred to as *"Jews,"* and the unbelieving were destined for destruction by the Romans in 66 A.D. – 70 A.D..

It is noteworthy to understand that Jesus was instructing the Judeans who were believers who were living (or visiting there at the feast days) in the province of Judea to flee to the mountains when they saw *"the abomination that maketh desolate that was spoken by Daniel the prophet"* (discussed in the previous verse). Again, note that this was **not** the Roman army entering into the temple – the exodus of the believers from Judea was to happen many months before the Romans ultimately surrounded the city of Jerusalem. If they waited till the Romans built their own wall around the city (which they did **in three days** to keep people from either entering or leaving), they could not have escaped – period.

If the history lessons that I have received are correct, the Roman Vespasian had come from Rome into Palestine all of the way to Judea, engaging in battle as he went through the land. His intention was to invade Jerusalem, but about that time the Roman Caesar died and Vespasian went north through the land of Palestine, exited it and went back to Rome and became one of the Caesars. Shortly thereafter, he commissioned Titus, a Roman General, to finish the job and go to Judea and take the city of Jerusalem, which he did between 66 A.D. – 70 A.D..

Now the important thing is to note that most people in the 21st century want to say that this referred to the people in Jerusalem when the Romans surrounded the city. But Jesus was very plain here. It was the people in **Judea**, not Jerusalem, that were to flee to the mountains. Of course, that included Jerusalem, but the admonition was to all of the believers throughout the entire province of Judea.

It is interesting that they were to escape to the mountains from any place in the land of Judea in which they were abiding. From Jerusalem, that would mean *"down,"* for Jerusalem was in the top of the mountains. That is why the Bible describes journeys in such terms as *"down from Jerusalem"* (if they were in Jerusalem – Acts 8:26), and *"up to Jerusalem"* if they were anywhere in Judea and going to Jerusalem – Acts 15:2.

In many places in history, it is stated that the believers in Judea (including those in Jerusalem) did indeed flee to the mountains (or to the area of Pella) and not a single believer perished in the onslaught that was brought on by the Romans. They listened to what Jesus had said and **did not** *"let that day overtake them as a thief in the* **NIGHT***."*

*"But ye, brethren, **are not** in darkness, that that **DAY** should overtake you as a thief"* [1 Thessalonians 5:4].

It did overtake the **unbelievers** as a thief in the night, as the avenues of escape were forever closed. They perished in the invasion of the Romans. Remember, that was for the 1st century A.D. people, not for us in the 21st century. If Jerusalem is ever again destroyed by the Romans, the people of other countries are not admonished to escape to the mountains. Why would I, living in America, want to go to the Judean mountains just because Rome decided to invade Judea today?

"Let him which is on the housetop not come down to take any thing out of his house" [Matthew 24:17].

It was a custom in 1st century Palestine to build houses with flat roofs, so that people could go up on top for things like prayer, if they wanted to be by themselves. We have an example of that when Peter went up on the house top to pray around meal time.

*"On the morrow, as they went on their journey, and drew nigh unto the city, Peter went up upon **the housetop** to pray about the sixth hour"* [Acts 10:9].

Some teach that there were stairs leading from the roof to the ground outside of the house – others deny that. However, that is almost irrelevant to the instruction. The primary point was **hurry** as the time would be so short that to fill up a back-pack would take more time than they had, and if they delayed, they would be caught and killed or become slaves of their enemy *("like a* thief *in the night")*. The instructions from Jesus were *"run for your lives, as quickly as you can, to the caves of the mountains for safety."* Does the song mean anything here, which originated with a thought in the old covenant, *Flee as a Bird to the Mountains?"*

"Neither let him which is in the field return back to take his clothes" [Matthew 24:18].

Jesus was not implying that the worker in the field, the farmer or the gleaner, was naked. Again, as in the preceding verse, he was instructing them as to the urgency of fleeing to the caves of the mountains and hiding from the approaching armies (plural). Like an emergency when one is caught in a burning house, flee with only the shirt on your back – just go and forget those things that are behind. The clothes that are referred to here are the outer garments, such as would be laid aside while one worked. Today, we would say, *"Forget your back-pact – run, run, run!"* Jesus himself said …

"The life is more than meat, and the body is more than raiment" [Luke 12:23].

There probably arc also *"spiritual applications"* to those verses, or at least some things about which are worthy to think very seriously. Consider that Jesus was speaking to Jews, the old *"Mosaic House"* to which they were still connected, and did not have anything for them any more; it was **immediately** passing away with the destruction of the temple and their way of life at the setting that Jesus had set before them, to happen in 66 A.D. to 70 A.D.. Also, any temporary **clothing** (covering of sins on a temporary basis?) that they had was to disappear and they were to be totally clothed with the Christ, clothing that would be permanent and never wear out. They were not to think about the physical things, but rather the spiritual things. Why?

"While we look not at the things which are seen, but at the things which are not seen: for the things which are seen are temporal; but the things which are not seen are eternal" [2 Corinthians 4:18].

Does that not also apply to us in the 21st century? In one of his parables, Jesus said that the *"field"* was the world (of the Jews). Can we make any spiritual application to the field in this verse?

> *"But woe to those who are pregnant and to those who are nursing babies in those days"* [Matthew 24:19].

In 66 A.D. the Romans and other nations' armies would set their feet in Judea with the intent of putting down the rebellion that the Zealot Judeans had initiated. The end was to be the complete destruction of the Mosaic system and the fall of the temple, of which there would not be left one stone upon another, so utter destruction. It thus ended in 70 A.D.. What of the people who were believers in Jesus?

They were told to immediately flee to the mountains, probably not any mountain that was close to where they were, but as far as they could get, not necessarily for protection, but probably more for the secrecy of the caves wherein they could dwell safely till the war was over.

The previous verses tell of the urgency of leaving Judea and fleeing and how fast they were to leave, not even to get some extra clothes, or return to their houses from the working fields, but immediately leaving the area, lest they be caught and become slaves or killed.

It was not to be a pleasant time. Really, it never is in time of war. A woe was pronounced upon the women who were pregnant. It is fairly easy for a man to run. It is much more difficult for a woman to run, but almost impossible for a pregnant woman to run. So, we should be able to see why a woe was pronounced upon the pregnant woman.

Another thing that would slow a woman down is having a baby that she had to carry. Maybe a lot of things had to be considered in such cases. If the mother of a baby had to flee so fast from her surroundings, it would not only slow her journey by having to carry the baby, but it would also be treacherous in that the baby would probably be crying and give away her secrecy in their flight. Also, she would have to stop occasionally and feed the infant, which would slow her fleeing from her home.

Are you getting the picture? All haste had to be made when the armies began their trek into Judea, and anything that would slow anyone was considered unwise or a warning of the dangers associated with whatever was a necessity to carry along (like one's baby). The next verse gives a little hope in getting some help for their flight away from the armies.

<u>Adam Clarke</u>, in his commentary, recorded the following …

> *"For such persons are not in a condition to make their escape; neither can they bear the miseries of the siege, Joseph says the houses were full of women and children that perished by the famine; and that the mothers snatched the food even out of their own children's mouths. See War, b.5c.10. But he relates a more horrid story than this, of one Mary, the daughter of Eliezar, illustrious for her family and riches, who, being stripped and plundered of all her goods and provisions by the soldiers, in hunger, rage, and despair, killed and boiled her own sucking child, and had eaten one half of him before it was discovered. This shocking story is told, WAR.b.6c.3, with several circumstances of aggravation."*

"But pray ye that your flight be not in the winter, neither on the Sabbath day" [Matthew 24:20].

The previous verse pronounced some *"woes"* on some of the people who were trying to escape the advance of the Roman army between 66 A.D. and 70 A.D.. However, this verse begins with the word *"but,"* showing a contrast. There was no woe on the people who were allowed to escape, but in order to escape the suddenness of the path of destruction, the believing Judeans had to have favorable conditions. Two are mentioned here, for which they must have prayed.

According to some, this chapter is dealing with the end of planet earth. If such is the case, why would anyone pray that it not be winter-time or on the Sabbath day? If all ended in the *"twinkling of an eye,"* how could there be winter or especially a Sabbath day?

In order to understand this verse by itself and also in the context, it is first necessary to understand who the *"ye"* were to whom Jesus was speaking. Was it not Peter, Andrew, James and John? Indeed it was. He was not speaking to you and me in the 21st century A.D.. Second, we need to understand that it was to be a *"flight."* The original word means to *"flee,"* or an *"escape."* One cannot *"escape"* if he is not already in danger. If one was in danger, then in order to *"be saved"* he had to flee or run for his life. That is what the disciples of pre-70 A.D. had to do in order to save their lives. The disciples that watched and observed the sign that Jesus gave, indeed did escape by fleeing to the caves of the mountains when the Romans and other armies conquered Judea and destroyed Jerusalem between 66 A.D. and 70 A.D.. Neither this verse nor this chapter has anything to do with us today in the 21st century.

The word *"winter"* comes from a Greek word that is translated in the <u>King James Version</u> by such wording as *"tempest, foul weather and winter."* The suddenness of the descent of the Roman army would necessitate the **immediate** fleeing of the believers. Immediately! Therefore, a storm would have hindered that escape and they would have been caught in the path of the Roman army and probably killed. So, the disciples were to *"pray"* that there was no storm when they had to flee so suddenly. Some did so pray and were allowed to escape and be saved from the destruction of the house of Judah.

The same would be true of their trying to escape on the Sabbath day. There were probably at least three reasons why the Sabbath day would not have been a day for them to try to flee.

➢ If some were inside of the gates to Jerusalem, the gates were closed and it would have made an exit very difficult. Knowing how fast the Roman army surrounded the city, it is no wonder how Jesus even talked about just one day.

- ➢ As Judeans, they were commanded not to go over *"a Sabbath days journey"* (which was about 7/8 of one mile). Fleeing their place of safety to the caves of the mountains would require a journey that exceeded that.
- ➢ See the next verse for the third reason for the believing Judeans of the 1st century to so pray.

"For then shall be great tribulation, such as was not since the beginning of the world to this time, no, nor ever shall be" [Matthew 24:21].

Those words of Jesus truly began to take on **significant meaning** to us in the 21st century who have been taught that the things of Matthew 24 are either happening now or will happen in our near future, or some yet distant time. Some people weave a strange web with such **mis**understanding in the other doctrines that they teach. The teaching about the **great tribulation** is one such teaching that sets the understanding of many in opposition to the teaching of Jesus. Let us examine it.

Notice that this verse begins with the word *"for,"* which comes from the Greek word *"gar,"* which primarily means *"because."* So, our understanding of the previous verse should become clearer as we understand why people were praying not to have their flight delayed when the Romans entered the territories of Galilee and Judea. Why? – because there was to be a *"great tribulation,"* and they wanted away from the cities of Judea. Now, we should be honest with ourselves and understand that this flight was to happen in the days of the early disciples between 66 A.D. and 70 A.D.. The next word is *"then,"* showing that it was consecutive, not thousands of years between. The time was identified. **It was *then*,** not 2,000 years in the future (in our time or in our future). It was the time for the believing Judeans to flee the arrival of the Roman army in the 1st century A.D.. As Paul said,

*"For **it is time** for judgment to begin with the household of God; and if it begins with **us** first …"* [1 Peter 4:17].

The *"mega pressure"* – the *"great tribulation"* – was to come on the Judeans during the 1ˢᵗ century A.D.. It is not something that is to happen in our lifetimes or in our future. The preachers who teach you such are twisting the words of the Messiah. How serious is it to twist and stretch what Jesus said? Well, I would not desire to be the one who did it. But, notice how it is twisted.

When the Roman army entered the territory, the believers were to immediately flee. Why? Because there was to be **the** great tribulation. It was to come upon the 1ˢᵗ century believers. Jesus further emphasized that it was upon **them** by stating that such great tribulation had never occurred before and **it would never happen again**. But you know what? The teachers today, in order to frighten you (whether you understand what Jesus said or not), tell you it did not happen in the 1ˢᵗ century, but that there is a great**er** tribulation awaiting us. Now that flatly contradicts what Jesus said. He said that such would happen to the 1ˢᵗ century people (then) and that there never would be such *"great tribulation"* again – **EVER!** And it will not ever be!

Observe what was prophesied by Daniel …

> *"And **at that time** shall Michael stand up, the great prince which standeth for the children of thy people; and there shall be **a time of trouble**, such as **never was since there was a nation even to that same time**; and to that time thy people shall be delivered"* [Daniel 12:1].

One other thing before we move on, and that is that the *"world"* of this verse is the Israelite world, not the entire planet. That can be seen by the original prophet in Daniel 12:1 when he called it the **nation** of Israel.

Other scriptures could be introduced here, but simply understand that the great tribulation of which Daniel spoke and the same great tribulation of which Jesus spoke are the same great tribulation and it was fulfilled almost 2,000 years ago. It is not in our time, nor in our future. I shall deal with the time element later in our studies.

> *"And except those days should be shortened, there should no flesh be saved: but for the elect's sake those days shall be shortened"* [Matthew 24:22].

This verse is following the context of the entire chapter. Let us hit the highlights thus far:

[v-1] – *"His **disiples** came to him."*
[v-2] – *"Jesus said unto **them**."*
[v-3] – *"The **disciples** came unto him privately."*
[v-4] – *"Jesus answered and said unto **them**."*
[v-6] – *"**You** shall hear of wars and rumours of wars."*
[v-9] – *"**Then** they shall deliver **you** up to be afflicted."*
[v-15] – *"When **ye** therefore shall see the abomination of desolation."*
[v-20] – *"Pray **ye** that **your** flight be not in the winter."*

Even the following verse says, *"If any man shall say unto **you**…"*. As you can see, the context has always been showing that Jesus was speaking to his disciples, in the 1st century A.D., not to us in the 21st century A.D.. We can learn a lot of what Jesus wants us to know by interpreting the chapter in the 1st century setting, even learning some **principles** that can help us in the 21st century, but we can learn nothing that is correct if we try to make the things that Jesus said to his disciples almost 2,000 years ago, apply directly to us today in the 21st century. Let us review one verse in the midst of the context thus far.

> *"And woe unto them that are with child, and to them that give suck in **those days**"* [v-19].

Those days came up again in this verse that we are now studying. ***Those days*** would be shortened because of the elects sake. ***Those days*** are not something in our day and time or any future time. They were the days in the 1st century when the Roman army and other armies that joined them devastated Judea and destroyed the Herodian temple and the Judean religious economy forever. Accept what Jesus said to his apostles and do not let the religious teachers (doctors?) of today tell you that those things are in your lifetime. It is time for people to quit twisting, misapplying and misinterpreting the scriptures. If you are a young preacher, now is the time to seriously consider these things. It is most embarrassing to have to do it when you get older.

It has generally been taught that there was not a single believer in Jerusalem when it finally fell to the Romans. It would be very difficult to prove such. In fact, does this verse right here indicate that the siege ended so that believers could survive? All of the Judeans were not killed in the siege. There were about 99,000 carried away as captives. Where in the Bible does it say that there would be no believers among than number? Come on now – where? Pregnant?

The believers who watched closely what Jesus said, and heeded to obey him, certainly fled to the caves of the mountains for safety from the invading armies. What about those who got caught inside the gates? Or, what about the believers who were slowed down; such as the women with small babies or were expecting immediately? For the sake of such people, the siege was shortened and some of the *"flesh"* continued to live. That was God's plan and **prophecy**.

> *"Then if any man shall say unto you, lo, here is Christ, or there; believe it not"* [Matthew 24:23].

It becomes more evident in this verse that Jesus was speaking to his apostles in the 1st century, because today, if someone comes to you and says, *"Here is Christ,"* how many of you would believe it? Or better yet, how many of you would take it seriously? Or better yet, how many of you would laugh the person to ridicule? You know by now that Jesus came in the 1st century, not today as you read this.

Now to get more serious, notice again that Jesus said, *"… if any man shall say unto **you**."* The *"you"* were the apostles of the 1st century. You should be able to repeat or memorize this clause because Jesus was only talking to his four apostles, Peter, Andrew, James and John. That is all — four! It was possible for some to claim to be the Christ during the 1st century, and in fact, history does record that there were many who appeared then and claimed to be the Christ. So, the warning of Jesus to his apostles about the claim of some being the Christ during the 1st century A.D. was a valid warning. It was claimed and the apostles were warned not to believe it.

Now if you think that you have it all figured out, think about this. If the *"second coming"* of Jesus in 66 A.D. to 70 A.D. was to be in the same FORM as it was when he left his apostles, why did Jesus have to warn them of the imposters? They had been with him for over three years. Did they not recognize him? Was Jesus telling his apostles that the FORM of his return would be different? Indeed it would be.

For a study of the word *"Christ,"* it is to be noted that the Greek means *"Messiah,"* and the Hebrew means *"anointed."* Jesus was certainly the Israelite Messiah and he certainly was the highest anointed of God.

There was one dimension in the Bible that was described as a king. There were many kings.

There was a second dimension that was described as a priest. There were many priests.

As far as I have researched, there was **only one that was both king and priest** and his name was Melchizedek.

*"And Melchizedek **king** of Salem brought forth bread and wine; and he was the **priest** of the most high"* [Genesis 14:18].

Jesus was to be a priest after the order of Melchizedek, so he would also be a king.

"The LORD hath sworn, and will not repent, Thou art a priest for ever after the order of Melchizedek" [Psalms 110:4].

There was another dimension that was described as a prophet. There were many prophets.

There is only one in the Bible that was **all three**, altogether **a king, priest and prophet**, and that was Jesus, the son of God. He is the only one to fill all **three dimensions**. The third dimension deserves a lot of study, but that would require an entire book within itself. Maybe you would like to do some studying on that subject. If so, I would appreciate your feedback.

Do not prostitute this passage **from the 1ˢᵗ century** to our time in the 21ˢᵗ century.

"For there shall arise false Christs, and false prophets, and shall show great signs and wonders, insomuch that if it were possible, they shall deceive the very elect" [Matthew 24:24].

In the preceding verse, Jesus said, *"**if** any man shall say unto you, lo, here is Christ"* do not believe him. Notice carefully the word **if**. Possibly, someone would say to them that the Christ was either here or there, because there would be those who arose who were false Christs (more than one).

Now this study really begins, Jesus **did not say** that there would arise men who claimed to be Christs. He **said** that there would arise **false** Christs. There is a major difference.

The word *"false"* modifies the noun, which in this case was *"Christs."* That means that there were actually some people who were *"anointed"* of whom would be present during that forty year period of which we have spoken so many times. But, just because they were appointed by man or God did not make them perfect. A couple of examples can be used here, Balaam was a prophet of God, but he was a **false** person. He wanted to take money from the king of a country that was an enemy of Israel and curse Israel for the money by which he could profit. Yes, he was God's prophet but he was *"false."* There is nothing to indicate that anything he said was false as a prophet. The word *"false"* modifies the **person**, not what the person teaches. In light of how much the term is used today, it might interest you to know that the term *"false teaching"* does not accurately occur in the Bible. Do any of us know it all? Do we not all make mistakes? Are we not all in a learning process? Is not something that each of us think, something that we consider false in our teaching? Does that make us a *"false teacher"* when we are honest and really trying to know the truth? It most certainly does not – even if we teach something that is false. Of course, when one closes his mind to learning the truth when it is pointed out, that would make us a *"false"* person. Look around and consider what others are teaching, it might be the truth.

Peter is another example that we can use here. Peter **taught** that the gentiles were acceptable to God. That was not false teaching. However, when Peter was associating with gentile believers and certain Judeans came from Jerusalem, Peter played the **hypocrite** and withdrew from the gentile believers. That made Peter a **false** person, even though what he taught was not false, but the truth. I received the following from a good friend of mine.

> *"Concerning your examples of a false teacher(?), another one is in Philippians where Paul was in prison and his enemies were preaching the gospel for the purpose of causing him harm. What they taught evidently was right, even if for the wrong reason*

because Paul said in verse 18, 'But what does it matter? The important thing is that in every way, whether from false motives or true, Christ is preached. And because of this I rejoice.' They were false teachers(?) while teaching truth."

There were also going to be during that 1st century, forty year period, many prophets. Some of them would be *"false"* prophets, just like Balaam. Not necessarily that they taught anything that was false, but that they themselves would be false. I hope that these three examples are enough to show you what a *"false person"* is and is not. One can teach truth and yet he himself be false. During that 1st century, forty year period, there were prophets of God and others who were anointed of God. Some would be righteous and some would be false. The apostles were warned of the false prophets and the false anointed ones, and told not to listen to them.

The next time that you would like to withdraw your association from or excommunicate a brother who teaches something different from you, remember that you cannot use any verse in the Bible accusing him of *"false teaching"* for such terminology is not to be found.

How are we to determine whether those anointed ones and those prophets who are mentioned in this verse were real? Simple enough – they could perform supernatural things.

    "... and shall show great signs and wonders ...".

The word *"sign"* is translated in the <u>King James Version</u> as *"miracle, sign, token and wonder."* Those false people could not only do and show signs, but they were to show *"mega"* (great) signs. If they were that great, the believers would be tempted to believe them. That is why Jesus had to warn the apostles not to believe them. If those four apostles **knew** what *"form"* that Jesus would appear in 70 A.D., then they **knew** that the *"false"* ones was not he. Crazy reasoning is it not?

The Greek word that is translated as *"signs"* is *"semeion."* And is defined by <u>Strong's</u> as *"an indication, especially ceremonially or* **supernaturally.**" By definition, it is shown that those were indeed prophets and anointed ones of God. However, as we have pointed out, they were hypocrites and false people. They had the power from God to do supernatural things, and they chose to set forth false signs.

Spiritual Israel was the elect. They were God's chosen, selection, election. The signs and wonders were so powerful, so strong, so capable, so mighty, that if it were possible, the very chosen of God would be deceived. However, the elect were forewarned not to believe those false prophets and anointed ones.

Josephus represents the false Christs and false prophets that appeared as *"magicians and sorcerers."* He said that they led the people out into the deserts and promised to work miracles to deliver them [Antiq. B.20 chapter 8, section 6].

But it was not possible for the chosen spiritual Israelites to be deceived by anything, for it was all foretold by Jesus here in this setting. Now, some might have deceived themselves, but there was enough information showing exactly what to look for to understand when the **presence** (parousia) of Jesus and God would be there in the conquest of the natural Israelite system between 66 A.D. and 70 A.D. to keep the believers from being deceived.

Again, understand that the setting for the fulfillment of all those things was the first century A.D. and has nothing directly for us in the 21st century. Do not let *"false"* teachers today deceive you as to the plain teaching of Jesus here in this chapter.

"Behold I have told you before" [Matthew 24:25].

Having been forewarned, there was no excuse for the apostles and those whom they taught, to be deceived. Jesus had told them before all of those things happened. Both were to come to pass and they could be deceived, but exactly the things to look for to know when his **presence** (*parousia*) would be there in the destruction of natural Jerusalem were being told to the apostles **before** they came to pass. They were to listen and heed the pre-instructions of Jesus so they would not be deceived and led astray and lost.

You will notice again that Jesus is addressing some of the apostles when he used the word "*you.*" That would certainly make the application to a pre-70 A.D. fulfillment as all of the apostles were dead by or at that time (possibly John was still alive, according to some in secular history). To us, this chapter is only a history lesson of about 2,000 years ago. It is not teaching anything that will happen in our day and time (unless by principle).

> *"Wherefore if they shall say unto you, behold, he is in the desert; go not forth; behold, he is in the secret chambers; believe it not"* [Matthew 24:26].

The word *"they"* refers to the false anointed ones and false prophets that were previously mentioned. As noted previously, the *"you"* to whom Jesus was speaking, were the apostles. So, it is proper to conclude that some of those false anointed ones and false prophets would probably be speaking directly to the apostles.

It was previously mentioned that there were indeed false prophets who led people into the desert(ed) places, promising them deliverance. Jesus' warning was not for them to follow.

The Greek word *"tameiois"* means *"a chamber on the ground floor (generally used for storage or privacy)."* However, the **presence** (parousia) of Jesus would be seen in the power of the invading armies and the complete overthrow of the natural Judean system between 66 A.D. and 70 A.D.. His **presence** was not hidden in a private place. The **parousia**, or presence, of Jesus was in the 1st century A.D.. It has nothing to do with a coming of Jesus in the 21st century or later. The apostles were told *"believe it not."* When someone today tries to tell you that this chapter refers to our time or some future time, *"believe it not."*

> *"For as the lighting cometh out of the east, and shineth even unto the west; so shall also the coming of the Son of man be"* [Matthew 24:27].

Albert Barnes lived from 1798 to 1870. It is probable that his commentaries were written in the 1860's. They are referred to as <u>Barnes Notes</u>. The following is a quotation of what he and others thought two centuries ago about this verse.

> *[For as the lightning cometh out of the east...] This is not designed to denote the QUARTER from which he would come, but the MANNER. He does not mean to affirm that the "Son of man" will come from the "east," but that he will come in a rapid and unexpected manner, like the lightning. Many would be looking for him in the desert, many in secret places; but he said it would be useless to be looking in that manner, it was useless to look at any particular part of the heavens to know where the lightning would next flash. In a moment it would blaze in an unexpected part of the heavens, and shine at once to the other part. So rapidly, so unexpectedly, in so unlooked-for a quarter, would be his coming. See Luke 10:18; Zech. 9:14.*

> *[The coming of the Son of man] It has been doubted whether this refers to the destruction of Jerusalem, or to the coming at the day of judgment. For the solution of this doubt let it be remarked ...*

> *1. That those two events are the principle scenes in which our Lord said he would come, either in person or in judgment.*
> *2. That the destruction of Jerusalem is described as his coming – his act.*

3. *That these events – the judgment of Jerusalem and the final judgment in many respects greatly resemble each other.*
4. *That they "will bear," therefore to be described in the same language; and,*
5. *Therefore, that the same words often include BOTH events, as properly described by them.*

*The words had, doubtless, **<u>a primary reference to the destruction of Jerusalem</u>**, but they had, at the same time, such an amplitude of meaning as also to express his coming to judgment.*

Two centuries ago, those Bible scholars were wrestling with *"is there any separation between the judgment and the coming of Jesus?"* They were on the very brink of the connection as you can see from his quotation. Had he just looked more closely at one scripture regarding *"the judgment,"* he would have known that the *"coming"* and *"judgment"* of Jesus were to happen at the same time and also to happen in the 1st century A.D., not separating the *"coming"* of Jesus in the 70 A.D. destruction of Jerusalem by the Romans and his *"judgment"* upon the Judahites at the same time and place. Here is the scripture (and others teach the same thing).

*"For **<u>the time is come that judgment must begin</u>** at the house of God; and if it first begin at us, what shall the end be of them that obey not the gospel of God "* [1 Peter 4:17]?

Yes, indeed! As Barnes said, the words, doubtless, a **primary** reference to the destruction of Jerusalem in 70 A.D. and at the same time, meaning also to express his coming in judgment at the very same time. There is no separation of 2,000 years in either verse. They do not refer to our time or to a future time.

I am aware that such conclusions are upsetting to some because of traditions that have been handed down in the various religious circles in which we have been *"brought up."* I am sorry about that, but we need to be honest with ourselves and if we need to change the way that we understand something, then so be it. Let us be open-minded and be willing to learn and change with our growth. Or, maybe that is the real reason – we are not growing because we are not looking at things with which we differ.

"For wheresoever the carcass is, there will be the eagles be gathered together" [Matthew 24:28].

There are many good scholarly quotations that put the time of this illustration in the destruction of Jerusalem by the Romans in 70 A.D.. Here is one of them.

*"The sayings of Jesus contained in this verse most probably reflects a proverbial saying familiar to **the people of his day**. Its purpose is to refute the arguments of persons who claimed that the Son of Man (or Messiah) had already arrived, and that he could be found in such and such a place.*

"The Greek word used here for eagle may also mean "vulture" or "buzzard," which is also true for the word used for eagle in the Hebrew Old Testament. But the meaning of "vulture" is better suited to the context.

*"The argument of the parable and **its application is as follows:** Just as surely as vultures flock about a corpse, so the coming of the Son of Man will be **recognized** by everyone. Therefore to ask when or where he will make his appearance is a senseless and useless question. When it happens, there will be no doubt"* [UBS New Testament Handbook Series].

The context is plain enough if we will but look at it. As to how the apostles to whom Jesus was speaking would know **when** he was to make his **appearance** (presence = *parousia*) known was when the carcass (the dead body of the unbelieving Israelites in the destruction of

Jerusalem in 70 A.D.) appeared, and the vultures were **present** that preyed on the Judahite leftovers (the Romans who took everything and everyone from the temple and city that was not destroyed in the siege). The apostles would then know the day and hour that God and Jesus' **presence** (parousia) was there. That is the way that every eye could see the **parousia** of God and Jesus. That was the **when** and that was the **manner** in which they would **see** him.

The **manner** of the coming of Jesus in 66 A.D. to 70 A.D. was the same **manner** of the coming of God in the destruction of Egypt in old covenant times.

> *"The burden of Egypt. Behold, **the LORD rideth upon a swift cloud** and shall come into Egypt: and the idols of Egypt shall be moved at **His presence**, and the heart of Egypt shall melt in the midst of it"* [Isaiah 19:1].

God's **presence** was **seen** in the destruction of Egypt, but there was no physical bodily presence. His **presence** was seen in the army that He sent to destroy Egypt, and when the army destroyed Egypt, **everyone could see the presence** of God. In actuality, there was a civil rebellion in progress and Egyptian would fight against Egyptian, but the idea is that God was in control and He could be **seen** in the destruction of Egypt.

The usual Greek word for *"coming"* in the *"new testament"* is *"erchomai."* The word that is used with reference to Jesus' appearance is not *"erchomai,"* but **parousia**. Again, let me remind the reader that **parousia** means **presence.** As God's **presence** was seen in the destruction of Egypt, so Jesus' **presence** would be seen in the destruction of rebellious Judea between 66 A.D. to 70 A.D.. There was no bodily presence of God's **presence** in Egypt, and there was to be no bodily **presence** of Jesus' **presence** in the destruction of Jerusalem, which ended in 70 A.D.. There will be more proof to be considered in coming comments, so stay with me.

As we continue with the thought of the *"parousia"* (presence, **not coming**) of Jesus in the destruction of the rebellious Judahites in 66 A.D. to 70 A.D., we will look at one of the most controversial verses in the entire Bible.

> *"And when he had spoken these things, while they beheld, he was taken up; and a cloud received him out of their sight. And while they looked steadfastly toward heaven as he went up, behold, two men stood by them in white apparel; Which also said, Ye men of Galilee, why stand ye gazing up into heaven? This same Jesus, which is taken up from you into heaven, shall so come in like manner as ye have seen him go into heaven"* [Acts 1:9-11].

Sometimes, it is easier to understand what a verse is teaching by understanding what it is **not** saying. I think that such might be helpful in this case. I know that what I am about to say is touchy, but please give it some very careful consideration.

The *"angels"* that spoke to the apostles **did not** say, *"This same Jesus, which is taken up from you into heaven, shall so come in like **form** as ye have seen him go into heaven."* Yet that is the way that 99% of the people today want to interpret the passage. They want a physical, bodily **form**. Look closely now and understand what they **did say**. They were talking about the **manner** of Jesus' (return) parousia (**presence**), **not the form** in which he went away, and **not the form** in which he would *"return."*

The *"manner"* of Jesus' going into heaven was *"with the clouds,"* so his future parousia (**presence**) could be *"seen"* when he was seen *"with the clouds."* Does the Bible teach anything about Jesus and *"the clouds?"* Yes, it begins with the old covenant.

> *"I saw in the night visions, and, behold, one like the Son of man **came with the clouds** of heaven, and came to the Ancient of days,*

*and they brought him near before him, And there was given him dominion, and glory, and a kingdom, that all people nations, and languages, should serve him: his dominion is an **everlasting** dominion, which shall not pass away, and his kingdom that which shall not be destroyed"* [Daniel 7:13-14].

There seems to be some translation problems, or at least a lack of understanding (especially on my part) concerning some *"new testament"* passages that deal with *"the kingdom."* It will take much study to get all of the problems worked out. But one thing is sure. The **everlasting** kingdom of Jesus **was present and future** to the time that the apostle Peter wrote his second epistle. The following verse proves it. As you look at the verse, consider that Peter was speaking to believers who lived prior to 70 A.D.

> *"For so an entrance **shall be** ministered unto you abundantly into the everlasting kingdom of our Lord and Savior Jesus Christ"* [2 Peter 1:11].

The believers between 30 A.D. and 70 A.D. **were not in the everlasting kingdom** of Jesus. To deny this is but to deny that the Holy Spirit has told us the truth. I do not want to accuse him of that. Do you?

But, at the coming **parousia** (presence) of Jesus, they would enter into his **everlasting** kingdom. That would be in 70 A.D.. More will be forthcoming as we study other verses.

> *"Immediately after the tribulation of those days shall the sun be darkened, and the moon shall not give her light, and the stars shall from heaven, and the powers of the heavens shall be shaken"* [Matthew 24:29].

Again, if we are studying closely, we can see why Matthew 24 is probably the most controversial chapter in the Bible. For example, in this verse, Jesus mentions **THE** tribulation. The tribulation period that is taught throughout the *"new testament"* has been applied by man to many different periods of time. The real question is, *"Do we want to believe the time element that Jesus gave of* **THE** *tribulation, or do we choose not to believe him?"* I accept what he said, so let us look at the time element that he set forth here.

He said that *"the tribulation"* would occur after **those days**. To what time period were *"those days"* referring? Let us look again at the preceding verses. I will not go all of the way to verse one, showing conclusively that it was the time for people of the 1st century A.D., but we will go back a little.

> *"But pray ye that **your** flight be not in the winter, neither on the Sabbath day: 21. For **then** shall be **great tribulation** such as was not since the beginning of the world to this time, no, nor ever shall be. 22. And except **those days** should be shortened, there should no flesh be saved: but for the elect's sake those days shall be shortened. 23. Then if any man shall say unto **you**, Lo, here is Christ, or there, believe it not. 24. For there shall arise false Christs, and false prophets, and shall shew great signs and wonders insomuch that, if it were possible, they shall deceive the very elect. 25. Behold, I have told **you** before. 26. Wherefore if they shall say unto **you**, Behold, he is in the desert; go not forth; behold, he is in the secret chambers; believe it not. 27. For as the lightning cometh out of the east, and shineth even unto the west; so shall also the coming of the Son of man be. 28. For wheresoever the carcass is, there will the eagles be gathered together"* [Matthew 24:20-28].

It will be **immediately** noticed (did you notice how I used the word *"immediately?"*) that Jesus had already used the term *"great tribulation"* (v-21). And, it is plain for those who want to see and are not self-deceived that the **great tribulation** was so great that such greatness had never happened before and would never happen again as long as the planet stands. It is also to be noted that Jesus used the words "*you*" and "*yours*" four times even in these verses that **immediately** (did you notice how I used that word "*immediately?*") preceded this statement by Jesus. **Those days** were the days at the ending of the lives of the apostles to whom Jesus was speaking. The **you** were the apostles. **Those days** were the days that preceded the destruction by the Romans in 66 A.D. and 70 A.D.. The **greatest tribulation** that would ever happen, occurred in the 1st century A.D., not in our time, nor in any **immediate** future to us (did you notice how I used the word "*immediate?*") or any time that is distant (not immediate) in our future.

Now we need to look closely at the first word in the verse that we are studying, which is **immediately**. It is translated from the Greek word "*eutheos,*" which is defined as "*shortly, soon, forthwith, straightway, immediately, directly, i.e. at once.*" There is no room for 2,000 years in the word; therefore, knowing that the "*great tribulation*" was to happen before 70 A.D., the other things that are spoken of in this verse would happen "*immediately.*" They are not things that will happen in the 21st century or beyond. Do not let modern day preachers deceive you – accept it exactly as Jesus told his apostles; in this verse, about 2,000 years ago.

> "*That is, **immediately after these tribulations**, events will occur that "may be properly represented" by the darkening of the sun and moon, and by the stars falling from heaven. The word rendered "immediately" – eutheoos – means, properly, "straightway, immediately," Matthew 8:3; 13:5; Mark 1:31; Acts 12:10; then "shortly," 3 John 14. This is the meaning here. Such events would "shortly" or "soon" occur. In the fulfillment of the predictions they would be "**the next in order**," and would occur "before long." The term here requires us to admit that, in order to the fulfillment of the prophecy, it can be shown, or it actually happened, that things "did" **soon** occur "after the tribulations of those days" which would be "properly represented or described" by the images which the Savior employs*" **[Barnes' Notes].**

What are those things that were to *"immediately happen after those days"* and how was it possible? Here are the things that were to happen **immediately**.

> *"... the sun (shall)be darkened, and the moon shall not give her light, and the stars shall fall from heaven, and the powers of the heavens shall be shaken."*

Let it first be said that according to all of the scientific information that I have read, the smallest star is larger than the earth. How could **all** of the stars fall to the earth, when, if even one star hits the earth, the earth would cease to exist? Would not the same problem occur if it were possible for all of the stars to fall to the earth?

> *"And the stars of heaven fell unto the earth, even as a fig tree casteth her untimely figs, when she is shaken of a mighty wind"* [Revelation 6:13].

It should become **immediately** (I hope that it does not take people 2,000 years to figure this out) apparent that Jesus was using what we refer to as a figure of speech. This figure of speech is referred to as a *"hyperbole."* The origin of the word is Greek also, which means *"excess."* Here is the English definition:

> *"An exaggeration or overstatement intended to produce an effect **without being taken literally**, as: He was centuries old; she wept gallons of tears"* [The Reader's Digest Great Encyclopedic Dictionary].

Some people want to try to interpret everything literally, but such method of interpretation is not only unknown to the Bible but is utterly impossible. To try to understand these things **literally**, creates all sorts of problems. I shall point out some of them, besides more than one literal star hitting planet earth. This realm of thinking may be different from yours, but hang in there and let us look more closely at how Jesus really did use those terms.

The first thing that we should notice is that it is plain that God used such figurative language in the *"old testament."* The dream that Joseph had is a case in point.

> *"And he dreamed yet another dream, and told it to his brethren, and said, Behold, I have dreamed a dream more; and, behold, the **sun** and the **moon** and the eleven **stars** made obeisance to me. 10. And he told it to his father, and to his brethren: and his father rebuked him, and said unto him, what is this dream that thou hast dreamed? Shall I and thy mother and thy brethren indeed come to bow down ourselves to thee to the earth"* [Genesis 37:9-10].

Another thing is plain. Man is capable of understanding the meaning of figurative language. When Joseph told his brothers and father of his dream, which included the **sun, moon and stars** bowing down him, his father understood that he was not to interpret it **literally**, for the literal sun does not bow down to anyone. He understood that he represented the sun in the dream that his son experienced. He knew that it was figurative and **not literal** language. When we examine other scriptures, we can understand that figurative language is used and that such language **cannot** be interpreted **literally**.

> *"1. The burden **of Babylon**, which Isaiah the son of Amoz did see --- 5. They come from a far country, from the end of heaven, even the LORD, and the weapons of his indignations, **to destroy the whole land**. 6. Howl ye; for **the day of the LORD is at hand**; it shall come as a destruction from the Almighty --- 9. Behold, the day of the LORD cometh, cruel both with wrath and fierce anger, to lay the land desolate: and he shall destroy the sinners thereof out of it. 10. For the stars of heaven and the constellations thereof shall not give their light: **the sun shall be darkened** in his going forth, and the moon shall not cause her light to shine. 11.*

And I will punish the world for their evil, and the wicked for their iniquity, and I will cause the arrogancy of the proud to cease, and will lay low the haughtiness of the terrible" [Isaiah 13:1-11].

In this passage from the prophet Isaiah, we see again some figurative language. To adequately explain those verses, would take much writing. I shall only hit the highlights that will be necessary to help us understand what the passage of Matthew 24 means, when it is filled with figurative language (as is the series of verses in Isaiah). We see some more figurative language concerning the stars, but that does not seem to be as problematic as when the sun did not give forth light. Notice that there is nothing in that figurative language that said that the sun was destroyed. There was to be a time that (in figurative language) the sun would be darkened, i.e. it would not give its light. That figure of speech indicated that God's face of approval would not be seen. When such occasions have occurred at various times throughout the Bible, it has meant that there was **not a literal darkness** on the land, but that *"the day of the LORD was at hand."* That expression always denoted God's judgment on a nation or nations. Let that point sink deeply into your mind. *"The day of the LORD"* is always the wording to show God's **judgment** upon a nation or nations. In the above quotation, the day of the LORD was God's judgment upon the Judeans at the hand of the Babylonians about 586 B.C.. Such is stated in figurative language in the text and context. Even Babylon is mentioned to show what all of the many words and phrases were that occurred in the context. The *"world"* that was being destroyed was the *"world"* of the Judeans (commonly referred to as the *"Jews"*). The *"world"* **was not** planet earth. The word *"world"* is used many times in the Bible, so consider that when it is used, it had particular reference to a particular *"world,"* not the way that we use the word *"world"* as reference to planet Earth. When Babylon destroyed *"the whole land,"* it was the land of the Judeans, not the whole of the planet Earth.

*"The images used here **are not to be taken literally**. They are often employed by the sacred writers to denote "any great*

calamities." As the darkening of the sun and moon, and the falling of the stars, would be an inexpressible calamity, so any great catastrophe – any overturning of kingdoms or cities, or dethroning of kings and princes is represented by the darkening of the sun and moon, and by some convulsion of the elements" [Barnes' Notes].

It would take an entire book to deal adequately with how the sun, moon and stars are used figuratively in the Bible. We have already seen how they were **not literal** in the case of Joseph's dream, and how the **impossibility** of all of the stars **literally** falling to the earth, and we must understand that there is as much evidence in the Bible that shows that the moon is also not used in a literal sense, but is used as a figure of something. I will not go into detail now of the biblical, figurative use of the word *"moon."* Please do some research for yourself if you so desire. I have written a book about the stars, moon and the sun, called, The Heaven's Declare The Glory Of God which can be obtained at Amazon.com - just type in Ron McRay and it will immediately show up.

To the Bible student, *"the tribulation"* occurred in the 1st century A.D.. It was *"immediately"* after the great tribulation of the 1st century that the sun, moon and stars did not give light, so the darkness occurred in the 1st century A.D.. It can be easily understood that the terms are used in a figurative sense. Recall the following section of the passage in Isaiah that was previously quoted.

> *"1. The burden **of Babylon**, which Isaiah the son of Amoz did see --- 5. They come from a far country, from the end of heaven, even the LORD, and the weapons of his indignation, **to destroy the whole land**. 6. Howl ye; for **the day of the LORD is at hand**; it shall come as a destruction from the Almighty. --- 9. Behold, the day of the LORD cometh, cruel both with wrath and fierce anger, to lay the land desolate; and he shall destroy the sinners thereof out of it."*

In connection with the darkness of the sun, moon and the stars of this context, Isaiah said that *"the day of the LORD (was) at hand,"* When God sent the Babylonians to destroy the Judeans in *"old testament"* times, it was called *"the day of the LORD."* When the term *"the day of the LORD"* is mentioned in other places throughout the Bible, it always means a time of destruction by some other nation. Putting both the darkness that was brought on by God and *"the day of the LORD"* together, we can understand better the following passage.

> *"The sun shall be turned into darkness, and the moon into blood, before that great and notable day of the Lord come"* [Acts 2:20].

The setting of that passage was the salvation that was being preached by the apostles in Jerusalem on the first Pentecost after the resurrection of Jesus from the dead. In it, the Judeans were being told that they had time to turn to God and not be destroyed, but that the day of destruction (darkness) would surely come (which it did when the Romans came and destroyed Jerusalem, the Judean economy and worship between 66 A.D. and 70 A.D.. That was the judgment of God. That was the *"great and terrible day of the LORD."* It happened in 70 A.D., it is not in our time or future time. The sun not shining in the passage in Acts is the same figurative language that was used by Isaiah in chapter 13. *"The day of the LORD"* was always the day of judgment and destruction of some people, somewhere, sometime in past biblical history. It was at the time of the destruction of Jerusalem in the 1st century A.D. that …

> *"... the powers of the heavens shall be shaken"* [Matthew 24:29].

To begin with, without consulting the **figurative use** of such language in the *"old testament,"* it would do us good just to use a little common sense. For example, is not God the most powerful of the heavens? If so, **was His power shaken**?

To understand the entire context, along with what *"heavens"* of which Jesus was speaking, let us read a quotation from the scholar, <u>Adam Clarke</u>:

> *"Commentators generally understand this, and what follows, of the end of the world and Christ's coming to judgment:* **<u>but the word immediately shows that our Lord is not speaking of any distant event</u>**. *But of something immediately consequent on calamities already predicted: and* **<u>that must be the destruction of Jerusalem</u>**. *'The* **<u>Jewish heaven</u>** *shall perish, and the sun and moon of its glory and happiness shall be darkened – brought to nothing. The sun is its religion of the church, the moon is the government of the state; and the stars are the judges and doctors of both. Compare Isaiah 13:10; Ezekiel 32:7-8, etc.* <u>Lightfoot.</u>

> *"In the prophetic language, great commotions upon earth are often* **<u>represented</u>** *under the notion of commotions and changes in the heavens.*

> *"The fall of Babylon is* **<u>represented</u>** *by the stars and constellations of heaven withdrawing their light, and the sun and moon being darkened. See Isaiah 13:9-10.*

> *"The destruction of Egypt, by the heaven being covered, the sun enveloped with a cloud, and the moon withholding her light. Ezekiel 32:7-8.*

> *"The destruction of the Jews by Antiochus Epiphanes, is* **<u>represented</u>** *by casting down some of the host of heaven, and the stars to the ground. See Daniel 8:10.*

> *"And this very destruction of Jerusalem is* **<u>represented</u>** *by the prophet Joel, (Joel 2:30-31) by showing wonders in heaven and in earth – darkening the sun, and turning the moon into blood. This general mode of describing these* **<u>judgments</u>** *leaves no room*

to doubt the propriety of its application in the present case" [Adam Clark's Commentary].

The *"present case"* term that he used means that the passage is to be understood and interpreted as to meaning the *"present"* time of the apostles of Jesus, **not future time** (such as the 21st century or later).

> *"And then shall appear the sign of the Son of man in heaven, and then shall all the tribes of the earth mourn, and they shall see the Son of man coming in the clouds of heaven with power and great glory"* [Matthew 24:30].

As I studied this verse, the very first thing that *"popped out"* at me was that the word *"then"* occurs twice in this verse. Thayer says that the Greek word *"tote"* means simply ***then, at that time***. Englishman's records 163 times of the use of this word in the *"new testament."* It is translated by the word *"then"* every time except seven times, where it is translated by the words *"and"* (1 time), *"still"* (1 time), *"when"* (1 time), and *that time"* (4 times), and in all cases, the word *"then"* can be substituted and mean the same thing. Another interesting thing is that it has already occurred five times in Matthew 24:9-23 and we have understood in all of those verses that it means **immediately following** whatever was said previously. It also occurs one more time in v-40. In the parallel chapters of Mark 13 and Luke 21, the word is always translated by the word *"then"* in nine verses.

Having said all of that, it was *"then,"* i.e. *"immediately"* in the 1st century that the *"sign"* was to appear, and it was *"then,"* i.e. *"immediately"* in the 1st century that *"all of the tribes of the earth would mourn."* That was in 70 A.D.. It is not in the 21st century, and will not be in our future.

To understand this better, we can study briefly about the *"earth"* that is mentioned. We see in the context both of the words *"heaven"* and *"earth."* How are we to interpret them? The answer again lies in the use of figurative language. Observe how they are used in the Bible.

> *"The vision of Isaiah the son of Amoz, which he saw concerning* **_Judah and Jerusalem_** *in the days of Uzziah, Jotham, Ahaz, and Hezekiah, kings of Judah. 2.* **_Hear, O heavens_**, *and* **_give ear, O earth_**; *for the LORD hath spoken, I have nourished and brought up* **_children_**, *and they have rebelled against me. 3. The ox knoweth his owner, and the ass his master's crib; but* **_Israel_** *doth not know,* **_my people_** *doth not consider. 4. Ah* **_sinful nation_**, *a people laden with iniquity; a seed of evildoers, children that are corrupters; they have forsaken the LORD, they have provoked the Holy One of Israel unto anger, they are gone away backward"* [Isaiah 1:1-4].

It can be seen here that the prophet(s) of God spoke of the rulers of the Judahites as *"heavens,"* and the other Judeans as *"earth."* This is the way in which figurative language is used. It is so used in Matthew 24, all of the *"tribes of the earth."* This was not all of the nations of the planet, but rather all of the *"tribes"* of the earth. He clearly had reference to the *"tribes of Israel,"* particularly of *"Judah and Jerusalem."* Why would they mourn in 70 A.D.? It was because of their unbelief in Jesus as the son of God, who would commission the Romans to destroy them. God would come *"riding on a swift cloud."* And Jesus would come *"on the clouds of heaven."* Again, nothing is here about the **form** of his appearance being literal, and the use of *"heaven and earth"* is **not literal** either. Why do we misunderstand these things? Primarily because we do not spend enough time studying the *"old testament,"* for one cannot understand the things in the *"new testament"* if he/she is not rooted and grounded **accurately** in the understanding of all of the figurative words and phrases of the *"old testament."* This is not the last time that *"heaven and earth"* will come up, but the future use of the phrase has its foundation in the figurative uses in the *"old testament."* Let us spend more time in a study in depth in those *"old testament"* scriptures.

"The sign of the Son of man in heaven" has different interpretations from various scholars. It may not be as easily understood as most people think. Let us examine some different viewpoints.

(1) One may take the expression *"in heaven"* to apply to the Son of man who is in heaven.

(2) Or, one may take the splitting of the words *"the sign --- in heaven"* as referring to the sign itself being in heaven.

(3) Or, one may take *"the sign of the Son of man"* as Jesus himself as being the sign. Such construction is used in the Bible. For example …

*"But he answered and said unto them, an evil and adulterous generation seeketh after a sign, and there shall no sign be given to it, but **the sign of the prophet Jonas.** 40. For as Jonas was three days and three nights in the whale's belly, so shall the Son of man be three days and three nights in the heart of the earth"* [Matthew 12:39-40].

You can obtain one of my books titled <u>Was Jesus Three Days and Three Nights In The Heart Of The Earth?</u> at AMAZON.COM, and also the Kindle version also. Just type in my name and it will come right up.

In those verses, it is easy to see (**perceive**, not literally see with the biological eyes) that the *"sign of the prophet Jonas"* was Jonas himself, *and by being in the "whale's belly"* for three days and three nights, Jonah himself was the sign of some future event.

If we were to take number 3 as being the correct interpretation, it would seem that we have a major problem, which is, of what would Jesus who was in heaven, be a sign? Was he not the fulfillment of all of the signs, rather than being a sign himself? Maybe it is correct, but I cannot see it. If you believe that he himself was the sign of something, would you please write me and tell me something upon which to base it?

Likewise, if we take number 2 as being the correct interpretation, it would seem again that we have a problem or problems. How could we understand of which *"heaven"* Jesus was speaking? Was it the heaven where God is supposed to dwell? Was it the *"third heaven"* of which the Bible speaks? Was it the "firmament" that was called *"heaven"* in the book of Genesis? Was it the heaven of which Isaiah 1:1-4 was speaking (which we have already discussed)? How could the 1st century believers have seen a sign if it was where God is said to dwell? First, in order for whatever the *"sign"* was, it had to be a sign that the 1st century believers could *"see"* or *"perceive."* Again, number 2 may be the correct interpretation, but I cannot see it. If you do, please correspond to me and give me some convincing arguments.

To me, number 1 seems to be correct, but with some explanation. Yes, the Son of man was in heaven. But the sign itself would not be in heaven.

My desire is that in the following personal remarks, **I be very kind**. If I remember correctly (it has been 58 years), it was in 1957 (and following years since his son Garner Ted married one of my high-school class-mates) that I had a radio program that immediately followed Herbert W. Armstrong. I would sit in the lobby of the radio station as the words of Mr. Armstrong went out on the airwaves. I was taking notes. Before I tell you what I said, let me say that Garner Ted produced the best material in refutation of the evolution of man from some one-celled thing. I will do what God said, and that is to *"render honor to whom honor is due."* He deserves honor for that excellent material.

Now back to the radio station. I made notes of what Mr. Armstrong said on the program and followed his radio program with my notes. Invariably, he would talk about this chapter that we are studying, i.e. Matthew 24. Here are the verses that he would use as a basis for his argumentation (and many more smaller ones).

"And ye shall hear of wars and rumors of wars; see that ye be not troubled; for all these things must come to pass, but the end is not yet. 7. For nation shall rise against nation, and kingdom against kingdom: and there shall be famines, and pestilences, and earthquakes, in diverse places" [Matthew 24:6-7].

These are all of the signs that he said would happen to indicate the time of the coming parousia (presence) of Jesus. Look at them …

1. Wars
2. Rumors of wars
3. Nation rising against nation
4. Kingdom rising against kingdom
5. Famines
6. Pestilences
7. Earthquakes

Then Mr. Armstrong would take the current events of 1957 (and more), any war that was going on at that time, any famine that existed in that year, any pestilence that was somewhere in the world, and especially of any earthquake that was of any size, anywhere on the planet. Yes, they were all happening in that year and subsequent years, somewhere in the world, and so Mr. Armstrong told his large listening audience that the *"coming"* of Jesus was near, any day and hour. He told his audience that they must **prepare immediately** for that time. It **did not come** at that time. Later, he wrote an article that said that 1975 was the time of the end. But it did not come then either. Herbert W. Armstrong has long since passed from this life. His son, Garner Ted Armstrong also died a few years ago. Now listen to me, each one of you readers – they both died without it happening and everyone that is living will die without it happening too. Yes **you - I'll say it again, YOU** will die and the people who continue to live for 5,000 years from now will die. You might as well get ready for such **because that is what the Bible says!!!!!!!**

And I think by now that you know the reason. The parousia (remember that word?) of Jesus that is spoken of in **Matthew 24** (and the remainder of the Bible) happened in the 1st century A.D.. It was **for the apostle's time**. It is not for our time. It is not for future time. It happened almost 2,000 years ago. But let us continue …

Above, we mentioned **seven** things that Jesus said would happen in the lifetimes of the four apostles to whom he was speaking, i.e, between 33 A.D. and 70 A.D.. When we study the question that they asked Jesus and try to harmonize those seven things, we have major difficulties. Let us look at what the apostles asked about the *"end"* and the *"coming"* of their Messiah.

> *"And as he sat upon the mount of Olives, the disciples came unto him privately, saying, Tell us, when shall these things be? And what shall be **THE sign**, of thy **coming** and of the **end** of the world"* [Matthew 24:3].

Do you see the problem? **The seven things mentioned in vv. 6-7 were not signs** of either the *"end"* of the age or of the *"coming" (presence)* of their Messiah. **The apostles did not ask Jesus about *signs (plural)*.** They only asked him about one sign, **THE** *sign,* and it was not any of those seven things of vv. 6-7. What was that *"one sign?"*

In response to the two questions from Jesus's apostles, Jesus informed them that the following men today interpret as signs (which were **really not signs**, just predictions of coming things) were events that they needed not to be concerned.

1. Not false Christs and false prophets
2. Not wars and rumors of wars
3. Not nation rising against nation
4. Not kingdom against kingdom
5. Not famines
6. Not numerous earthquakes

7. Not tribulation and persecution
8. Not the stumbling of many regarding the faith
9. Not the increase of iniquity
10. Not love's decline
11. Not the gospel being preached in the whole world

If none of those events were **THE** **sign** of the consummation of the Hebrew age, but merely birth pains **preceding THE sign** about which the apostles were asking, why should we concern ourselves with those things in our area in the 21st century, as some tend to do today? But even then, all of those happenings were to find their fulfillment in the apostles' generation in the 1st century A.D., otherwise *"they"* could not *"see"* them.

That to which Jesus related at this point in his discussion was **not the single sign** the apostles sought, but they were **plural things** (not signs) that would precede **THE sign**. They asked what would be **THE sign and THE time** of the immanent destruction of the city and the temple. Therefore we must seek for the *"single"* sign to which Jesus referred in his response to their questions. And, while we do so, we cannot go beyond that specific generation and introduce concepts that were irrelevant to them. To do so would violate **every** principle of sound, contextual interpretation.

Therefore, the events that Jesus presented at this point in his reply were **not** the specific sign for which the apostles were told to look. The specific sign and the specific time that were relevant to their generation were yet to be identified. Mark 13 and Luke 21 are parallel accounts of this same event. Luke unmistakably tells of **THE sign**.

> *"But when ye see Jerusalem compassed with armies, then **know** that her desolation is at hand"* [Luke 21:20].

This verse indicates a change of emphasis. Herein Jesus addresses the apostles specific time question and Luke recorded that he said to them, *"… when **you see**."* Nothing that he said at that point was relevant to another generation or another place. What he said was definitely related to the generation of the four apostles and the fulfillment of the desolation of Jerusalem as he had prophesied earlier.

So, the answer to the apostles' *"sign question"* was Jerusalem being encompassed with armies, which Jesus said that **they would see**. It was a singular answer and had no inference to any other event that would occur in their generation or in any other generation in the future. They asked for **THE** sign and they received an answer that was relevant to the prophecy and to the generation in which that specific prophecy would be fulfilled, i.e. the 1ˢᵗ century A.D..

It is important also to note that Jesus was emphatic about this matter and said, when referring to Jerusalem; *"her desolation,"* previously addresses the city in the feminine gender when he prophesied against her in Luke 19:41-44. He described her desolation in graphic detail.

> *"Now as He drew near, He saw the city and wept over it, saying, 'If you had known, even you, especially in this your day, the things that make for your peace! But now they are hidden from your eyes. For the days will come upon you when your enemies will build an embankment around you, surround you and close you in on every side, and level you, and your children within you, to the ground; and they will not leave in you one stone upon another, because you did not know the time of your visitation'."*

We can be certain that Jesus spoke directly to and about Jerusalem in the apostles' generation because of Luke's account. Compare the King James Version reading to the following American Standard Version reading …

"And when he drew near, he saw the city and wept over it, 42. Saying, If you had known in this your day, even you, the things which belong unto peace! But now they are hidden from your eyes. 43. For the days (plural) shall come upon you, when your enemies shall cast up a bank around you, and compass you round, and keep you in on every side, 44. And shall dash you to the ground, and your children within you; and they shall not leave in you one stone upon another, because you knew not the time of your visitation."

From the context, we can see that Jesus not only answered the apostles specific sign question, he insisted that they regard that particular sign as **the** sign that they asked for because he said, *"when you see ... then know."* Jesus said to the four apostles, *"This is it. This is what you want to know. This is the answer to your question."* When the armies surround the city, you can be confident that you have the answer to your sign question. Know for sure that this is the one and only sign that you will see.

Throughout his reply to the four apostles, Jesus never veered away from what he spoke of initially – the desolation of the city and the temple. He even addressed the city in a very loving, tearful way. Desolation of the city and temple, though necessary, disturbed Jesus and by revealing those things to the four, he would, if they were ever watchful, redeem them physically from being entangled in the abominable devastation that was about to befall that part of the Hebrew nation.

Luke was very emphatic about who should recognize the sign of which Jesus spoke. Jesus specifically said that those to whom he was talking at that time were the ones who should see those things and watch for their occurrence. He did not speak to or of anyone else. It was **that generation** that would witness all of the events that he revealed, including **the specific sign**, and they would succumb to their impact if they failed to heed his warnings and flee at the appropriate time. So, therein are the answers to the apostles' *"time and sign questions"* – that generation in Jesus' presence about 33 A.D..

Jesus set out to answer the apostles' questions and adds nothing more to that discourse. There were only the two questions to which they wanted answers – the **time** question and the **sign** question. They asked nothing else and he introduced nothing else.

The Greek word for *"end"* that is used in Matthew 24:8-14, is *"telos"* and means *"accomplishment"* or *"fulfillment."* The only accomplishment or fulfillment of which the apostles wanted to know, and which was prophesied by Jesus, was that of the Hebrew era. That was the only *"end"* that concerned them and **they wanted to know only the time and the sign that heralded its imminence**. [I have used some thoughts of Bob Chapman, and I wanted to thank him for those thoughts.]

As we continue to study v-30, it should be taken into account that we are approaching the zenith of the teaching of Jesus concerning his parousia (do you still not really understand that word? Shortly, it will be printed in AMAZON.COM.) in the destruction of the Judahite system of things, particularly by the Roman army between 66 A.D. and 70 A.D.. This is not the place to give up, for in this verse and the next few that follow, Jesus makes things very plain to those who want to think for themselves and truly understand these things exactly as Jesus' apostles did about 33 A.D. when he was speaking to them. Do not give up – stay with me and Jesus!

We have already studied the word *"then"* as it occurs twice in this verse. There is a reason for that. The use of the word twice denotes succession. Note the succession …

1. **Those days** (the destruction of Jerusalem in the 1st century)
2. *"The tribulation of **those days**"* (v-29)
3. *"**Immediately after** the tribulation of those days"* (v-29)

4. *"**Then** shall appear the sign"* (v-30)
5. *"**Then** shall all the tribes of the earth mourn"* (v-30)

We have already studied about the appearance of the sign, but I would like to add one more thought here. The Greek word, from whence came the translation of *"appear"* is *"phaino,"* which means to *"shine or to lighten."* Why would Jesus use any other expression, since he had already used the illustration of *"lightening"* that shined from the east to the west?

After the appearance of **the (one) sign** of the end of the age and the parousia (presence) of Jesus, then *"all the tribes of the earth shall mourn."* Who and why?

One of my readers wrote the following sentence to me. *"The word **earth** can and should be translated from the Greek word **ge**, meaning land ... meaning the land of Judea."*

We have already studied about the *"earth"* as being the Judean world, not the planet. What about the *"tribes?"* The word comes from the Greek word *"phulai,"* which means *"an offshoot, i.e. a clan or race."* It is translated in the <u>King James Version</u> by either the word *"kindred"* or *"tribe."* The reference is obviously **not** to *"nations"* (*goyim or ethnos*), but rather to the twelve *"tribes"* of Israel. After the complete destruction of the temple and the Judean economy in 70 A.D., the divisions of any survivors were no longer considered as the divided *"tribes"* as they had been for centuries. So, the mourning of the tribes refers to the tribes of Israel mourning because of the armies surrounding the city of Jerusalem to destroy it. Why would the Chinese *"nation"* mourn over the destruction of Jerusalem in 70 A.D.? We need to stay within the bounds that Jesus set out for the apostles when he told them this, about 33 A.D..

"The Son of man (huion tou anthroopou)" has obvious reference to Jesus. We will continue to discuss the things concerning Jesus in this verse.

While there are some connections in scriptures, we now are at a point where I must spend a short time with another word. That word is *"erchomai."* We have been discussing the word *"parousia"* rather consistently, which means *"present,"* in contrast to the English word *"absent."* The Bible even speaks of satan as having a parousia or presence in only one verse, 2 Thessalonians 2:9, while the word parousia = presence occurs twenty-one other times in the *"new testament."*

I have studied these words for some time, but in my own mind, I need much more study, as you probably do also. Forgive me for not knowing much, and especially in my study of these two words. But since the next word in this verse is *"erchomai,"* let us study it for a little while.

The subject switches from the *"sign"* of the Son of man to the actual *"coming (erchomai)"* of Jesus. We have studied *"the sign,"* now we must try to understand what the actual *"coming of the Son of man"* means.

After Jesus said *"then shall all of the tribes of the earth shall mourn,"* our question should be *"why were they mourning?"* We have already discussed the answer, but let us be reminded that Jesus was coming to **destroy** the Judeans, their temple, and their entire system and economy in 66 A.D. to 70 A.D..

When the word *"erchomai"* is used in what we call the *"new testament,"* it apparently usually refers to **destruction**. In this case, it was the **destruction** of Jerusalem, completed in 70 A.D.. The Greek word primarily means *"to come or go, in a great variety of applications, literally or figuratively."* Obviously in this verse, it would **not** be to *"go,"* but rather to *"come,"* so the word *"coming"* is a very good translation. The Son of man, Jesus, was coming and all of the *"tribes"* (not all nations) of the *"earth"* (**ge** = land of the Judeans) would mourn over the coming of Jesus in the Roman armies to **destroy** Jerusalem and

The Sign Of The End Revealed

the Judeans. The house of Judah was about to come to an end by being stoned and burned.

As the Egyptians would see (perceive) God's coming to **destroy** them in the expression …

> *"The burden of Egypt. Behold, the LORD rideth upon a swift cloud, and shall come into Egypt: and the idols of Egypt shall be moved at his presence, and the heart of Egypt shall melt in the midst of it"* [Isaiah 19:1] …

… so the Judeans would see (perceive) Jesus coming to **destroy** them. Yes, the contemporary generation of Jesus' fleshly presence and that of his apostles would *"see"* the Son of man *"coming"* in that 1st century A.D.. That coming of Jesus is **not** for our generation, neither for any future generation. Are you getting tired of me saying those things? I am sure that you are but that is the only way to finally get those points over, and for a few of you, you will shrug them off because you have gotten so far rooted in the old untruth in your preacher's traditions. I wish I could help you but your mind is so far made up that you just will not listen. Even if Jesus were here and told you that, you would not believe him. But, he just did - did he not? The quicker that people understand what the apostles understood when Jesus was speaking to them, the quicker that they will be able to really comprehend what the Bible actually teaches. Then and only then can we apply to our lives what we must in the 21st century.

We have been taught so many erroneous things concerning the Bible, that I believe that if you believe that the *"coming of the Son of man"* **in this verse applies to <u>our</u> generation, that you will probably swear up and down that Elijah went up to the heaven where God dwells, in a chariot of fire, pulled by horses of fire, by means of a whirlwind. Correct?**

www.EschatologyReview.com   113

But, I have another book available for you to read that will get rid of that false idea. It is called <u>Is It Appointed For Man Once To Die?</u> and it is available at AMAZON.COM. Just type in Ron McRay in the blank. Kindle is available too.

We have already spent much time on Matthew 24:30, but it is necessary that we spend some more time in its study. This verse and the next few that follow are the pinnacle of the teaching of Jesus in this chapter concerning things that would happen before all of those who were biologically alive when he was speaking, would die. So, it is very important that we take our time on these verses, for they are the most misunderstood in all of the three chapters of Matthew 23, 24 and 25.

Let it be clearly understood here that the ten northern tribes, called *"the house of Israel"* had been taken into captivity by Assyria and scattered throughout the nations in the eighth century B.C.. So, the **tribes** of the *"land"* that mourned were the tribe of Judah, the tribe of Benjamin and the tribe of Levi (or at least the portion of them that were not taken captive by Assyria when the house of Israel was taken captivity). It was the major portion of the three tribes that would *"see"* the *"coming of the Son of man"* to **destroy** Jerusalem between 66 A.D. and 70 A.D.. Of course, it included any of the other tribes who had trickled back into the land.

Notice that Jesus said plainly that the tribes of the earth (land) would *"... see the Son of man coming in the clouds of heaven with power and great glory."* Did Jesus tell the truth or did those three tribes who resided in Judea in the 1st century A.D., actually *"see"* (*perceive"*) the **coming** of Jesus to **destroy** the Judean system through the Roman army? I will go with Jesus telling the truth that it happened in the 1st century A.D. and will not happen in our lifetime or a future time.

The Greek word *"epi"* is much better translated as *"on"* or *"upon."* The words *"with"* and *"in"* are not the primary meaning of the word. Jesus was to come *"on"* the clouds, just as God came riding *"upon"* a cloud in Isaiah 19:1. The **coming** of both was for the purpose of **judgment** and **destruction**.

Obviously, the coming of God on a cloud is figurative language, for He is not confined to such a small space, literally. The coming of Jesus on the clouds is also figurative language. If one considers that Jesus would literally come on the clouds in a literal (changed) body that he occupied while he walked on the planet, how small would the clouds (plural) have to be for him to be *"on clouds"* (plural)? Really, it does not make sense at all unless we **do not** take the expression literally, but figuratively, just as the coming of God upon a cloud was figurative.

This event, whether one thinks of it as an event that happened in the 1st century or an event that might happen in our lifetimes, or some future time, is usually referred to as the second coming. Let us dispense quickly of a study of this subject by pointing out that the term the second coming does not occur anywhere in the entire Bible. Did you know that? Check it out for yourself.

And, of course, people always want to talk about Acts 1:11, which is one of the most abused passages of scripture in the entire Bible. And so will I.

> *"Which also said, Ye men of Galilee, why stand ye gazing up into heaven? This same Jesus, which is taken up from you into heaven, shall so come in like manner as ye have seen him go into heaven."*

The first thing that should be noticed is that the word *"heavens"* (ouranos) is used three times in this verse. Let us look at their occurrences backwards.

1. The apostles saw Jesus go *"into heaven."*
2. Jesus was *"taken up from them into heaven."*
3. The apostles were *"gazing up into heaven."*

Looking at number one, it is certain that the apostles saw Jesus taken into heaven. Did the apostles see the heaven where God dwells? If so, they saw things that others, as mortal men, have never seen. If not, what is the heaven to which they saw Jesus ascend?

Looking at number two, it is plainly stated that Jesus was *"taken up from* (the apostles) *into heaven."* We should not have any problem understanding that, only to ask the same question – what is the heaven into which he went when he was taken up from them?

Looking at number three creates some problems. The apostles were gazing up into heaven. Did they see **into** heaven? If so, into which heaven did they see? To which heaven were they gazing?

When one does a closer study of the *"old testament,"* he will find that the space where the birds fly is called *"heaven."* Also, the place where the stars are located is called *"heaven."* Also, the place where we believe that God dwells is called *"heaven."* In fact, it is stated that Jesus ascended *"**far above all** heavens."*

Since the exact same Greek word is used three times in this verse, all meaning the same; which *"heaven"* is under consideration? Let me pose a thought that might make all of these very clear.

1. The apostles were gazing **into** the *"air"* (heaven), the place where the birds fly.
2. Jesus was taken up from the apostles **into** the *"air"* (heaven), where the birds fly.
3. The apostles saw Jesus ascend **into** the *"air"* (heaven), where the birds fly.

The Greek word *"ouranos"* simply means *"the sky."* It is only by extension that it is used as *"heaven"* and there are many implications of the word throughout the Bible. The apostles were steadfastly looking into the sky. Jesus ascended into the sky. The apostles saw Jesus ascend into the sky. And then a **cloud** obscured him from their sight, so they could not have seen him go any further. If you think that it was a literal cloud, it had to be close enough for them to see with their biological eyes and we all know where the uppermost and the lowest (fog) clouds are in relation to the ground.

Another very interesting thing is that in the Greek manuscript, in all three instances, before the word *"heaven,"* the word *"ton"* occurs (yes, every time). The word *"ton"* means *"the,"* which is in English the definite article, i.e. not *"**a** heaven,"* but *"**the** heaven."* There was only one particular heaven at which and into which they were looking and into which Jesus ascended. It was *"the sky."*

Let us move forward in our study of Acts 1:11. Here is the quotation again.

> *"Which also said, Ye men of Galilee, why stand ye gazing up into heaven? This same Jesus, which is taken up from you into heaven, shall so come in like form as ye have seen him go into heaven."*

Did you read it closely? That is what is wrong with most Bible readers. Well, just to be sure, let us read it again.

> *"Which also said, Ye men of Galilee, why stand ye gazing up into heaven? This same Jesus, which is taken up from you into heaven, shall so come in like manner as ye have seen him go into heaven."*

Do you see any difference in the two quotations? Well, you should. If you do not, go back and read both of them again and notice that there is one word that is different, and it means everything in understanding this verse. Before you proceed further, please be sure that you can see the one word that is different in the quotations. Now, having found it, which one is correctly quoted from the <u>King James Version</u>?

The word *"manner"* comes from a Greek word, *"tropos,"* which means *"a turn, i.e. (by implication) **mode or style**."*

When we use the word *"mode"* in the English language, we are speaking of the *"method or style"* of the transportation. For example, my wife left on a trip and will return in the same **manner**. In that example, I am not using the word **manner** to describe the FORM in which she traveled. The form might have been an airplane, or an automobile, a train, or some other *"form"* of transportation.

The English definition of the word *"manner"* is, *"A way of doing or **a way in which something happens** or is done; mode."* The Reader's Digest Great Encyclopedia Dictionary. Note that the definition **does not include the** FORM.

On the other hand, The English definition of the word *"form"* (which does not occur in the passage), is: *"The shape or contour of something as distinguished from its substance or color, external structure. 2. The body of a living being with regard to its shape, figure"* IBID. Note that the passage is not referring to the *"shape or figure"* of Jesus, but is referring to the *"manner"* (the way) of Jesus' departure and return, and that was *"with the clouds,"* **not** a biological, changed body.

The angels told the apostles that the same *"manner"* of Jesus' departure would be the same *"manner"* of his return. The angels **did not tell of the form** of Jesus' departure, **nor the form** of his return. That being the case, why do nearly all of the preachers of the 21st century speak of the *"form"* of Jesus' return, rather than the *"manner"* of his return?

Jesus's departure was in some form that the apostles could see with their biological eyes. But there was **not** a statement made that he would *"return"* in the same form in which he left. Rather, the *"manner"* of his departure was that *"a cloud received Him out of their sight."* So, the *"manner"* of his return was that he would be *"seen"* in or with the *clouds*. Remember to look closely and not read in words that are neither in the Greek nor the English. The word is **manner – not form**.

Much could be said about Jesus' coming with the clouds. The original word for *"cloud"* is *"nephele,"* pronounced *"nef-el'-ay."* In Acts 1:9, Jesus was said to be removed from the visibility of the apostles by *"a (single) cloud"* in the <u>King James Version</u>. In the *"new testament"* the word is defined as *"cloudiness"* and may mean a totally cloudy, overcast (or fog) condition into which he ascended, or a mere cumulous cloud that obscured their view of him. There is no sure way to tell.

Then another question arises. Why is the Greek word *"epi"* translated by the English word *"in,"* when it means *"on, upon or over?"* As we have seen, God came riding **on** a cloud in His destruction of Egypt. It would certainly be important to see the son of God coming **on** the clouds, as being parallel to that of his Father, rather than the word that is incorrectly translated as *"in"* here in Matthew 24:30.

We can admit that Revelation 1:7 does indicate that the Son of God would come *"with"* the clouds, meaning accompanying or amidst, but there are so many constructions with the word throughout the *"new testament,"* that it would be very difficult to show that it meant anything different than the many other times that he would come *"on"* a cloud. It is not always clear when the plural is to be distinguished from the singular.

The word *"cloud"* is used both in a literal sense of the moisture that is in the sky, and it is always used **figuratively**. For example …

> *"Wherefore seeing we also are compassed about with so great a* **CLOUD** *of witnesses, let us lay aside every weight, and the sin which so easily besets us, and let us run with patience the race that is set before us"* [1 Thessalonians 4:14].

In connection with the word *"cloud"* as it is used in the above verse, notice the following one ---

> *"For if we believe that Jesus died and rose again, even so them also which sleep in Jesus will God bring with him"* [1 Thessalonians 4:14].

How do we know for sure that some or all of the *"great **cloud**"* of witnesses, were not the ones that God would *"bring with Him?"* Is that the *"cloud"* that Jesus would come *"**with** the clouds"* of Revelation 1:7? The word *"cloud"* appears twenty-one times in the *"new testament"* in the <u>King James Version.</u>

Much could be said about Jesus' coming in or with the clouds, but this is not the place to expand much on that aspect. You are encouraged to do some study, both in the *"old testament"* and in the *"new testament"* about the *"clouds."* We shall take one more look at Jesus' coming **with** or **in** the clouds. Let us notice some verses that either parallel or deal with the same subject. The first one is a parallel account of this verse, which is recorded by Mark.

> *"And then shall they see the Son of man coming **in** the clouds with great power and glory"* [Mark 13:26].

At this point, you will need to recall the things that we covered on Mark 13:25 or go back and study it very, very carefully. For you see that Mark 13 and Luke 21 are the same account as is viewed by this chapter in Matthew, so it also helps to look at those accounts. The original Greek word here in Mark 13:25, is *"in"* the clouds.

It is interesting to note the antecedent to the word *"they"* in this verse in Mark. It refers back to the *"stars"* and the *"powers in the heaven"* in that verse. Do the stars *"see?"* Do the *"powers"* see? Yes, according to this verse in v-26, both see. We have already shown from other scriptures that the terms are used figuratively, and it is true in this case.

It was the *"people"* who would see him. Therefore, the only logical conclusion is that the *"stars"* and the *"powers"* were the people. Study that logically and go over it a couple of times.

And, the people would *"see"* him coming in the destruction of Jerusalem in those three and one-half years. It was the *"perception"* of his coming that they would see. They would know that he had prophesied about the **destruction** of Jerusalem about forty years earlier, and it was that contemporary generation to which he spoke that would *"see"* (perceive) his coming to **destroy** Jerusalem. Review earlier comments about his coming *"in the clouds* (plural)." Let us look at another verse that was recorded by Matthew.

> *"But Jesus held his peace. And the high priest answered and said unto him, I adjure thee by the living God, that thou tell us whether thou be the Christ, the Son of God. 64. Jesus saith unto him, Thou hast said: nevertheless I say unto you,* **Hereafter** *shall* **ye see** *the Son of man sitting on the right hand of power, and* **coming in the clouds** *of heaven"* [Matthew 26:63-64].

Again, we **see** (notice that the word *"see"* here is used as perceive, not seeing with the biological eye) the coming of Jesus in judgment, to **destroy** Jerusalem, which included those who murdered him. The high priest was an Israelite (descendant of Jacob = Israel), and was told that he would see that *"coming"* of their Messiah. That would be in the biological lifetime of the high priest to whom Jesus was speaking, not 2,000 years or more in the future. If you will take the time to read it, Mark records the same conversation in Mark 14:61-62. There is only one other at which we shall take a look - then move on.

> *"Behold,* **he cometh with clouds**; *and every eye shall see him, and* **they also which pierced him**; *and* **all kindreds of the earth** *shall wail because of him. Even so, Amen"* [Revelation 1:7].

There is a difference in the Greek word in this verse. Here it is *"meta,"* which means *"accompaniment,"* that is, it can be and should be translated by the word *"with,"* which in this case, the translators correctly rendered it.

"All kindreds of the earth" is the same group of people of which Jesus was speaking in Matthew 24:30, where we are studying. However, Matthew used the expression, *"all the tribes of the earth mourn(ing)"* – *"kindreds"* and *"tribes"* referring to the Israelite tribes that were in the **land** of Judea when the Romans intruded it in order to **destroy** them between 66 A.D. and 70 A.D..

Would Jesus be returning **with** (maybe) a *"great cloud of witnesses"* to which we have already referred? What about his Father? Have we not already seen (perceived) such in at least three passages to which we have referred?

> *"And Enoch also, the seventh from Adam, prophesied of these, saying, Behold, the Lord* **cometh WITH ten thousand of his saints**, *15.* **To execute judgment** *upon all, and to convince all that are unGodly among them of all their unGodly deeds which they have unGodly committed, and of all their hard speeches which unGodly sinners have spoken against him"* [Jude 14].

> *"For if we believe that Jesus died and rose again, even so them also which sleep in Jesus will God* **bring WITH him** [1 Thessalonians 4:14].

Are these two verses dealing with the great *"cloud of witnesses"* – the word *"clouds"* being used figuratively but not literally? It is imperative that we understand that the *"coming"* and the *"clouds"* are not literal (in the flesh bodies) in Jesus' return to destroy Jerusalem.

> *"And he shall send his angels with a **great** sound of a trumpet, and they shall **gather together** his elect from the four winds, from one end of heaven to the other"* [Matthew 24:31].

We have much more **figurative language** in this verse, as we have had in most verses since the beginning of the chapter. First of all, let us look at the word *"angels."*

The Greek word is *"angelos,"* hence a transliteration of the word would be *angel,* but that is not the definition of the original word. It means **a messenger** and is translated in the <u>King James Version</u> as a messenger and practically translated as *"angel."* In this verse, we do **not** have what people describe as *"heavenly angels"* with *"wings,"* but Jesus was speaking of the apostles, prophets, inspired teachers and all believers as taking the message of the gospel to the Israelite world in the 1st century A.D.. By the acceptance of the gospel, the elect were gathered together by the process that is described by another Greek word, *"ekklesia,"* meaning *"ek=out and kaleo=to call,"* hence, the *"called out people,"* that people usually (erroneously) referred to as *"church."*

It is interesting that the expression, *"he shall send"* is the Greek word *"apostello,"* from which the English word *"apostle"* is derived. It means *"to send forth or out on a mission, either literally or figuratively."*

The word *"sound"* is not found in the original but it is implied. Of what benefit would a trumpet be if it did not make the desired sounds?

When reading from the *"old testament,"* it is understood that the *"blowing of **A** trumpet"* was for the purpose of calling people to an **assembly**.

> *"And if they blow but with **ONE** trumpet, then the princes, which are heads of the thousands of Israel, shall **gather themselves** unto thee"* [Numbers 10:4].

*"But the Spirit of the LORD came upon Gideon, and he blew **A** trumpet; and Abi-ezer was **gathered** after him. 35. And he sent messengers throughout all Manasseh; who also **was gathered** after him: and he sent messengers unto Asher, and unto Zebulun, and unto Naphtali, and they came up to meet them"* [Judges 6:34-35].

*"And it shall come to pass in that day, that **THE** great trumpet shall be blown, and **they shall come** which were ready to perish in the land of Assyria, and the outcasts in the land of Egypt, and shall worship the LORD in the holy mount at Jerusalem"* [Isaiah 27:13].

*"Declare ye in Judah, and publish in Jerusalem; and say, Blow ye **THE** trumpet in the land; cry, **gather together**, and say, **Assemble yourselves**, and let us go into the defensed cities"* [Jeremiah 4:5].

*"O ye children of Benjamin, **gather yourselves** to flee out of the midst of Jerusalem, and blow **THE** trumpet in Tekoa"* [Jeremiah 6:1].

*"Set ye up a standard in the land, blow **THE** trumpet among the nations, prepare the nations against her, **call together** against her the kingdoms of Ararat, Minni, and Ashchenaz"* [Jeremiah 51:27].

*"Blow **THE** trumpet in Zion, sanctify a fast, **call a solemn assembly**: 16. **Gather the people**, sanctify the congregation, **assemble** the elders, **gather** the children, and those that suck the breasts: let the bridegroom go forth of his chamber, and the bride out of her closet"* [Joel 2:15-16].

*"In a moment, in the twinkling of an eye, at **THE** last trump: for **THE** trumpet shall sound, and the dead shall be raised incorruptible, and we shall be changed"* [1 Corinthians 15:52].

This last verse shows that the great gathering was unto Jesus. **THE** trumpet was sounded in 70 A.D. and the **great gathering** of the people happened in the coming of the kingdom of Christ. This verse proves it.

*"The scepter shall not depart from Judah, nor a lawgiver from between his feet, until Shiloh come: and unto him shall **the gathering of the people** be"* [Genesis 49:10].

What does that do with the time element that was taught by the writers of the *"new testament?"*

For example, 2 Thessalonians gives us a time element and the essential character of the sound of **THE** trumpet and at that sound a **great gathering** of people shall gather. It is a lengthy reading, but is very much of necessity that we read the entire short chapter, in view of the misapplications and misunderstandings of the verse that is in context with all of the others that we have studied.

*"Now we beseech you, brethren, by the **coming** of our Lord Jesus Christ, and by our **gathering together** unto him, 2. That ye be not soon shaken in mind, or be troubled, neither by spirit, nor by word, nor by letter as from us, as that the day of Christ **is at hand**. 3. Let no man deceive you by any means: for that day shall not come, except there come a falling away first, and that man of sin be revealed, the son of perdition; 4. Who opposeth and exalteth himself above all that is called God, or that is worshipped; so that he as God sitteth in the temple of God, shewing himself that he is God. 5. Remember ye not, that, when I was yet with you, I told you these things? 6. And **now** ye know what withholdeth that he might be revealed in his time. 7. For the mystery of iniquity **doth already work**: only he who now letteth*

will let, until he be taken out of the way. 8. And then shall that wicked be revealed, whom the Lord shall consume with the spirit of his mouth, and shall destroy with the brightness of his coming: 9. Even him, whose coming is after the working of satan with all power and signs and lying wonders, 10. And with all deceivableness of unrighteousness in them that perish; because they received not the love of the truth, that they might be saved. 11. And for this cause God shall send them strong delusion, that they should believe a lie: 12. That they all might be damned who believed not the truth, but had pleasure in unrighteousness. 13. But we are bound to give thanks alway to God for you, brethren beloved of the Lord, because God hath from the beginning chosen you to salvation through sanctification of the Spirit and belief of the truth: 14. Whereunto he called you by our gospel, to the obtaining of the glory of our Lord Jesus Christ. 15. Therefore, brethren, stand fast, and hold the traditions which ye have been taught, whether by word, or our epistle. 16. Now our Lord Jesus Christ himself, and God, even our Father, which hath loved us, and hath given us everlasting consolation and good hope through grace, 17. Comfort your hearts, and stablish you in every good word and work" [2 Thessalonians 2:1-17].

I have shown from previous studies the subject of the great gathering unto Jesus. While I have used the <u>King James Version</u> all of my life, sometimes I have to stop and apologize for it. This is one of those cases. The phrase in v-1, *"gathering together"* comes from one Greek word, the **form** of which is used only here and one other place in the entire *"new testament."* The definition is *"a gathering together"* or *"an assembling together."* It refers here to what is usually referred to as *"the second coming of Christ,"* although the term *"second coming"* is not found in the Bible – that is right – it is not found, not even one time in the entire Bible.

Before further study of this phrase, it is necessary to look at the expression *"is at hand"* in v-2, for it is in this phrase that the translators made a horrible mistake. As far as I know, with the limited number of other translations at my disposal, all of the others render the phrase as *"has already happened"* or some equivalent. Let us look at a few of them.

> *"… that you may not be quickly shaken from your composure or be disturbed either by a spirit or a message or a letter as if from us, to the effect that **the day of the Lord HAS COME**"* [NASV].

> *"… not to be quickly shaken in mind or excited, either by spirit or by word, or by letter purporting to be from us, to the effect **that the day of the Lord HAS COME**"* [RSV].

> *"Please don't be upset and excited, dear brothers, by the rumor that **this day of the Lord HAS ALREADY BEGUN**"* [TLB].

> *"… not to be so easily confused in your thinking or upset by the claim that **the Day of the Lord HAS COME**"* [TEV].

> *"… not to be easily unsettled or alarmed by some prophecy, report or letter supposed to have come from us, saying that **the day of the Lord HAS ALREADY COME**"* [NIV].

> *"… not to be soon shaken in mind or troubled, either by spirit or by word or by letter, as if from us, as though **the day of Christ HAD COME**"* [NKJV].

As far as I know, the <u>King James Version</u> is the only (mis)translation that does not translate the word correctly. But in so mistranslating it, it has caused much confusion among those who read and/or study the Bible. Make no mistake, the time element shows **closeness** of the day, but that it was correcting the notion of the first century believers that it had *"already begun"* or *"already happened."* That brings up a lot of questions, does it not?

That *"day"* was the **destruction** of Jerusalem and the Judahite system by the Romans in 66 A.D. to 70 A.D.. It is not referring to some time in our day or some future time to us. Do not leave us now, as more proof is coming up as Jesus continues to answer the **when** question that his apostles had asked of him. Notice in v-7 that things were *"already at work"* for the *"second coming"* to take place *"soon"* after Paul wrote the letter to the Thessalonians.

I thought a very long time about whether I should follow the rabbit trail of the Greek word that is rendered in 2 Thessalonians 2:1 as *"gathering together,"* and decided that it would be in the reader's best interest to side-tract just a little. We will return to study more about this passage later.

Are the following taught in the Bible?

1. We should assemble on Monday for **one hour**, encouraging each other.
2. We should assemble on Tuesday for **two hours**, exhorting each other a little **more** than we did on Monday?
3. We should assemble on Wednesday for **three hours**, mutually helping each other **more** than we did in Tuesday?
4. We should assemble on Thursday for **four hours**, and exhorting each other **more** than we did in Wednesday.
5. We must assemble together on Friday for **five hours**, encouraging each other **more** than we did on Thursday.
6. We surely must assemble on Saturday for **at least six hours** and exhort each other **a lot more** than we did on Friday ---

--- because Sunday is the *"day that we saw approaching."* **Or is it**? Let us look at the **only other time** that the **form** of the Greek word *"episunagomen"* occurs, other than in 2 Thessalonian 2:1 (there translated as *"gathering together"*).

*"Not forsaking the **assembling** of ourselves **together** as the manner of some is: but exhorting one another; and so much the **more** as ye see **the day** approaching"* [Hebrews 10:25].

If we interpret *"the day approaching"* in Hebrews 10:25 as *"Sunday,"* then the above scenario of a gathering on each day of the week, *"more"* each succeeding day, would be the obvious necessity.

But, with the early believers on the run from the approaching **destruction** of the Judaic system by the armies up to 70 A.D., and by all of the persecutions, trials, afflictions and tribulation that went before and during that event, surely we do not see the ekklesia (the called out people of Jesus stopping in one place, building a building in which to assemble, putting up a sign, opening a bank account, assembling together in the building every day, thereby telling the Judeans who were after their lives, **Here we are, come get us**. Such would have been beyond the thinkable to the 1st century group of believers.

In 2 Thessalonians 2:1, the one Greek word that is rendered in the King James Version as *"gathering together,"* in Hebrews 10:25 it is rendered by *"assembling together."* There is no difference, and the time was the (so-called) *"second coming"* of Jesus in 70 A.D. and it was **the day** that the 1st century believers *"could see the day approaching."* It was the day that God was going to *"gather together His elect from the four winds, from one end of heaven to the other."* It was the *"great gathering"* of all of Jesus' believers.

Encouragement and exhortation to faithfulness was needed more and more the closer to 66 A.D. that the believers came. It was going to be a very difficult time for them, but they would be rewarded for their **watching** and faithfulness, when Jesus returned to **destroy** the Judean system by 70 A.D..

Hebrews 10:25 has nothing to do with anyone in the 21st century, or anytime to follow. It all happened nearly 2,000 years ago. It was **the**

day (not *"a day"*) that the **1ˢᵗ century Hebrews** (not *"us"*) could see approaching. I could write an entire book on these two verses, but we need to stay with our study of Matthew 24.

To be fair, I suppose that I ought to say a little more concerning Hebrews 10:25. Let me refresh your memory as to what the verse actually says.

> *"Not forsaking the **assembling** (of ourselves) **together**, as the manner of some is; but exhorting one another: and so much the **more**, as ye see **the day** approaching."*

Now, I do not want to take more time than necessary, for we shall not discuss this particular verse, but I will ask that you read the entire context, for there is one verse in the context that sets the parameters of **the time element** that Jesus set. Observe very closely.

> *"For **yet a little while, and he that shall come will come**, and **will not tarry**"* [Hebrews 10:27].

Look closely at that verse, especially at all of the things that I have put in **bold** letters. There is one thing that the Greek manuscript includes that the King James Version leaves out. It is the word **very**. I will quote the verse again, but this time, using three different translations, the verse will be quoted as the original Greek should have been translated.

> *"For yet a **very** little while, He that cometh shall come, and **shall not tarry**"* [ASV & NAS].

> *"For in **just a very** little while, He who is coming will come and **will not delay**"* [NIV].

What does that do with **the time** of its occurrence in **a very little while** from the time that the writer wrote the book of Hebrews? Do you believe that the book of Hebrews was written in the 1ˢᵗ century or in the

21st century? If it was written in March of 2015, then *"in a very little while,"* Jesus would return. If it was written in the 1st century, then Jesus made his second appearance nearly 2,000 years ago. Come on now – let us be honest with ourselves and God.

The great *"assembling together"* or *"gathering together"* into the kingdom of Jesus happened nearly 2,000 years ago or do you think that Jesus' kingdom does not exist yet? You cannot have it both ways. I am afraid that many of us are just plainly not serious about a consistent study of the Bible. It is time for us to put our thinking caps on and get serious and accept the Bible for what it says, not what we **think** that it says. I am ready – are you?

God was to *"gather His elect"* in the first century A.D.. 2 Thessalonians 2:1 says that it had not happened when Paul wrote the letter, and when the writer of Hebrews wrote of the great *"gathering of the elect"* [Hebrews 10:25,37], he said that it would be only a *"very short time"* after he wrote the letter. Now, we have Jesus, Paul and the writer of Hebrews saying that the great *"gathering"* happened in the first century A.D.. Why do we not accept what the three of them wrote? We have a lot of religious baggage that needs discarding. Let us begin now and realize *"unto him (Jesus) shall the gathering of the people be,"* as the *"old testament"* recorded, and unto him it happened in the 1st century. If you believe the Bible, it is not an arguable point of view. To be pleasing to God we must accept it as His Son and the apostles gave the **time element** of its happening – 1st century A.D..

Well, we finally made it to the last part of v-31. The gathering of the elect (or more closely defined and translated as *"chosen,"*) was to be done from the *"four winds"* and *"from one end of heaven to the other."* What do those expressions mean?

Maybe if we approach it backward, it will help us to understand the proper method of interpretation. What is *"heaven"* that is listed twice in the King James Version? If it is where God is usually said to dwell, then does it mean that in 70 A.D. God gathered all of the elect from the place where God dwells, that there were none on the planet? Does the *"heaven"* where God dwells have **two** ends to it (or more, if north, east, south and west are concerned)?

Albert Barnes was struggling with the passage being fulfilled by 70 A.D. when he wrote …

> *"If this refers to the **destruction of Jerusalem**, it means, shall send forth his messengers – whatever he may choose to employ for that purpose: signs, wonders, human messengers, or the angels themselves – and gather Christians into a place of safety, so that they shall not be **destroyed with the Jews**"* [Barnes' Notes].

Of the *"four winds,"* the thought is the uppermost part of the earth. Let us only notice two passages that show how the prophets used the expression. God said it this way …

> *"Then said he unto me, Prophesy unto the wind, prophesy, son of man, and say to the wind. Thus saith the Lord God; Come the four winds, O breath, and breathe upon these slain, that they may live"* [Ezekiel 37:9].

> *"Fear not: for I am with thee: I will bring thy seed from the east, and gather thee from the west; 6. I will say to the north, Give up; and to the south, Keep not back: bring my sons from far, and my daughters from the ends of the earth"* [Isaiah 43:5-6].

Concerning the expression *"from one end of heaven to the other,"* let us notice one verse from the parallel chapter of Mark 13.

> *"And then shall he send his angels, and shall gather together his elect from the four winds, from the uttermost part of the earth to the uttermost part of heaven"* [Mark 13:27].

<u>Albert Barnes</u> explained it this way.

> *"The expression denotes that they shall be gathered from **all parts of the earth** where they are scattered. The word "heaven" is used here to denote the "visible" heavens or the <u>sky</u>, meaning that through "the whole world" he would gather them"* [Barnes Notes].

I believe that it is easy enough to see that Jesus was using the *"winds"* and the *"ends of heaven"* in a figurative sense, not a literal sense (i.e. if one is open-minded enough to take a serious look at it). The chosen elect were not literal *"winds"* to begin with, so how could they be collected from them?

> *"Now learn a parable of the fig tree: When his branch is yet tender, and putteth forth leaves, ye know that summer is nigh"* [Matthew 24:32].

Maybe I have missed something here, but as far as my studies have led me, the *"fig tree"* was used **as a figure** (not literal) of the rebellious Israelites – in this particular case, the rebellious **two tribes** referred to were the rebellious Judeans. Because of their rebellion, God was going to destroy them by means of primarily the Roman army between 66 A.D. to 70 A.D..

When the righteous of the Israelites were referred to **figuratively** (not literally), it was by means of the use of the *"olive tree."* This is not the place to take the time to show the difference, but in your private studies, you can put the *"fig tree"* in one column and the *"olive tree"* in another column and put all of the scriptures that you can find in the proper column and you will have many days of study. But, let us get back to the verse at hand.

You will recall that the context is dealing with the **destruction** of Jerusalem. The Judeans were to be **destroyed**. The rebellious harlot was to be stoned and burned. The object of God's wrath was upon the *"fig tree."* So, Jesus used it here to show how close the time was for the **destruction** of that tree (Judahites – commonly referred to as *"Jews"*). Within forty years, within that current, contemporary generation, the **barren** *"fig tree"* would be **destroyed**. The apostles were told those things so that they and the people that they told would know of the time when the **destruction** was coming, i.e. the time that the *"fig tree"* was to wither up by the roots. Again, **that time element was in 70 A.D., not in our time or any future time to us.**

Jesus talked to everyone in parables. He did **not** explain them to the rebellious Judeans, but did explain them to the believers (when asked). Notice in this verse that he told his apostles to *"learn"* the parable. He then explained the parable. Then he said *"likewise,"* thus explaining the real (unseen) truth that he wanted his apostles to understand.

 A couple of interesting things are said in this verse. First, we would normally use the word *"it"* when referring to the *'"fig tree,"* but the Greek word is accurately translated by the word *"his."* That should have given the apostles a clue that Jesus was going to explain something that was connected to people. Secondly, the Greek word *"apo"* suggests that it was *"from"* the *"fig tree"* that they were to learn something, not simply because Jesus was trying to teach them something.

There was not (nor is not) anything difficult to understanding the parable itself. When spring was in the air and the buds were turning to leaves, they understood that (the) summer (Greek is *"heat")* was very, close by. We know that to still be true today, for we see it every spring day. What did Jesus mean by using in parabolic form the physical, literal (seen) *"fig tree?"* The answer is found in the next verse.

> *"So likewise ye, when ye shall see all these things, know that it is near, even at the doors"* [Matthew 24:33].

Jesus was still speaking to his apostles when he used the word *"ye."* He was not speaking to you or me in the 21st century. Therefore, there were to be some of his disciples still biologically alive when those things came to pass.

As we noticed in the previous verse, the time of summer could be seen when the fig tree was putting on leaves. So, likewise, the apostles could see the time of the **destruction** of the *"fig tree"* (the Judeans) by the sign that their Messiah had given them. As *"all those things"* were being completed, then the disciples were to **know** that the end was near. How near? Not a long way off – not in the 21st century or later, but very near, in the 1st century A.D., while some of the disciples were still alive.

> *"Whosoever therefore shall be ashamed of me and of my words in* **THIS** *adulterous and sinful generation; of him also shall the Son of man be ashamed,* **when he cometh** *in the glory of his Father with the holy angels. (1) And he said unto them, Verily I say unto you, That there be some of them that stand here, which* **shall not taste of death***, till they have seen the kingdom of come with power"* [Mark 8:38-9:1].

It is important to notice that v-1 begins with the word *"and,"* which denotes that the two verses belong together and that the sayings of Jesus were connected together. Sometimes, when men put chapters and verses to the original texts, they seem to disconnect the thoughts of the writer, but while such may seem to be so in this case, it is not so in these two verses. The *"coming"* of Jesus to **destroy** the Judeans and the arrival of the kingdom of God with His power would happen before **some** of those who were biologically alive when Jesus spoke to them, were dead. Did Jesus lie about that? Was the Son of God mistaken? Have you seen any 2,000 year old people around lately? No? If only we believed what he said, we would **know** as did the apostles, that all of those *"things"* came to pass in the 1st century, by 70 A.D..

It is argued by some that the phrase *"it is near"* should be *"he is near."* But, it really makes no difference, because the *"coming"* of Jesus was the coming of *"it,"* i.e. the **destruction** of the Judeans and their legalistic system by 70 A.D.. *"It"* or *"he"* as *"at the doors,"* and that shows the immediacy of the event, and that event would be *"seen"* (perceived) and *"known"* by the disciples to whom Jesus was talking while he was biologically alive.

As the disciples could *"see"* the arrival of summer by the budding of the fig tree, so the same disciples could *"see"* the arrival of *"it"* or *"he"* (Jesus) by observing *"all these things"* that he had just told them. By now, to any open minded believer, it is indisputable that Jesus was speaking of the **destruction** of Jerusalem, between 66 A.D. to 70 A.D., not something in the 21st century or beyond. But, Jesus gives more proof of the time element. He gets more emphatic as to the answer of the apostles as to **when** would be THE sign of his presence at the end of the Judean age.

"Verily I say unto you, THIS generation shall not pass, till all these things be fulfilled" [Matthew 24:34].

Due to the extreme importance of that verse in understanding what Jesus was teaching, this will be longer than usual. Please consider it closely, and if you are so inclined, please read the remainder of the book – there is still some good information to come. Thank you.

Among the scholars, it is almost universally accepted that all of the verses of Matthew 24, through this verse, applies to the events that transpired in the first century, ending in 70 A.D.. Although such is true, there are some who try to **change some wording** in this verse so as to make changes in following verses, which will bring about false conclusions. Such is the case with the word *"generation."*

The Greek word that is translated as *"generation"* is *"genea,"* and defined as *"a generation, by implication, **an age**."* If that is all that was known, possibly any age could be ascertained. However, we should notice two things.

1. The apostles had asked about the sign **WHEN** the **destruction** of the temple was to occur and the **end of the age** (that accompanied the destruction of the temple). We know the answer was in 70 A.D..
2. The second thing is that Jesus said very plainly that it was **THIS** **generation**, not *"some"* generation.

There have been many attempts to discredit what Jesus said very plainly in this verse, in order to try to prop up someone's propaganda and agenda, especially if it could frighten someone into thinking that Jesus could come in the next few minutes, *"so get your affairs in order right now, **give me all of your money, buy my million dollar books**, do not worry about tomorrow, everything around you, or the condition of the planet, or your children or grandchildren, for the end is **right around the corner**,"* i.e. *"it is at the doors."* If that is true, why do they want your money, for if time and the planet ends, there will be no place to spend it. **Every generation** for almost 2,000 years have been saying and looking for the supposed *"second coming of Jesus,"* when in reality it happened while some who were alive when Jesus was biologically alive. Some of them were still alive in 70 A.D. when the temple fell. It did happen in **this** generation who were alive when Jesus was alive. It will not happen again. Do not let the deceivers and a *"den of thieves"* allow you to believe differently than what Jesus said very plainly. In case you are a little confused, due to the deceitful *"preaching"* of some in our century, notice a couple of more things.

We have already studied Matthew 23:36-37, which states …

*"Verily I say unto you, All these things shall come upon **THIS** generation. 37. **O Jerusalem, Jerusalem**, thou that killest the prophets, and stonest them which are sent unto thee, how often*

would I have gathered thy children together, even as a hen gathereth her chickens under her wings, and __ye__ would not."

Jesus pronounced his *"woes"* on the Judean leaders in this chapter (read all of Matthew 23 again). He ended his indictment of the Judahite's 1st century religious leaders with this shocking surprise …

"Behold, __your__ house __is__ left unto you desolate" [v-38].

If God left it desolate 2,000 years ago, why do we think that it is occupied today by the *"Jews?"* The temple was desolate, deserted, burned and destroyed in 70 A.D. by the Roman armies.

There are many other scriptures that show conclusively that the original word that is translated in this verse as *"generation"* means the *"contemporary"* people who were alive when Jesus was alive. Let me add something about Matthew 24 from Eusebius, the Christian historian from the late 3rd century A.D..

"The whole body, however, of the church at Jerusalem, having been commanded by a divine revelation, given men of approved piety there before the war, removed from the city, and dwelt at a certain town beyond the Jordon called Pella. Here, those that believed in Christ, having removed from Jerusalem, as if holy men had entirely abandoned the royal city itself, and the whole land of Judea; the divine justice, for __their crimes__ against Christ and his apostles, finally overtook them, __totally__ destroying the __whole generation__ of these evil doers from the earth … these facts, as well as the whole tenor of the war, and each particular of its progress, when finally __the abomination of desolation__, according to the prophetic declaration, stood in the very temple of God, so celebrated of old, but which was now approaching its __total downfall__ and final destruction __by fire__; all this, I say any one that wishes may see accurately stated in the history written by Josephus" [Eusebius' Ecclesiastical History, Book 3, Ch. 5].

When one observes the phrase *"this generation,"* he must ask himself this question, *"which generation?"* The word *"generation"* in <u>Thayer's Greek-English Lexicon of the NT</u>, is the Greek word *"genea,"* which is defined as …

> *"The whole multitude of men living at the same time."*

Also we find in William F. Arndt and Wilber Gingrich, <u>A Greek-English Lexicon of the NT</u> and <u>Other Early Christian Literature</u>:

> *"… basically, the sum total of those born at the same time, expanded to include all those living at a given time. Contemporaries."*

I will not spent much time in this and the next paragraph because the change in wording by some people, trying to uphold their agenda, instead of teaching what Jesus did, is not only inadequate but totally misleading.

I have noticed that some Bible commentators dance around the meaning of the word *"generation."* Some say that Jesus was speaking to a generation that was not going to exist until thousands of years in the future. Others claim that the entire Jewish **race** was in view. Those are **not** sound biblical interpretations. The Greek word *"genos"* (rather than *"genea"*) is best translated *"race."* The word that Jesus used here is not *"genos,"* but *"genea,"* and they have totally different meanings. He was speaking of the generation (*genea*) that was biologically alive when he was alive, not some race (*genos*) of people in the 21st century (or any century between or afterward). Do not be deceived. Do not close your mind. An understanding of this verse is crucial.

Matthew24:34 is one of the most interesting and most often **twisted** passages in the entire Bible. It will help us to understand the verse, by looking at many of the various translations of the verse, especially regarding the word *"fulfilled"* in the <u>King James Version</u>. I do not have all of the translations at my disposal, but of the ones that I have, it might be an indication that the <u>King James Version</u> might be the **only** translation that has the Greek word *"genetai"* translated by the word *"fulfilled."* Let us look at the <u>King James Version</u> first, then some of the other prominent translations.

> *"Verily I say unto you, This generation shall not pass, till all these things be **fulfilled**"* [<u>King James Version</u>].

> *[Verily I say unto you, This generation shall not pass away, till all these things be **accomplished**"* [<u>American Standard Version</u>].

> *"Truly I say to you, this generation will not pass away until all these things **take place**"* [<u>Revised Standard Version</u>].

> *"Truly I say to you, this generation will not pass away until all these things **take place**"* [<u>New American Standard Version</u>].

> *"Then at last this age **will come to its close**"* [<u>The Living Bible</u>].

> *"Assuredly, I say to you, this generation will by no means pass away till all these things **take place**"* [<u>New King James Version</u>].

> *"Remember that all these things **will happen** before the people now living have all died"* [<u>Today's English Version</u>].

> *"I tell you the truth, this generation will certainly not pass away until all these things **have happened**"* [<u>New International Version</u>].

To any honest thinking individual, how can there be any doubt? What do the words ***fulfilled, accomplished, take place, will come to a close, will happen, have happened*** mean? Cannot a second grade student tell us old people what the words mean? Is there anything in these words in any of the translations that mean anything other than that **all of the things that were listed between Matthew 24:1-33 happened in the 1ˢᵗ century A.D.**? They all took place before the **contemporary** people in Jesus' days had died biologically. They were all accomplished. They will not happen again. The things of Matthew 24 are not for our generation in the 21ˢᵗ century, nor for any future generation of people. **That age came to a close**, as <u>The Living Bible</u> stated it. This verse forever nailed it down that all of the other verses taught the same thing, i.e. that by 70 A.D., everything that Jesus had said in chapter 23 and thus far in chapter 24, happened and were completed in the 1ˢᵗ century A.D.. But for further surprises to some people, it does not stop with v-34, for the remainder of chapters 24-25 still deal with the same coming of Jesus to **destroy** the rebellious Judeans between 66 A.D. and 70 A.D.. How can such a simple saying of the Son of God be twisted so much by so many people? **And why?**

There is no need to discuss further the meaning of *"pass away,"* for one of the translations even put it plainer, *"have died."* Seven of the eight that were quoted above say "***THIS* generation**," not *"some generation."* Read the translation from <u>Today's English Version</u> again.

> *"Remember that all these things **will happen** before the people now living have all died. Heaven and earth shall pass away, but my words shall not pass away"* [Matthew 24:35].

Let us just skip this verse. No, I am not joking – I am serious now. **Let us just skip this verse!** You are probably asking why we should do that. Well, because 99% of the people that study Matthew 24 skip it. Why? It is either because they do not know what to do with this one verse, or it does not fit in with their theology (?). What do I mean by that?

It is mistakenly theorized that Matthew 24 is divided into two sections, one dealing with what happened in 70 A.D. and the other part dealing with our time in the 21ˢᵗ century or beyond. Those who make this mistake will tell you that the section that deals with the destruction of Jerusalem by the Romans in 70 A.D. is verses 1-34. Then they will tell you that the second section deals with the (erroneous) *"second coming"* is verses 36-51. **Where is v-35?**

Does v-35 deal with the destruction of Jerusalem in 70 A.D.? Then it belongs with the first section and should be verses 1-35. If it deals with the second section, then it should be verses 35-51. But they just leave it out completely because it does not fit and they do not have a clue as to the meaning.

The truth of the matter is that there are **not** two sections in Matthew 24. Jesus was still talking about *"all these things"* that were to happen before all of the people died who were alive and listening to him. So, what does the verse mean?

I do not want to spend much time here either, as I have already covered the subject of *"heaven and earth"* in previous verses in Matthew 24. Why should they have one meaning in previous verses and a different meaning in this verse? Go back and read the comments on verses 29-30, with which I have previously spent much time.

The *"heaven and earth"* was the Judahite economy. It is a figure of speech, and has nothing to do with a **literal** destruction of any **literal** heaven and earth. If so, which heaven would be destroyed? The Bible talks about at least three heavens, but in this verse only one of them would be destroyed. Again, go back and read the comments of verses 29-30. The Judeans, their leaders (heaven) and the followers (earth) were going to be destroyed. Take time right now to get your Bibles out and read Isaiah 1:1-4 and you can see the *"heavens and earth"* that was going to be destroyed. That is the context of not only the **first 34 verses of Matthew 24**, but is also the context of the remainder of the chapter. The quicker that people understand that, the easier it will be for them to understand the whole Bible. Do not let people who are out for a following or material gain, mislead you into thinking that this verse (and following verses) is a change of topic with Jesus.

The apostles had asked Jesus to explain **when** these things would happen. His answer was that it would happen before that contemporary generation had died. He used figurative language throughout his response for them to understand **when** it was going to happen, and in this verse, very implicitly stated that **it was going to happen – they would pass away**. But what he was **saying** (before this verse and after this verse) would happen and they could depend on it. So he continued to talk about **that day** in the next verse.

"But of that day and hour knoweth no man, no, not the angels of heaven, but my Father only" [Matthew 24:36].

Jesus continued in this verse to talk about **that day**, not *"another day."* He was still answering the question that the apostles had asked him – **when** was the *"time of the destruction of Jerusalem and the end of that age?"*

What is it that confuses people who study this chapter? It is probably that Jesus said in v-34 that it would happen in the 1st century A.D. and in this verse (v-36) that he did not know when. At least one question is in order. How could he know that it was to happen in the 1st century generation (before they died) and at the same time not know? Is that the problem with people not understanding? Well, let me see if I can help a little, by using a personal illustration.

Sometime early in 1957, my wife, LaVeta became pregnant. Calculations were made by the doctors and the **when** of the arrival of our first daughter was determined to be in November (which it was). Predictions of the **time element** was good so far. But, as we questioned the doctors further about **the day** in November and the exact **hour** on that day, they said that they knew **the time**, but did not know *"of that day and hour."*

That illustration should be ample evidence as to how Jesus could know that it was to happen in his generation, and yet not know the exact day or the exact hour. I knew the year and month of the arrival of my daughter, but I did not know *"of that day and hour" of her arrival*. **Nowhere does it ever indicate that the Son of God never knew the WHEN of the destruction of Jerusalem and the end of the Mosaic age**. Contrary to that, **he did know** – it was to be within forty years (a biblical generation), and he stated such in v-34. The apostles had asked **when**, and he told them **when**, but did not know the **exact** day and hour. Why do you think that he constantly told them (the apostles and believers of his day) to *"watch"* if he did not know that the time was when they were still biologically alive and would *"see"* the day and hour? There was no need for them to *"watch"* if **that** *"day and hour"* was 2,000 or more years in the future.

I had to watch for the **beginning** and progression of the *"birth pangs,"* and Jesus told his apostles in v-14 what was the **beginning** of the **birth pangs** but he did not tell the exact time of the *"birth."* Now if you really want something to think about, when was the *"birth"* into the spiritual kingdom of God? Was it before the *"birth pangs"* of v-14? Or was it in 70 A.D.? You will have to study that out for yourself as Matthew 24 is not the place to discuss the subject more fully. I guess that one more question is in order. *"Is not 2,000 years a long time between the beginning of the birth pangs and the birth?"*

Let us summarize this verse. No **man** knew – the heavenly **angels** did not know, Jesus did not know the *"day and hour,"* but those who listened to the Son of God knew the **when** – it was before most people living when he was living would die – i.e. the first century A.D.. We can look back into history and know that it was in 70 A.D.. I will end this verse study by asking a question.

Since you and I have hind-sight, and can know that it all happened in the 1st century, **can you** (even with hind-sight) point out to me the *day* *and hour"* of *"***that day***?"* I thought not! Only the Father knew and only the Father knows right now. Did I stick my neck out too far with that statement? If so, please respond with the proof. I am open to a scholarly discussion.

Before we leave Matthew 24:36, which connects with the next verse (v-37), let us notice that the Greek word *"ekeinos"* means **that one**, and is specific. It was not just referring to *"a day,"* but specifically to **that** day of which the apostles had asked, namely, **that day** when the temple would be destroyed and **that day** when the *"end of the age"* occurred.

If Jesus' response was no more than *"I don't know the day or the hour,"* why did he waste all of the verses from v-5 through v-35, and just answer them plainly. *"You asked me **when** – I don't know **when**!"?* The answer lies in the fact that all of those verses were concerning the time, consequently, *"**that** day and hour"* of the fall of Jerusalem and the end of the Mosaic age. It was the same *"**that** day"* to which he had been referring from v-3. It was not another time, it was the same time.

> *"But as the days of Noe were, so shall also the coming of the Son of man be"* [Matthew 24:37].

The <u>King James Version</u> here does not spell the name Noah as we usually spell it, but it is the same person who was saved from the destruction of the flood by being in the ark that he built. The following is a quotation of the beginning of the evil people being destroyed in the flood.

> *"And it came to pass, when men began to multiply on the face of the earth, and daughters were born unto them, 2. That the sons of God saw the daughters of men that they were fair; and they took them wives of all which they chose. 3. And the LORD said, **My spirit shall not always strive with man**, for that he also is flesh; **yet his days shall be an hundred and twenty years.** 4. There were giants in the earth in those days; and also after that, when the*

*sons of God came in unto the daughters of men, and they bare children unto them, the same became mighty men which were of old, men of renown. 5. **And saw that the wickedness of man was great in the earth, and that every imagination of the thoughts of his heart was only evil continually**. 6. And it repented the LORD that He had made man on the earth, and it grieved him at his heart. 7. And the LORD said, **I will destroy man whom I have created from the face of the earth**; both man, and beast, and the creeping thing, and the fowls of the air; for it repenteth me that I have made them. 8. **But Noah found grace in the eyes of the LORD**"* [Genesis 6:1-8].

If we think about the situation in Noah's day, it is probable that Noah knew the time of the flood. The best probable interpretation of the expression *"yet his days shall be an hundred and twenty years"* is that it was **not** dealing with the biological lifespan of any particular man, as Noah was already 600 years old and lived another 350 years. In reading the entire verse, it seems very likely that God knew how wicked the world had become and determined to destroy them all (except Noah and his family who found favor with Him). It would take some time for Noah to build the ark to house all that God was to put into it, besides the eight people, and that period was one hundred and twenty years. However, Noah did not know *"the day and hour"* of his entrance into the ark or the flood.

Noah **knew** that the flood was coming. He **knew** that he had to build the ark. He did exactly as God told him. **That day** that God put him into the ark did not *"overtake him as a thief in the night."* Probably all of the other people were laughing at Noah for building such a big ship out in the middle of dry land *"until it began to rain."* **That day** did overtake the wicked, unbelieving world *"as a thief in the night."*

The parallel is that the same condition would exist when Jesus would make his appearance to destroy the unbelieving, wicked Judeans which was finalized in 70 A.D.. **That day** would not come on the believers *"as a thief in the night,"* but it did come on the unbelieving Judeans *"as a thief in the night."* The believers were prepared and the unbelievers were not prepared. Recall the parables that their Messiah gave to them about ten virgins, one-half of them were prepared and one-half of them were not prepared. The ones that were prepared went into the marriage feast, and ***the door was shut*** (like the door of the ark was shut by God) so as to exclude those who were unprepared. This verse has both the type and the antitype in it. One (the type) occurred in Noah's day, the other (antitype) occurred in the 1st century A.D. in Jerusalem.

> *"For in the days that were before the flood they were eating and drinking, marrying and giving in marriage, until the day that Noe entered into the ark"* [Matthew 24:38].

The Greek word *"gar"* is translated *"for"* and means *"to assign a reason."* The next Greek word, *"hos"* is translated by the word *"as"* and means *"in the same manner."* So the setting is in place to make the comparison. In the days before it began to rain in the days of Noah, the people did not believe that there would be a flood. They went on their merry way, believing that *"their God"* would not destroy them. *"In the same manner,"* the people living in 66 A.D., before the Roman army surrounded Jerusalem and then actually entered the city, did not believe that God would let their way of *"religious life"* and *"His city"* and *"His temple,"* along with those caught in the siege, to be destroyed. They went on their merry way, eating and drinking. Did we not read where it was stated …

> *"And I will say to my soul, Soul, thou hast much goods laid up for many years; take thine ease, **eat, drink, and be merry**. 20. But God said unto him, Thou fool, this night thy soul shall be required of thee"* [Luke 12:19-20].

They did not believe until it became a reality. They believed then, but it was too late, for the *"door was shut"* when *"Noah entered into the ark."* The parallel gets more interesting when the Greek is observed, for it does not say *"the day that,"* but rather **that day**. Note that the term **that day** is used in this verse as it was in the previous verse.

If we were living in the days of Noah and did not believe that there was a coming flood, what would we do? We would continue to do whatever we had been doing. We would continue to eat and drink. We would continue to get married and we would continue to have babies. By the way, the Greek word that is translated as *"giving in marriage"* is *"gaster,"* and primarily means *"the stomach,"* hence the way that the King James Version translates the word as *"belly, with child, and womb."* It denotes that the women still became pregnant and continued to raise a family, not realizing that their children would be destroyed in the flood. Had they believed and known that the flood was coming, many would not have been married and certainly no loving person would have brought children into the world that was to be destroyed by the flood. How would you have liked to have lived then and had been an eye witness to the drowning of all of your children?

"In like manner," before the Roman army surrounded Jerusalem, and for many years before that, the unbelievers continued their daily routine of eating and drinking, of finding a wife, and bringing children into the Judean world that were to be destroyed by the Romans. How would you have liked to have lived then, not believing what Jesus said about the destruction of Jerusalem, the temple and the end of the Jewish age before some of them died, only to bring more children into the world, knowing that they were going to be murdered by the Romans a few years later?

I would like to think that if I lived when Jesus said those things, that I would have believed him and that I would not marry, and certainly would not bring children into the world. Did he not already warn the **believers and the unbelievers ...**

> *"And woe unto them that are with child, and to them that give suck in those days"* [Matthew 24:19]?

It not only would be very, very difficult for the believing women to escape from the onslaught of the Roman army, but it would have been more difficult for the women who were caught inside the city to see their children starve to death (believers or non-believers). Josephus even recorded (and named) a woman who ate her own child for hunger and offered some of her own child to the Roman soldiers. Woe to anyone with child in those days – believers or unbelievers.

I think that we should consider one more thing. After **that day** that Noah entered into the ark, they still had a week before the rain began. They could knock on the door of the ark and cry, *"Lord, Lord, open unto us,"* but it would do no good. Jesus told another parable about the same thing that would happen in 70 A.D..

> *"When once the master of the house is risen up, and hath **shut the door**, and ye begin to stand without, and to knock at the door, saying, **Lord, Lord, open unto us**; and he shall answer and say unto you, **I know you not** whence ye are"* [Luke 13:25].

When the Roman army surrounded Jerusalem, they had a short time to cry to God to let them escape, but it was of no more avail than those standing without the ark. On both occasions, all death and hell broke loose and in both cases, they perished. That is what unbelief will do. Do you believe in God, the Almighty and His Son Jesus? Do you believe what they have said?

Does it seem like I am *"beating a dead horse to death"* by repeating these things? Well, sorry! I must follow as Jesus has lead, and he has continued in various terms and illustrations to emphasize the importance of his Olivet discourse, for on this chapter hung all of the fulfillments of all of the prophecies of the prophets. He continued in the next verse, so we will continue with the next verse also.

"And knew not until the flood came, and took them all away; so shall also the coming of the Son of man be" [Matthew 24:39].

Jesus continued the thought of the previous verse in talking about Noah and the people of that generation when the flood came.

They did not *"believe"* that there was to be a flood. And, of course, they could not *"know"* that the flood was coming, for such had not happened before.

But, at the point where Noah entered into the ark *"and the door was shut,"* they did realize that something dreadful was possibility going to happen to them.

But a step further shows us that beginning seven days after Noah entered the ark, it began to rain and the storehouse from below the earth released its water and at that point *"faith"* was no longer a valid option, for it had become a reality, then they **knew!**

The word *"all,"* always has to be interpreted in light of the context in which it occurs. Here Matthew is not writing about Noah and his family, for (in the sense that it is here used for drowning and being destroyed) they were not *"taken away."* Read the passage again and know for certain that the ones who were *"taken away"* were not the good people. The ones who were *"taken away"* were the bad people, and they were *"taken away"* for **destruction**.

When you have time, you might want to research all of the parables of Jesus and notice the word *"taken"* or some associated wording, and see how he used it. It might surprise you to see in those cases that the phrase is used correctly and sometimes we use it backwards, referring to the wrong people or action. I do not want to pursue that rabbit trail in this verse.

Surprise, surprise, surprise! At the coming of Jesus, the same mental condition would be prevalent among most people. They were not believers, and therefore they had no way of knowing for sure that God would actually allow the temple to be destroyed by the Romans in 70 A.D.. But what a surprise it was when in the space of about 72 hours, the Romans had built an outside wall around Jerusalem, and the *"door (of escape) was closed."* They **knew** then that something terrible was about to happen. No room for belief anymore, for the time of **destruction** had set in. It had become a reality. They **knew**! But it was too late. We will study more about this topic when we view the next chapter.

> *"Then shall two be in the field; the one shall be taken, and the other left"* [Matthew 24:40].

The word *"then"* introduces to us again the time element. It was immediately following the events that came before in this chapter. It also connects to the previous verse that speaks of Noah and the people who were **destroyed** in the flood. The illustration here is the second illustration – Noah being the first – showing the suddenness of the *"coming"* of the Israelite Messiah in 70 A.D. **to destroy** the unbelieving Judahites.

This illustration is of workers in a field. The indication is that one was working correctly and the other one was either not working at all (which is the best probability), or working incorrectly. Jesus used the illustration of only **two**, whereas in the illustration of Noah, he used the entire world. One was taken (for destruction) and the other left. Many are desirous of using this verse to prove their *"rapture"* theory, but careful study will show that it backfires on them.

In Noah's day, *"he took them all away"* to destruction – not to save them. Likewise, in this illustration, *"the one shall be taken"* **for destruction**, not for salvation. Both were in the same field (i.e. both belonged to God). One was removed **for destruction** and the other was left in the field (kingdom). The same thing can be seen in the following parable.

> *"Another parable put he forth unto them, saying, The kingdom of heaven is likened unto a man which sowed good seed in his field: 25. But while men slept, his enemy came and sowed tares among the wheat, and went his way. 26. But when the blade was sprung up, and brought forth fruit, then appeared the tares also. 27. So the servants of the householder came and said unto him, Sir, didst not thou sow good seed in thy field? From whence then hath it tares? 28. He said unto them, an enemy hath done this. The servants said, Wilt thou then that we go and gather them up? 29. But he said, Nay; lest while ye gather up the tares, ye root up also the wheat with them. 30. Let both grow together until the harvest: and in the time of harvest I will say to the reapers,* **Gather ye together FIRST the tares, and bind them in bundles to burn them:** *but gather the wheat into my barn"* [Matthew 13:24-30].

Before the *"saved"* were gathered together, **first** the tares (the disbelievers) were gathered together **for the purpose of burning them – destroying them**. This verse in Matthew and some of the parables deal with *"taking away"* (after they had been gathered together) the unbelievers *"being taken away"* **for destruction**, not to rapture the good away first.

It has been my observation over 60 years that if people are going to read the Bible, that they should pay much closer attention to what it truly says.

> *"Two women shall be grinding at the mill; the one shall be taken, and the other left"* [Matthew 24:41].

There is no Greek word or words for the phrase *"women shall be."* So, to understand why the translators put the phrase into the context, especially regarding women instead of men, we must go to the Greek word that is translated by the word *"one"* in this verse. The Greek word for *"one"* is *"mia"* and in this sentence an ***irregular feminine*** word, so it can be understood that the subject would be women. Also, later in the verse, the word *"other"* occurs. It is the same Greek word *"mia"* and denotes another woman, so the word to begin the sentence, *"two"* is a correct translation.

The previous verse tells of someone (working) in the field, probably referencing men. This verse talks of someone *"grinding"* at the mill or *"in the mill-house."* What is interesting about this is **the time of year** that is being indicated, which is the harvest time. Men at work were reaping the grain and the women were grinding it. It would take an entire book to deal adequately with the feast days, but let this short paragraph indicate to you that the *"coming"* of their Messiah to destroy them is indicated to be in the September/October time of year, the time of the harvest. This was the time of the *"gathering"* of the wheat into the barn and the time of the burning of the tares. This was the coming of the Roman army to **destroy** the city and system of the Judahites. We can look back and know what year, for such is recorded by the historians. It was 66 A.D. to 70 A.D.. The second illustration in this verse (the first one in the previous verse) says the same thing in different wording.

The idea is still the same in this verse as in the previous verse – one woman was *"taken"* for **destruction**, not taken for salvation. The one that was *"left"* was for salvation. It would be helpful to re-read the comments on the previous verses to find further information.

All of the translations at my disposal translate the last word as *"left,"* and I would not want to argue much with that many Greek scholars. The unbelievers were *"taken"* and **destroyed** *"first"* and the believers were *"left"* to be taken into God's barn. If He was talking about the end of planet earth, all would be gone, no one left.

"Watch therefore: for ye know not what hour your Lord doth come" [Matthew 24:42].

I will begin a study of this verse with the word *"ye."* It refers to the audience that Jesus had all of the way through this chapter. The ones to whom he was speaking were his apostles, the ones who were biologically alive when he was biologically alive in the 1st century A.D..

It was to them that he said to **watch**. Now why in the world would he tell them to watch if the *"coming"* of the Lord was not to occur for 2,000 years or more?

It was interesting in my research to learn that the Greek word *"gregoreuo"* literally means *"to stay awake."* The King James Version translates the word by the words, *"be vigilant, wake and watch or be watchful."* Recall the parable of the ten virgins and they were to *"watch,"* i.e. they were to *"keep awake"* and be ready for the arrival of the bridegroom. We will study more on that subject when we get to the next chapter.

The word *"therefore"* comes from an original word that connects (conjunctionally), i.e. these three verses are connected and it means *"accordingly."* As they saw the season of the *"coming"* of the Lord, they were to *"watch accordingly,"* i.e. the closer the time came, the more they were to be watchful. They knew when, they knew that it was in their generation in the 1st century A.D., but they did not know the *"day and hour."* If they understood Jesus to be talking about something in the 21st century, they would have asked him, *"Why Lord, must we watch? We will have been dead for 2,000 years. Why not say something that will be around and alert the people who are alive in the 21st century about watching, instead of telling us to watch?"*

It is only by implication that the Greek word that is translated as *"ye know"* can be used, for its primary meaning is *"to see."* Obviously any *"seeing"* would not be with the naked eye, but a **perception** of the *"coming of the Lord."*

The *"coming of the Lord"* was for the purpose of **destroying** the unbelievers and those who were not *"watching."* So, the apostles were admonished to *"keep awake"* and be *"ever alert,"* and *"so much the more as (they saw) the day approaching."*

> *"But know this, that if the Goodman of the house had known in what watch the thief would come, he would have **watched**, and would not have suffered his house to be broken up"* [Matthew 24:43].

Again, by means of another illustration, Jesus was instructing his apostles concerning his return. He was still telling the apostles to *"watch,"* that the time of the *"coming of the Son of man"* would be **in their generation**, not an event that would happen two millennia later in 2015 A.D.. Those who *"watched"* would be prepared and when the bridegroom came, they would be allowed to go to the wedding feast. Those who went to sleep and were not prepared would not be allowed to enter after the door was shut. There are at least three things in this verse that are very interesting.

> ➤ The first is that the expression, *"the goodman of the house"* simply means *"the head of the household."*
> ➤ The second is that the word *"house"* primarily means *"an abode,"* but by implication it means *"a family."* Is there a very real application here by the Master that the Judean family was about to be *"broken?"* Whether he meant to use the *"house"* as an illustration that the Judahite *"family"* was going to be broken is uncertain, but we know that the end result is the same. They were going to be **destroyed** in 70 A.D..
> ➤ The third is that the Greek word *"egregoresen"* is translated as *"he would have watched."* We have inherent in this word the

same thought that we have previously covered, i.e. he would *"have kept awake."*

It is with serious interest that we look at the word *"watch."* There were twelve hours in the Judaic day. Consequently it would be correct to say *"the third hour of the day,"* or *"the sixth hour of the day,"* or *"the eleventh hour."* But, the night divisions were different. It was divided into *"watches,"* each one having three hours. So the *"second watch"* would be from 9 PM till 12 midnight. Other passages say things …

> **"*The night is far spent, the day is at hand:*** *let us therefore cast off the works of darkness and let us put on the armour of light"* [Romans 13:12] …

… which, if connected to this verse, means that the thief could come and **destroy** in the **last watch of the night**, i.e. between 3 AM and 6 AM. But, the exact *"day and hour"* he would not know, and could not know. Other passages say things like the following …

> *"Yet I am writing you a new command; its truth is seen in him and you, because the **darkness is passing and the true light is already shining**"* [1 John 2:8 – N.I.V.] …

… indicating that **the day** of the age without end was **at hand** in the first century A.D. when John wrote.

Comparing this instruction with the previous illustrations, if the people had known the *"watch"* in which the flood was coming, they would not have allowed their families to drown. And if those working in the field had known the approximate time of the coming event, they would have both been ready because they would have been *"watching."* Once more – both women who were grinding would have been *"watching"* and both of them would have been saved from the **destruction**.

There has been no change of topic since v-1. It was concerning the destruction of the temple and the end of the Mosaic age that the apostles had inquired of Jesus and he told them that it would come before all of those who were biologically alive had died, but the exact day and the exact hour he nor they would know. But he did give them **THE sign**. He did not stop answering their question in v-34. He gave them warning about the division of the believers and unbelievers all of the way to the end of this chapter and on into chapter 25. We will see that when we get there.

> *"Therefore be ye also ready: for in such an hour as ye think not the Son of man cometh"* [Matthew 24:44].

The word *"therefore"* comes from compounding two Greek words that technically means *"through that thing."* It was through **that** illustration that the Messiah had just completed his instruction to his apostles about *"watching"* for the *"coming of the Lord,"* that he said, *"through that thing,"* i.e. the suddenness of the coming, you must *"be ready."* Since Matthew had already recorded the basis for what is in this verse, there is really not much else that needs to be said.

The Lord told his apostles that they *"also"* were to be (become) ready for the arrival of the Son of man. Why were they to be ready for the coming of their Messiah, if they were dead? Would it have not been better had not Jesus told them to be (become) ready for the violent deaths by which they would die – if his coming was 2,000 years yet into the future?

They did not know the exact day and hour, and he here told his apostles that *"in such an hour as the think not"* he would come (be **present**). They could not and did not know the exact hour, so they had to *"watch"* and be *"ready,"* for the coming of the Christ would be a reality during the lifetimes of some of those who were listening to him speak. **Look at this next passage very closely!**

> *"Whosoever therefore shall be ashamed of me and of my words in* **this** *adulterous and sinful generation; of him also shall the Son man be ashamed,* **when** *he cometh in the glory of his Father with the holy angels. (9:1) And he said unto them, Verily I say unto you, That there be some of them that stand here, which shall not taste of death, till they have seen the kingdom of God come with power"* [Mark 8:38 – 9:1].

It is unfortunate that a chapter heading interrupted the thought. There should be no separation between the two verses. It did come between 66 A.D. and 70 A.D.. It is not something for which we are to look in the 21st century – it was something for the apostles of Jesus to look for in their lifetimes.

The phrase *"as ye think not"* shows that they were *"thinking."* Why would they not be thinking about the return of their Messiah? He told them that he was definitely coming back and that it would be in the generation that was then alive. It was definite – *"the Son of man cometh!"* They were told to look for it. They did look for it. It did happen in the first century A.D.. To deny that, is to deny everything that Jesus said throughout all three of these chapters in Matthew. I will not deny what he said. I will accept it, even though I might not understand everything about that 1st century coming of the Son of man (who was Jesus). He said that it would happen in the 1st century. It did happen in the 1st century. In reality the only choice that we have is to believe what Jesus said or not believe it. I choose to believe him. I pray that each of you reading this will believe him also.

> *"Who then is a faithful and wise servant, whom his lord hath made ruler over his household, to give them meat in due season"* [Matthew 24:45].

As we study this verse (and the next six verses), it might seem somewhat controversial, however, all that I ask of you is to give the comments a fair hearing. Keep an open mind.

To emphasize the seriousness of the *"coming"* of the Son of man within forty years from the time that he spoke those things (ending in 70 A.D.), he began with this verse, the first of three or four parables (even though they are not called parables).

This verse and the next six verses are instructions from Jesus in a story form, commonly termed by Bible students as a parable. It concerns the *"ruler"* that the lord of the ruler had made him such over some household. The literal meaning shows that the purpose was for the ruler to give food at the proper time to the household. Let us consider it more closely.

The word *"then"* is not used here as a sequential idea, but rather who could Jesus conclude to be faithful and wise. So, we need to ask ourselves *"to whom"* was he speaking? Again, we are reminded that he was speaking to his apostles, and had been from the very beginning of this chapter. He was asking his apostles if they would be faithful and wise, not if or perhaps someone out there, unknown to them, and later on to be manifest whether they were to be faithful or not. He was not asking if we, in the 21st century would be faithful or not. Objectively, the word that is translated as *"faithful"* means *"trustworthy."* Could the apostles to whom Jesus was speaking be trusted to do the work for which he selected them? They were not predestinated to be trustworthy; they had a choice, just like Judas had a choice. Every man has a choice. If mankind did not have a choice of being faithful or evil, then there is no room for scriptures like *"choose ye this day whom ye will serve"* [Joshua 24:15].

The word *"wise"* (phronimos) means *"thoughtful, discreet (implying a cautious character)."* Were the apostles to whom he was speaking thoughtful and cautious?

I remember about fifty plus years ago, reading a commentary on the book or Romans by R.L. Whiteside about the Greek word *"doulos."* It really made an impression on me as a young believer. It is not really correct to simply translate it by the word *"servant,"* but more correctly by being a *"slave,"* i.e. *"a slave servant,"* whether voluntary or involuntary. Of course, the apostles were voluntary slaves as we are voluntary slaves.

The great Master of the apostles was asking the apostles to whom he was speaking if they would be cautious, thoughtful and trustworthy to do the job for which he had chosen them. For the most part of the next forty years, they had the glorious gospel of the Son of God on their shoulders to take to the world. Would they be wise and faithful – have a cautious character and be trustworthy?

As we continue to study v-45, we are confronted with what some may regard as a very controversial statement. If this is a parable, and I believe that it is – and if Jesus was speaking to his apostles, which I believe that he was, then who would be the *"lord"* in the passage? The *"lord"* (figuratively, in parabolic form) would be either the Almighty God or it would have to be Jesus himself. Which one would you chose?

I would not pick Almighty, for I do not believe that He ever has nor ever will place anyone *"over His house,"* with the exception of placing Jesus over part of His household for awhile. However, it gets more complicated if we interpret it as Jesus giving the apostles the *"rule"* over **his own household**. That would mean that the Messiah had a household.

Yes, I know, as you do, that there are other passages that speak of the *"household of God"* and *"My Father's house,"* and in that context is not speaking of the Son of God. But, when the passage comes up that says …

> *"But Christ as **a son over his own house**; whose house are we, if we hold fast the confidence and the rejoicing of the hope firm unto the end"* [Hebrews 3:6].

... we now have two verses that teach that Jesus had a *"house"* or *"household."* And the writer of Hebrews tells whose the *"house"* was. What do we think now? How controversial is it to think about something of which we have not thought much about before? To study this subject in more detail, obtain my book that is entitled, <u>The Relationship Of The Church, The Kingdom And House To Eschatology</u> at AMAZON.COM or the Kindle version. Type Ron McRay in the blank spot.

I am always open to be taught, but it seems to me today that Jesus did have a *"house,"* and that *"house"* was made up of believers between 30 A.D. and 70 A.D.. All of the while that the *"house"* belonged to Jesus, it was still included in the *"house"* of Almighty God. The Bible certainly teaches that God gave to His Son some people and that the ones that God gave to him would not be lost. This is called by the Greek word, *"ekklesia"* (which erroneously is called the church). It was only **one body**, regardless of where they met together or not. It had a beginning point and such is alluded to in Matthew 16:18. No organization!

> *"And I say also unto thee, That thou art Peter, and upon this rock I will build my ekklesia (church); and the gates of hell shall not prevail against it."*

Concerning the apostles, Jesus said ...

> *"I have manifested thy name unto the men which thou gavest me out of the world: **thine they were, and thou gavest them me**; and they have kept thy word"* [John 17:6].

> *"While I was with them in the world, I kept them in thy name: those that thou gavest me I have kept, and none of them is lost but the son of perdition, that the scripture might be fulfilled"* [John 17:12].

"That the saying might be fulfilled, which he spake, Of them which thou gavest me have I lost none" [John 18:9].

You have read enough in our studies of this chapter to understand that I believe that Jesus turned *"his house"* over to the Father; that the Father could be *"all in all"* in 70 A.D. with the destruction of the temple, the Judahites and the salvation of those who belonged to Jesus.

"And when all things shall be subdued unto Him, then shall the Son also himself be subject unto Him that put all things under him, that may be all in all" [1 Corinthians 15:28].

In the <u>King James Version</u>, we see the word *"ruler."* It conveys to us in the 21st century the wrong idea. The Greek word is defined as *"to place down (permanently), i.e. (figuratively) to designate."* Yes, the apostles were in the position of being *"over"* the believers, in that they **served** them, not bossed them. They followed in the footsteps of Jesus, who always taught people the right thing, led them by his example, and corrected their errors, but never forced them to do things. Even the King of kings was a leader of sheep, not a boss (not one who made decisions for *"anyone"* but himself), anyone who was a pastor, deacon, elder, minister or pope in some ~~church~~ and made any decision at all except for himself.

The believing community today in the 21st century does not need generals on white horses telling the privates what to do. What is needed is for them to get down from the bosses slot, degrade themselves to being buck privates, and **serve** those who follow. Yes, they need to take the privates by the hand and say, *"Come on, let me lead you and show you by example what needs doing."* Yes, we need leaders and servers but never a modern pastor. **Never!** Never a located preacher!

Then we find the phrase, *"to give them meat in due season."* The word *"meat"* simply means **food** – not animal meat. The believers must have been fed by the apostles. The feeding was to be done in *"due season,"* which means *"an occasion, i.e. set or proper time."* We can see this happening as the writings of the apostles did not come on the first Pentecost after the resurrection of their Messiah (Acts 2), but they were *"gradually"* written as the need arose. The apostles did not have all of the food that was necessary to feed the believers for forty years. Even if they did, we can see places where they sometimes did not understand what they preached. This brings to mind one of the most misunderstood and wrongly taught verses in the Bible.

> *"Study to show thyself approved unto God, a workman that needeth not to be ashamed, rightly dividing the word of truth"* [2 Timothy 2:15].

This teaching by the apostle Paul is the same instruction that Jesus gave in the parable that we are discussing. Let us look more closely at other translations.

> *"Do your best to present yourself to God as one approved, a workman who does not need to be ashamed and who correctly handles the word of truth"* [NIV].

> *"Be diligent to present yourself approved to God as a workman who does not need to be ashamed, accurately handling the word of truth"* [NASU].

> *"Do your best to win full approval in God's sight, as a worker who is not ashamed of his work, one who correctly teaches the message of God's truth"* [TEV].

First, notice that the apostle Paul was telling the preacher, Timothy, to do what he did. The thing that Paul was **NOT** telling Timothy was to do any kind of *"study."* The Greek word *"spoudazo"* means *"to make effort, be prompt or earnest."* Most other places in which the Greek word occurs in the Bible, it is translated as *"give diligence."* Maybe in the 17th century the word *"study"* meant such to that generation, but the word *"study"* in the 21st century carries an entirely different meaning. You can see by the other translations what it really means by such wording as *"do your best,"* and *"be diligent."* All that the first part of the verse means, is for Timothy to do his *"dead level best"* to be pleasing to God – nothing about studying the Bible (in fact, all of it was not written yet when Paul wrote to Timothy). Do we need to study more? Absolutely, but we need to quit prostituting this verse to try to make it mean something that it does not.

Secondly, the term *"rightly dividing"* is usually taught as meaning to know where to divide the *"old testament"* from the *"new testament."* Such is not the meaning, for at that time, not all of what we call the *"new testament"* had been written. Also, the meaning is expanded by looking at the other translations, with such wording as *"correctly handles – accurately handling"* and *"correctly teaches."* The definition is *"to make a straight cut – to expound correctly the divine message."* The idea is to teach a person what he needs and when he needs it. If one needs teaching about faith, do not each him about something else. If another person needs to be taught something about kindness, do not spend your time talking to him about forgiveness. There is a place for all of those, but when you teach people, *"cut it straight"* with him, tell him what he needs in order to be right with God. It has almost always been the case that some will **not** *"cut it straight"* with another, for being afraid of offending him and losing his popularity with the person, or worse yet, having his money cut off. All it takes is just **one person** and the preacher has just got fired. Do you remember the following scripture?

> *"The prophets prophesy falsely, and the priest bear rule by their means; and my people love to have it so: and what will ye do in the end thereof"* [Jeremiah 5:31]?

The prophets were not *"cutting it straight"* with the people when they prophesied falsely. However, the reason that the prophets did that was because the people *"loved to have it so."* And guess what the priests did? They took the money and kept their mouth shut. Have you seen preachers like this? Or, have you even seen preachers who are fully supported full time? Eventually it amounts to the same thing.

Does not false teaching make light the yoke upon man and removes God's fear from His conscience – and with that, man is ready to be content?

Every believer, regardless of how unpopular he becomes, or if the people cut off all of his money and he has to flop hamburgers at McDonald's, he should *"cut it straight"* with all people. Be honest with yourself and before God.

To make an application to us today – at the proper time that they need it, give to each person the proper food at the proper time (*due season*).

> *"Blessed is that servant, whom his lord when he cometh shall find so doing"* [Matthew 24:46].

I see no reason to spend much time on this verse. Jesus continued the thought of the servitude of his apostles and said that the person to whom he was speaking (**that** servant), would be blessed (*"fortunate, extremely blessed, well off"*) if he was giving the people their needed spiritual food as they needed it. The word *"so"* means *"in this way."*

Again, he introduces his coming, which we have already noted to be coming in 66 A.D. to 70 A.D. to **destroy** the temple and city of Jerusalem along with the Judean system.

> *"Verily I say unto you, That he shall make him ruler over all his goods"* [Matthew 24:47].

Jesus was still talking to his apostles. That is why he used the word *"you."* He then proceeded to talk of what he would do for *"them"* if they were rendering to the people of the 1st century their daily food (*"in due season"*). He was interested in their continued faithfulness to their calling.

The translated word *"verily"* comes from the Greek word *"amen."* When used at the end of a sentence, it means *"so be it."* When used at the beginning of a sentence, it declares that what is being said is **trustworthy** and can be simply translated as *"surely."*

As far as the Greek word *"kathistemi"* is concerned, we have already studied it a few verses back. It is translated as *"he shall make him ruler."* Figuratively, it means *"to designate, convoy or constitute."*

"Over all his goods," seems to indicate that the faithful apostles would receive from the Messiah a power to dispense all of the blessings of the new covenant; and his word would ever be accompanied with the demonstration of the Holy Spirit to the hearts of all that heard it.

In the next verse, the Lord told what would happen to any of the apostles who became wicked and did not remain trustworthy to the calling to which he gave to them. So, the time element is still before the apostles in Jesus' use of this parable, which each apostle must have applied to himself. Since it dealt with the apostles and their feeding the people with spiritual food *"in due season,"* it obviously refers to the 1st century A.D..

> *"But and if that evil servant shall say in his heart, My lord delayeth his coming"* [Matthew 24:48].

The word *"but"* shows that this thought is the opposite from what went before. That which was in the previous verses was the good servant (*slave*) who cared for the other bond-servants. This verse introduces the following verses that deal with the opposite character. Jesus was speaking to his apostles, and the application was specifically for them (yet we know that the extension to other believers would also be true).

Again, Jesus was speaking to the same apostles. He told them what would happen to them if they were faithful. In these verses, he is telling them what will happen to them **if** they were **not** faithful. It seems as if we are running into the subjective area with the Greek wording, and that would involve the word **if**. They did not have to be evil, but *"if"* they were, they would be punished.

The word that is translated as *"evil,"* probably could at this point be better translated as *"worthless,"* and would fit into his parables about the *"worthless"* fig tree (that had no fruit on it), which was representative of the worthless Judeans. We know from hind-sight that they were **destroyed** between 66 A.D. and 70 A.D. (withering from the roots up, just like the fig tree).

The Messiah gave another parable about a master taking a long journey and what happened to the *"worthless"* servant when he returned. Of course, the parable was not only representing Jesus as the Lord who took the long (delayed) journey, but also the *"worthless"* Judeans who did not believe that God would let Jerusalem and the temple be destroyed by 70 A.D.. However, the same thing was taught by the Lord in Luke 12. It is not the parallel of Matthew 24, for that would be Luke 21. Without any comment (for the lack of space), allow me to just quote the verse and you can see the parallel.

> *"Let **your** loins be girded about, and your lights burning; 36. And ye yourselves like unto men that wait for their lord, when he **will return** from the wedding: that when he cometh and knocketh, they may open unto him immediately. 37. Blessed are those servants, whom the lord when he cometh shall find **watching**: verily I say unto you, that he shall gird himself, and make them to sit down to meat, and will come forth and serve them. 38. And he shall come in the second watch, or come in the third watch, and find them so, blessed are those servants. 39. And this know, that if the goodman of the house had known what hour the thief would come, he would*

*have watched, and not have suffered his house to be broken through. 40. Be ye therefore ready also; for the Son of man cometh at an **hour** when ye think not. 41. Then Peter said unto him, Lord, speaketh thou this **parable** unto us, or even to all? 42. And the Lord said, Who then is that faithful and wise steward, whom his lord shall make ruler over his household, to give them their portion of meat in due season? 43. Blessed is that servant, whom his lord when he cometh shall find so doing. 44. Of a truth I say unto you, that he will make him ruler over all that he hath. 45. But and **if** that servant say in his heart, My lord delayeth his coming; and shall begin to beat the menservants and maidens, and to eat and drink, and to be drunken; 46. The lord of that servant, will come in a **day** when he looketh not for him, and at an **hour** when he is not aware, and will cut him in sunder, and will appoint him his portion with the unbelievers. 47. And that servant, which knew his lord's will, and prepared not himself, neither did according to his will, shall be beaten with many stripes. 48. But he that knew not and did commit things worthy of stripes, shall be beaten with few stripes. For unto whomsoever much is given, of him shall be much required: and to whom men have committed much, of him they will ask the more"* [Luke 12:35-48].

Since there was to be about a forty year period from the time that the Lord said that the things of which he was speaking would take place, patience and watching would gradually get farther and farther from the minds of the people. They would quit *"being awake"* and some doing evil things, saying that *"the Lord delayeth his coming,"* meaning *"I think it has been so long that he is not going to keep his promise."*

But the Bible is very plain about the subject, *"The Lord is not slack concerning his promise."* The word *"slack"* strictly means *"tardy."* Jesus told them plainly that his return would happen in *"that generation"* that was then alive – not 2,000 years or more into the future. We need to quit looking for that event. It happened almost 2,000 years ago and was completed in 70 A.D.. He was not one second late (tardy). It came on the exact day and hour that God had planned for it to come, even though the apostles were not permitted to know the exact day and hour in 33 A.D. when their Messiah was speaking this to them. As the *"day and hour"* drew near (closer to 70 A.D.), could they know then that it was *"at hand?"* I will discuss this later.

> *"And shall begin to smite his fellowservants, and to eat and drink with the drunken"* [Matthew 24:49].

This follows the words *"and shall begin,"* which are sequential words that denote what was said of the evil servant in the previous verse.

The words *"to smite"* does not mean to kill, as some think, but rather, among other words, means to *"hit with repeated blows, like scourging; by implication, to punish. Figuratively, it means to offend the conscience."* Whether it is used here as a figure, is controversial, but I believe that both a literal and a figurative interpretation is appropriate in this case. If an apostle should become evil, he would be among the flock of God and able to offend the consciences of other believers (co-slaves = fellowservants), or he may go further and go back to the Mosaic law system and actually persecute them.

The phrase *"to eat and drink with the drunken"* can be interpreted figuratively, according to Greek scholars. However, I think that the best interpretation would be to take the phrase literally. Either way was bad for that evil servant. **But, notice the key point, this man that was *"evil"* was a *"servant."*** He was not one on the outside. So it was possible for the apostles to turn back again to their former way of life in the Mosaic system and persecute their fellow believers. The consequences of so doing such were not good for them.

> *"The lord of that servant shall come in a day when he looketh not for him, and in an hour that he is not aware of"* [Matthew 24:50].

We have already discussed the meaning of *"the lord"* in this parable, as well as who the *"servant"* was. We also have looked closely at the *"day and hour"* in which those things would happen, and noted that no one except the *"Father of the Lord and Savior Jesus Christ"* knew **the exact time** that Jesus told this parable to illustrate what he had been teaching throughout this chapter.

The expression *"he looketh (not) for"* is a little more emphatic by understanding the Greek word (*prosdokao*), which means *"to anticipate, by implication, to await."* The 1st century believers were told to stay awake, watch for him, await his return, to anticipate his coming. In this case, the evil servant (remember that this one was a servant) kept putting off that *"day and hour"* and it came upon him *"like a thief in the night."*

The expression *"he is (not) aware of"* comes from the Greek word *"ginosko,"* which means *"to know."* But, had not Jesus just shortly before this told them that they did **not** *"know"* the *"day and hour,"* even though they knew that it would happen in their generation (a generation was considered as forty years)?

> *"And shall cut him asunder, and appoint him his portion with the hypocrites: there shall be weeping and gnashing of teeth"* [Matthew 24:51].

The expression *"shall cut (him) asunder"* comes from one Greek word, *"dichotome."* It is variously translated in different translations, but the primary meaning of the word is *"to bisect,"* which usually means *"to cut into two pieces"* (which some translations render it). However, by extension, it means *"to flog severely"* and may connect with the thoughts expressed in another place by Jesus when he said that some would be *"beaten with few stripes"* and others would be *"beaten with **many** stripes."* Obviously that extension seems to be used in a figurative sense.

A couple of other words find interest here. The first one is the Greek word *"tithemi,"* which primarily means *"to place,"* and further *"to place in a passive or horizontal posture."* Here I must only conjecture. The *"hypocrites"* would, at the arrival of the Son of God, be placed with the crowd of unbelievers, but recognizing that they were being condemned of God, that they would bow or prostrate themselves before the God of both heaven and earth (*"every knee shall bow?"*).

The second is the Greek word that is translated as *"hypocrites."* We have all heard accurately that it is best defined as *"an actor under an assumed character."* Figuratively, then, it would mean what we call a hypocrite (notice how closely the Greek word is – *"hupokrites,"* with only the changing of two letters, pronounced almost the same).

There were Christians in the 1st century who looked pious and faithful, but that *"look-alike"* was just the *"play actor."* They, themselves, were evil people, stealthily sneaking in among the flock to steal the spirits of the believers. And their Messiah had already said that *"if it were possible, they would deceive the very elect."* Somebody was among them and they were deceiving and being deceived, as we have previously studied. The difference here is that one was openly *"beating his fellow believers"* while the other one appeared to be good to his fellow believers. In the end, the portion (*"meros"*) would be the *"sharing"* of the same fate.

The word *"there"* is not a fill-in word or used simplistically in a sentence as we usually do. It denotes a *"place."* The *"place"* where the hypocrites and openly rebellious would be, would be separate from the true believers, and punishment would be the rule of the day (in that place).

"Weeping and gnashing of teeth" denotes the lamentation or wailing of a person in grief and pain of being *"cut asunder."* Also the *"gnashing"* of the teeth implies a grating or grinding of the teeth in pain. Under painful conditions today, we can understand that fairly well, but it

would not be the same without narcotics 2,000 years ago. Probably there was a little anger also.

> *"Now when they heard this, they were cut to the quick, and they began gnashing their teeth at him"* [Acts 7:54].

I am at the fork in the road again. Which way shall I go? The choice is to follow the teaching of the Lord, as Matthew 25 is but an extension of this verse and Matthew 24 and begins with the word **then**, denoting the same period. Everyone should be able to see the connection.

The other choice that I have is to go to the parallel thoughts that were set forth by Mark and Luke regarding this same subject and look at how they clarified some things that Matthew did not cover as well. What will I do? The preponderance (one side weighs more than the other) is that I really should stay with Matthew until Jesus finished his teaching completely. There is one danger in so doing – that some reading this will quit reading before we get through this next chapter and then study Mark's account and then Luke's account of the same Olivet discourse as did Matthew, thereby missing some very clear, compelling evidence and additions that clarify more for us to understand. I do not know the future, so I will pray that all of you will continue with me to get *"the whole story."*

Chapter Three

MATTHEW 25

This is vitally important! This verse should be Matthew 24:52 as there should **not** be a division between 25:1 and 24:51. This is a **continuation** of the Olivet discourse.

> "**THEN** *shall the kingdom of heaven be likened unto ten virgins, which took their lamps, and went forth to meet the bridegroom"* [Matthew 25:1].

As mentioned, to begin here instead of taking the other rabbit trail was a very, very difficult decision to make, but it was not difficult for the 1st century believers. For when they were reading the treatise that Matthew had written, probably they knew nothing of the one that Mark had written, or the one that Luke had written, so they just kept right on reading after the last verse of chapter 24 (especially that their language had no chapters or verses).

The second thing is that, while it is convenient for us to find something or to refer to others quickly where we want them to read, the chapters and verses that we have in Matthew (or the remainder of the Bible) were not present. It was like a letter that was to be read from start to finish as one composite.

So, in this case, a very large mistake was made by the division of the chapter where it is located, for chapter 25 is but an extension of chapter 24. In other words, all of chapter 25 should be chapter 24. Again, we are now reading **Matthew 24:52**. Let me quote the last three verses together, as Matthew recorded them.

> *"The lord of that servant shall come in a day when he looketh not for him, and in an hour that he is not aware of, And shall cut him*

> *asunder, and appoint him his portion with the hypocrites: there shall be weeping and gnashing of teeth. __THEN__ shall the kingdom of heaven be likened unto ten virgins, which took their lamps, and went forth to meet the bridegroom"* [Matthew 24:50 – 25:1].

See? If there are no verse or chapter separations, it becomes much easier to see the connection that Jesus made. He did not change the subject.

The subject of the coming of their Messiah in 66 A.D. to 70 A.D. was to **destroy** the rebellious Judeans, the destruction of Jerusalem and the ritualistic Mosaic system. He had instructed the apostles to *"watch"* and *"remain awake"* for they did not know the *"day and hour"* of that coming.

As we said, this verse begins with the word *"then."* The Greek word that is so translated is the word *"tote,"* and means *"when then."* The Son of God was still speaking to the 1st century believers about his coming in that generation (within a forty year period), i.e. by 70 A.D.. Again, let me emphasize, Jesus did not change the subject of Matthew 24 – rather he told them the following parables of *"watchfulness"* and *"staying awake"* and *"being ready"* because they did not know the *"day and hour"* even though they knew that it would be while some of them were still biologically alive [Matthew 24:34 – 9:1 already quoted above].

It is here that the *"kingdom of heaven"* is introduced. That there is a technical difference in *"the kingdom of heaven,"* *"the kingdom of God"* and *"the kingdom of Christ,"* it is necessary, in my understanding, that we comprehend that they are all connected together. But let us look at the definition of the Greek word that is used here, which is *"ouranos."* It is defined as *"(through the idea of __elevation__); the sky; by __extension__, heaven; by __implication__, happiness, power, eternity; __specifically__, the gospel."* Boy, that is a mouthful, is it not? With that definition, it should cause us (when we have time) to look at all of the verses that have the word *"ouranos"* as the root word from which we get the word *"heaven"* and do a very good word study, to see which avenue would be best suited to translate the correct idea of any particular verse in which it occurs. Which one would be good here where the *"kingdom of heaven"* is mentioned? Do not give up now as it gets more interesting. We will still discuss the kingdom in what follows.

Whether you refer to the *"kingdom of Christ"* or the *"kingdom of God,"* you are referring to the *"kingdom of heaven,"* for both of the kingdoms of Jesus and God were/are heavenly kingdoms. Jesus was continuing to tell his apostles about his completed coming in 70 A.D. and what the kingdom of heaven would be like at that time.

The illustration that he used here was *"ten virgins."* It is interesting that he used a *"one on one"* principle here, as just as many as went into the marriage feast were the same number as were locked out. All of his parables do not use the *"one on one"* illustration. The two previous ones did, as there were *"two"* in the field and the *"one on one"* illustration was used; and there were *"two"* grinding in the millhouse, and the *"one on one"* illustration was again used there. So, this illustration shows that he was still speaking of the same event and time – only he expanded it from one to **<u>five</u>**.

The Greek word for *"virgins"* is *"parthenos,"* and is defined as *"a maiden, by implication, an unmarried daughter."* However, the translators do not always follow their rules. The word *"virgins"* does not always describe a female. For example, look closely at the following verse.

> ***"<u>These are they which were not defiled with women; for they are virgins.</u>** These are they which follow the Lamb whithersoever he goeth. These were redeemed from among **<u>men</u>**, being the firstfruits unto and to the Lamb"* [Revelations 14:4].

Now, who is to say that the ten virgins that were mentioned in Matthew 25:1 were not either female and/or male? Does not even the English word imply either male or female? The idea is not so much as to the sex of the individual under consideration but the *"pureness"* or *"faithfulness"* of the person(s). But even the pure and faithful men and women who were believers in the 1ˢᵗ century could be caught napping and not ready. Acts 21:9 certainly referred to the female for they were *"daughters of Philips."* And the final thought in this paragraph is that the verse says that they were redeemed *"from among men."* The word *"men"* here does not denote a male. It is the Greek word *"anthropos,"* which simply means *"a human being."*

Notice first that there was no distinction made. All ten were virgins. Secondly, all ten took their lamps. Thirdly, all ten went forth to meet the bridegroom. But something was seriously wrong. I will get to that part shortly.

One thing that is often overlooked is that each one took his (or her) own personal lamp (or torch). Since people were considered *"the light of the world,"* could the illustration be that what they took was their own working efforts to be the light of the world, rather than a literal lamp – that this part of the parable was also a figure of speech? The context seems that this might be the better explanation – especially since the Greek says "**THE** lamps." Maybe it has something to do with them being *"the **light** of the world."* I will return to that later in this parable.

The term *"went forth"* is translated by so many variable words and the primary meaning of the Greek word is *"to issue,"* that I am not going to argue with the forty-seven scholars who translated the King James Version in the way that they translated the phrase. However, the general picture that we get as we hear the parable read by the preachers, suggests that all ten of the virgins were somewhere very close to the door into which the bridegroom was to go, not that they *"went forth"* to meet the bridegroom from wherever he was coming. That Jesus was coming in that 1ˢᵗ century is without question to anyone who has an open mind that has not been flooded with false concepts, who are honest, open-minded, real searchers of the Bible. From where did the

Messiah come? And if they *"went out"* to meet him, how far did they go? You see, I leave some questions open-ended – you will have to think for yourselves.

A very interesting proposition arises in Jesus's use of the word *"meet,"* which comes from the Greek word *"hupantesin,"* which is defined as *"an encounter"* (which may be the word that the translators selected) or as *"an occurrence or in order to fall in with."* Could that have anything to do with *"and those who sleep in Jesus will God bring with Him?"* But let us just assume that the superficial meaning of the parable is correct – all ten of the virgins went to meet the bridegroom (Jesus). Question? Does the Bible teach that God was coming **with** Jesus at the same time? Did anyone see God in the flesh with his Son who was/is supposed to literally come in the flesh? Oh!

There seems to be no doubt with the scholars/translators that the word *"bride-groom"* is the correct translation of the Greek word *"numphios."* The problem lies in the English definition of a *"bride-groom."* It is defined as *"a man who is newly married man to his bride **or** is about to be married."* Which was it in this parable? Jesus was coming and going into and from the marriage feast, depending upon which parable at which you look. The ones that were ready went in with him to the marriage feast, and the door was shut to those who were not prepared. At any rate, know for certain that the parable **is a continuation** of the same discourse that Jesus made in Matthew 24.

> *"And five of them were wise, and five were foolish"* [Matthew 25:2].

Again, the 50% illustration is used by Jesus. Five were to be punished and five were to receive blessings. Be reminded again of the *"one on one"* illustrations that were already used by the Master in the last verses of Matthew 24 – two in the field, *"one taken, one left"* – two grinding in the millhouse, *"one taken, one left."* While all three show a 50% ratio, not all of Jesus's parables use that exact ratio.

The Greek word for *"five"* is *"pente,"* from which we get some of our English words, such as *"**Pente**-gon"* – the five-sided building in Washington D.C.. Also, it comes from Bible words such as *"**Pente**-cost"* – in that usage, it was *"fifty"* days after Passover.

It gets very interesting now. A study of the Greek word that is translated as *"foolish,"* which is *"moros,"* indicates that it is probably from where the English word *"moron"* comes. The definition of the Greek word itself is *"dull or stupid; heedless, blockhead, (apparently) absurd."* Is that not very interesting? Now that you know the definition, does *"foolish"* really describe the condition of five of those virgins? I think that it is too easy on the description. They were not only foolish, but they were also heedless, dull and stupid, and the next verse shows why.

The Greek word *"phronimos"* is translated as *"wise."* It certainly denotes wise, even more so *"discreet (implying a cautious character), but also thoughtful."* The best word here would be *"thoughtful,"* in contrast to the foolish ones who were heedless and *"dull of hearing."* The next few verses will show why *"thoughtful"* would be a better translation. Their Messiah was still telling them to be ready and watch, continuing his instructions to *"watch"* from Matthew 24.

> *"They that were foolish took their lamps, and took no oil with them"* [Matthew 25:3].

Now we know why one of the definitions of *"foolish"* is *"blockheads."* They were not thoughtful. They were dull and heedless to the coming rejection. We would say that anyone who took a lamp with no oil was *"stupid,"* and that is one of the definitions.

They did not have electricity, so they had to burn some kind of fuel. The Greek word may even describe olive oil, especially since olives grew there and they were accustomed to olive trees. This discourse was on the Mount of Olives and we usually refer to it as the Olivet Discourse.

They did take their lamps, but were stupid and dull enough in their thinking as to not take anything to burn in their lamps. When their lamps went out, guess where they were? They would have been in total darkness – the term *"darkness"* was used of the rebellious Judeans of that time. These were **NOT** *"watching and ready"* as Jesus had instructed them in the previous chapter.

> *"But the wise took oil in their vessels with their lamps"* [Matthew 25:4].

The word *"but"* indicates the opposite. Such was quite true. The foolish took no oil to burn in their lamps, while the wise did take oil to keep their lamps burning.

"Vessels" comes from an original word that simply means *"a receptacle,"* probably what we consider to be a pail or bucket, possibly with a *"bent"* to it, like a gasoline can. The wise virgins had their lamps, they were burning, and if the fuel got low they had plenty in reserve. They were thoughtful and heeded what their Master had said in Matthew 24. Sure, by now, all of us can understand that this chapter is but a continuation of Matthew 24 and concerned the two responses to the apostles' questions regarding the things that were to be completed by 70 A.D. when Jerusalem and the temple were destroyed. **Only the principle** of being thoughtful and ready to die applies to us in the 21st century.

> *"While the bridegroom tarried, they all slumbered and slept"* [Matthew 25:5].

We do not want to contradict what the Son of God said in the previous chapter, when he said that those things would *"happen in this generation"* – i.e. the 1st century A.D., the people who were biologically alive and listening to him speak were to see, perceive and experience all of the things that are mentioned in these three chapters. Therefore, we cannot interpret this verse as that Jesus *"tarried"* for 2,000 years and is still tarrying. The fulfillment of all of his words occurred about 70 A.D..

The *"tarrying"* was only for the space that involved forty years. He was going to return. They were instructed that it would be in *"their generation"* [Matthew 24:34] while some were *"still living"* [Mark 9:1].

The Greek word for *"tarried"* is *"chronizo."* It is from the word that we obtain English words such as *"chron-ological."* The definition is *'to tarry, to linger, to delay, to take time."* It certainly deals with **time**.

Jesus had promised to return in their lifetimes. Did he keep his promise? If he did not, then he is a liar, a false prophet and we might as well just throw our Bibles away! The longer that he delayed that return, the more people lost their faith in him and in his promise and begin to say …

> *"… **where is the promise of his coming?** for since the fathers fell asleep, all things continue as they were from the beginning of the creation"* [2 Peter 3:4].

It will be necessary at the proper time to study more in detail concerning 2 Peter 3, but understand now that it cannot contradict what Jesus plainly taught here and in these parables. The passage above is not asking where the promise was, for it is evident that they knew it or they would not have been asking the question. The full question was, *"Where is the **keeping** of the promise of his coming?"* Peter's response to those who were going back to law-keeping is found in v-9 of the same chapter.

> *"**The Lord is not slack concerning his promise**, as some men count slackness; but is longsuffering to us-ward, not willing that any should perish, but that all should come to repentance."*

Note that the word *"promise"* is not plural, i.e. not *"promises."* Only **ONE** promise is under consideration and that promise was *the promise of his coming.* There was not one coming against Jerusalem in 70 A.D. and a **SECOND COMING** sometime thousands of years later (today or later). There was **a coming** in judgment against Jerusalem and the destruction of the temple in 70 A.D. but there is no record at all in the Bible of another coming. Did you get that? No second coming. In fact, the Bible never, never, never used the phrase *"second coming!"* Period. He made a promise in Matthew 24 and said that the time was in that current, contemporary generation with him. It happened in 70 A.D. but the entire Bible was written **BEFORE** that event of 70 A.D.. So, that **one** coming was to come to pass just like Jesus and the apostles said – **soon, shortly, at hand**, etc. In hind-sight, we know that it came between 66 A.D. to 70 A.D.. Did he keep his promise? Absolutely! As we have said so often, it is not something in our day in the 21st century – it happened nearly 2,000 years ago. Get this now – When the Master said …

> *"Verily I say unto you, This generation shall not pass, till all these things be fulfilled"* [Matthew 24:34] …

… he knew that his Father would know the exact day and hour that his return would be in that 1st century generation. And he knew that his Father would keep His promise. In fact, he knew, since he knew that his Father knew the *"day and hour,"* that his Father would be **prompt** in keeping His promise. In fact, in 2 Peter 3:9 (that is quoted above), Peter said that God was not *"slack"* in that one promise. The word means *"tardy."* The return of their Messiah would happen in the exact day and hour that the Father had established, even though the apostles did not know the exact day (at the time that Jesus was saying these things).

Even though **he tarried about forty years**, his return was right on schedule – it was not tardy – it was right on time – it was not one second late. Why did he delay? V-9 tells us that it was because he did not desire anyone to be punished. He wanted the gospel to be preached to the entire Israelite world and then he would cause the end to come. Remember that is what he said in Matthew 24:14.

> *"And this gospel of the kingdom shall be preached in all the world for a witness unto all nations; and **then** shall the end come."*

Such preaching in all of the Judean world was accomplished in that generation before 66 A.D..

> *"For the hope which is laid up for you in heaven, whereof ye heard before in the word of the truth of the gospel; 6. **Which is come unto you, as it is in all the world**; and bringeth forth fruit, as it doth also in you, since the day ye heard of it, and knew the grace of in truth"* [Colossians 1:5-6].

> *" If ye continue in the faith grounded and settled, and be not moved away from the hope of the gospel, which ye have heard, and **which was preached to every creature which is under heaven**; whereof I Paul am made a minister"* [Colossians 1:23].

As you can see, this is **not** something for which our generation is to expect. Again, it happened nearly 2,000 years ago. Jesus said in Matthew 24:14 (quoted above) that when it was preached to all of the world, *"**THEN** shall the end come."* Did he not tell his apostles the truth? If he did tell them the truth, the end came in the 1st century, regardless of what the television, radio and pulpit evangelists tell us. I believe what Jesus said – what about you? If you differ with me, that is alright. If you differ with the Master's teaching, you have a major problem. I will still love you. Be honest with yourself and God.

While Jesus tarried about forty years, some believers slumbered and slept. The unbelievers were as dead, since they gave no heed to understanding, expecting, anticipating and watching for the return of their Messiah. They did not know him. That is the meaning of this part of the parable that says that **ALL TEN** virgins slumbered and slept while their Lord delayed his return.

I always thought that slumbering and sleeping were the same. If they were the same, why are both mentioned? In the English language the word sleep shows soundness whereas slumber shows **light** sleep or kind of like cat-napping. In the Greek language, there are two words with two different meanings. The first one, *"slumbering"* simply means to nod (and of course it could or could not mean that they *"totally"* nodded off to sleep at times). The second one, *"slept,"* means *"to lie down to sleep."* The two words are a little different, because the **intent** was to go to sleep, in which case, they were totally ignoring the Lords command to *"stay awake"* (see previous comments). This seems to fit the five foolish virgins. They did not need oil in their lamps – it was better sleeping in the dark.

One thing that we must not overlook is how the word *"darkness"* is used throughout the *"new testament"* regarding the time of its occurrence. The Bible not only uses the term, it also implies it, as it does in this parable. It says that they needed *"lamps,"* and one does not need them in the daylight. Such expressions as *"the night is far spent, the day is at hand,"* also indicate the time of the return of their Messiah to be at the end of the system of *"darkness"* and the dawning of the new day. And, yes, *"the day was at hand"* in the 1st century A.D. – it is not for us in our century or future centuries.

> *"The night is far spent, **the day is at hand**: let us therefore cast off the works of darkness, and let us put on the armour of light"* [Romans 13:12].

While the apostles still lived, *"the darkness was passing away."*

> *"Again, a new commandment I write to you, which thing is true in him and in you, because the darkness is passing away, and the true light is already shining"* [1 John 2:8 NKJV].

Eventually, the cry went forth that *"the bridegroom cometh"* and it might have come from anyone other than from at least one of the ten virgins. So, it is possible that at least one of the ten virgins was *"nodding,"* enough to awaken.

One very interesting thing here is that Jesus told them that they would know when the hour came for his return, **even though they did not know it** at the time that he was giving **this Olivet discourse** in these three chapters.

> *"And at midnight there was a cry made, Behold, the bridegroom cometh; go ye out to meet him"* [Matthew 25:6].

Again, we see that the cry of the coming of the bridegroom was said to be in the nighttime. Just because the cry was made at midnight, does not mean that he actually returned at midnight. The Greek word for *"midnight"* is *"mesos"* and means *"the middle,"* which does not mean at exactly twelve o'clock. For example, we might say, *"While we were in bed trying to sleep, a thunderstorm came up in the middle of the night,"* not even knowing the exact hour of the thunderstorm. But, it was before daylight. There is another Greek word that is used, which is *"nuktos,"* which only means sometime in the night.

For the unbelievers, it would come *"as a thief in the night."* Their condition is always thought of as *"darkness."* The darkness was always contrasted to the light. The believers were of the light and in the light.

> *"For yourselves know perfectly that the day of the Lord so cometh as a thief in the night. 3. For when **they** shall say, Pease and safety; then sudden destruction cometh upon **them** as travail upon a woman with child, and **they** shall not escape. 4. But **ye**, brethren, are not in darkness, that that day should overtake **you** as a thief. 5. **Ye** are all the children of light, and the children of the day: **we** are not of the night, nor of darkness. 6. Therefore let*

us not sleep, as do others: but let *us* watch and be sober" [1 Thessalonians 5:2-6].

For the believers, the coming of Jesus would be when the darkness was passing away and the true light was already shining. It would not be nighttime nor darkness for the believers. It would be the beginning of a new day after sundown. They were constantly warned to *"stay awake"* and expect the return of their Messiah in their lifetimes.

> *"And take heed to yourselves, lest at any time your hearts be overcharged with surfeiting, and drunkenness, and cares of this life, and so that **day** come upon you unawares"* [Luke 21:34].

> *"The night is far spent, **the day** is at hand: let us therefore cast off the works of **darkness**, and let us put on the armour of **light**. 13. Let us walk honestly, as in **the day**; not in rioting and drunkenness, not in chambering and wantonness, nor in strife and envying"* [Romans 13:12-13].

The coming of the Lord was very close when John wrote …

> *"Again, a new commandment I write unto you, which thing is true in him and in you: because the darkness is past (**literally, 'is passing away'**), and the true light now shineth"* [1 John 2:8].

The only other very interesting thing in the verse is that the word *"cometh"* is not in the original Greek.

"Then all those virgins arose, and trimmed their lamps" [Matthew 25:7].

This verse begins with the same Greek word with which chapter 25 begins, i.e. *"tote,"* and denotes successive time, not some delay or missing time for thousands of years. As soon as the cry was made that the bridegroom was appearing to the ten virgins, it was at the very next moment that they all arose and trimmed their lamps. No gap. [Look again at Matthew 25:1, and its use there as it connected v-1 to the last verse of Matthew 24.]

All ten of the virgins had *"slumbered and slept."* The awakening for those who were not watching had taken place, all of them arose. What can be ascertained is that it was probably not one of the ten that made the announcement of the appearance of the bridegroom (in fact, other passages indicate that the announcement came from another source). Even v-6 indicates that the cry was made to all ten virgins, for all ten had *"slumbered and slept."*

For the explanation of *"ten virgins"* and *"lamps,"* see v-1. It is interesting that another thing might be added – that many years later, the apostle Paul wrote to the believers in Corinth and told them that he was …

> *"… jealous over you with Godly jealousy: for I have espoused you to one husband, that I may present you as a **chaste virgin** to Christ"* [2 Corinthians 11:2].

The Greek word *"kosmeo"* is translated in the <u>King James Version</u> as *"adorn, garnish, trim."* Obviously, in this story, the proper word would be to *"trim"* the wick on a lamp that had oil in it, for the lamps would burn better with a properly trimmed wick. The Greek word properly means *"to put in order."* They all trimmed their lamps. They all put their lamps in proper working order. That is, when five of them discovered something. The next verse tells us what they discovered.

> *"And the foolish said unto the wise, Give us of your oil; for our lamps are **gone** out"* [Matthew 25:8].

We have already been told, in verses 1-2, that one-half of the ten were wise and the other one-half were foolish. So, even though the number

www.EschatologyReview.com

186

five is not used in this verse, we know that five were wise and five were foolish in this parable of the Lord.

This must be a parable of the Lord, otherwise anyone who is not a *"virgin"* cannot even be considered for the *"kingdom"* that is mentioned in these two verses. Such would **never** *"taste of my supper"* said Jesus. Have you considered that it just might be speaking of the *"Lord's supper,"* since Jesus was speaking of **his** supper? You may obtain a copy of my book, titled The Lord's Supper at AMAZON.COM . Just type in RON MCRAY on the blank spot and it will come up automatically (and Kindle).

> *"For I say unto you, That none of those men which were bidden shall taste of my supper"* [Luke 14:24).

Would that leave about 75% the world over that are not even considered for the kingdom of God? This is a story by Jesus. It is a story that illustrates wisdom and stupidity. It is a story of the coming of the Son of man to his marriage feast.

We now know what all ten of the virgins discovered. The wise ones discovered that they had made preparation *"enough"* to have replenishment of the oil supply in their lamps that were going out, so no reason to be concerned. We also know that the foolish ones discovered that because of the delay of the bridegroom and their not listening to the admonition that the bridegroom had previously given that they were always to be prepared. They did not bring enough oil and their lamps were going out.

The King James Version here is not accurate with the Greek wording. The King James Version indicates that the lamps of the foolish had **already** gone out, but the correct rendering is *"our lamps are going out"* – *not already gone out!* One may wish to compare other translations of this phrase.

The watchfulness, faithfulness and righteousness of the wise could **never** be transferred to the foolish. Even though there was an attempt by the foolish to borrow the wisdom of the righteous virgins, it was not possible. They asked for oil and they received none. The Greek word *"ek"* and the expression *"of your oil"* indicated that the foolish virgins were not asking for **all** of the oil of the wise virgins, just some *"out of"* the *"vessels"* [v-4] that the wise had carried with their lamps. Is there not a lesson for us to have wisdom and always be ready to do good – whenever the occasion arises? For a refresher of the words *"foolish, wise and oil,"* see v-4.

At any rate, the division had already been suggested in the difference between the *"wise"* and the *"foolish."* Does it not indicate already that there was a separation coming that was based already on the separation of their *"foolishness and wisdom?"* Before this chapter is finished, the Lord would give another parabolic expression showing this very separation, *"as a shepherd divideth the sheep from the goats."*

> *"But the wise answered, saying, Not so; lest there be not enough for us and you: but go ye rather to them that sell, and buy for yourselves"* [Matthew 25:9].

Really? The words *"not so"* are **not** to be found in the original! The five wise virgins **responded** to the request for some of their oil and in that response was simply an affirmation that they did not have enough for themselves and the five foolish virgins who had no extra oil.

It matters not how much righteousness and faithfulness that wise people have to do, the unwise cannot be justified by the righteousness and faithfulness of wise people. While the righteousness of Jesus was imputed to the faithful, the righteousness of one individual cannot be loaned or given to another person. Each person is accountable to God for his or her mindset and actions.

The word *"lest"* is translated from the Greek word *"mepote,"* which means *"not ever."* The application to us today is that what you do can *"not ever"* be credited to me.

> Another thing that is unusual is the Greek use of a double negative in the Greek words *"ou me,"* which strengthens the denial, like saying *"not at all."*

Maybe the word *"but"* is implied in the translation, but there is no corresponding Greek word from which to translate it. There were simple directions on how the unwise could obtain their oil – the same way that the wise got their oil.

There is really not much to say about the remainder of the verse. Possibly a more accurate translation would be to *"instead of obtaining oil from us, **travel instead** to **market** and **purchase from the oil dealer** for yourselves – we cannot supply your oil."*

> *"And while they went to buy, the bridegroom came; and they that were ready went in with him to the marriage: and the door was shut"* [Matthew 25:10].

The stupid virgins took the advice of the wise virgins and went to the market to purchase some oil for their lamps that were going out (even in the dark). While they were gone from the place where the marriage was apparently to take place, the bridegroom came and went into the place where the Lord's marriage supper occurred and also the marriage itself of the bridegroom.

We must keep in mind that Jesus was still talking to the same four apostles on the Mount of Olives. The subject continued to be about his coming in the Roman army in 66 A.D. to 70 A.D. to get married and to destroy the unwise unbelievers. This parable is a **continuation** of that thought from Matthew 24. We are not waiting on the marriage of the

Lamb of God today, for he got married in 70 A.D.. When Jesus said in Matthew 24:34 that …

> *"… I say unto you, **This generation** shall not pass, till **all these things** be fulfilled."*

He not only was including all of the verses that preceded that verse, but all of the verses that followed it, all the way to the end of chapter 25 (including this verse). He was the bridegroom and he came in that 1st century generation exactly as he said that he would. If you believe what he said in these two chapters, there is no way that it is a debatable subject. It is only a matter of whether we want to believe him or ignore him. This does not refer to any coming of Jesus in the 21st century or beyond. It transpired in the 1st century exactly as he said that it would.

Those that were ready (faithful, watching and prepared) went in **with him** to the marriage supper of the Lamb. The unwise **had separated themselves** from the entrance (door) into eternal life. Anyone who has ever been separated from God **separated himself**.

> *"But **your** iniquities have separated between you and your God, and **your** sins have hid his face from you, that he will not hear"* [Isaiah 59:2].

"And the door was shut." There was forever a **final separation** between the wise and foolish, those who were ready and those who were unprepared. It was shut *"forever"* for both the good and the bad. Jesus had delayed and given the unbelieving Judeans forty years to repent – now, *"time shall be no more,"* i.e. there was no more time left for them, time had run out. It was time to enter or forever to be locked out. Again, that happened by 70 A.D.. This verse is not for us in the 21st century, except to learn from it that we must always be prepared (not for his coming, but for our death, which will forever seal our destiny). It was judgment day for the Judeans. Solomon said …

*"For **the living know that they shall die:** but the dead know not any thing, neither have they any more a reward; for the memory of them is forgotten"* [Ecclesiastes 9:5].

You and I know that we will die, but we do not know when. So, we should live every day and hour as if it were our last day and hour on this planet – **it might be!**

"Afterward came also the other virgins, saying, Lord, Lord, open to us" [Matthew 25:11].

The five foolish virgins who were not prepared, ready, watching and **expecting** the bridegroom, wanted into the marriage area also.

The Greek word *"husteron"* that is translated by the word *"afterward,"* literally means *"eventually."* Get the story in mind. They **went** to get oil, so the same time that it took for them to **go**, also took for them to **return**, including the time they spent in the transaction at the market. So, it took some time. **Eventually**, they arrived back and wanted the door opened. But they found that it was permanently closed (as the door was forever closed in the ark in Noah's day to the unbelievers).

One very interesting thing in this verse is the occurrence of the Greek word *"loipoi,"* which is the **masculine plural**. While we usually think of a virgin as a female, here the word that is translated as *"other,"* denotes that the remaining ones were males. Well, we know that both male and female can be virgins, so there is no respect of persons. The thought primarily though is on the continued faithfulness to Jesus during those forty years of transition – 30 A.D. to 70 A.D.. To refresh our memory, the apostle Paul said that he was …

*"… jealous over you with Godly jealously; for I have espoused you to one husband, that I may present you as a **chaste virgin** to Christ"* [2 Corinthians 11:2].

In this parable, the word *"lord"* comes from a Greek word, *"kurios,"* which means *"supreme in authority, a controller, by implication, a respectable title."* Such was great for the bridegroom of the parable, but since Jesus was more than a mere mortal, and that he was to be the **spiritual** bridegroom, about to marry the faithful (in 70 A.D.), the **application** to the word *"lord"* here would of necessity have to be that he was *"supreme in authority."* Those *"other"* virgins, the remaining ones, would have to abide by the decision of the one with **all authority** and be forever left out, for *"the door was shut."*

> *"But he answered and said, Verily I say unto you, I know you not"* [Matthew 25:12].

A deeper study of the Greek manuscript will show that when a **response was expected**, the bridegroom told the foolish virgins that he could **see** (know) right through them and that they were false and were not really the virgins that they claimed to be. The word *"not"* is an *"absolute negative!"*

The original statement by Jesus was that there were **ten virgins**. In the outcome, there were only five that were faithful, and the unfaithful ones were found out. He had at one time known them, but now he no longer knows them. The application of the parable is that Jesus was the bridegroom and there were some that would remain faithful to the end and be saved (Matthew 24:13). But there would be a *"great falling away"* and those that were virgins, that ceased to be virgins by their unfaithfulness, would no longer be known by Jesus.

> *"Let no man deceive you by any means ; for **that day** shall not come, except there come **a falling away**, and that man of sin be revealed, the son of perdition"* [2 Thessalonians 2:3].

That day is the same *"that day"* at which we have looked many times in our study of Matthew 24. It was to happen in that 1st century generation. What good would it do for the four apostles to wait for 2,000 years so see such an event? Are we not supposed to believe that every generation has had its falling away? Go back and study the notes in those chapters concerning *"that day."* The five foolish virgins had fallen away and when they asked entrance into the marriage, the response was *"no"* and the door was forever shut. Half the people were lost who were alive when Jesus told the parable. What about half of the people in every generation for 2,000 years? Very wrong interpretation. There is a contrast here with another verse.

> *"And then will I profess unto them, I **never** knew you; depart from me, ye that work iniquity"* [Matthew 7:23].

The previous verse said, *"Many will say to me in **that day** ..."* *"That day"* is the same day of the verse that is being discussed and the same *"that day"* that is used throughout the three chapters to **only** four apostles. If you are really interested in this point, just take your Bibles and read these three chapters again and mark all of the times that the expression *"that day"* occurs. Remember that it was the time of the coming of Jesus (the bridegroom) in 70 A.D.. *"That day"* came nearly 2,000 years ago. It is not going to happen in our time or future time. Remember that these two chapters are referring to the same topic of conversation between Jesus and his apostles about the *"when"* of his **coming** and the *"what"* concerning the **sign** and the end of the **age** (not the planet).

Matthew 7:22-23 concerns those who were **never** virgins. Jesus had **NEVER known them**. So, in the Bible, there is a difference between those that Jesus did **not** know and those that he **never knew**. Some never believed in him, while others believed and fell away. If one believes the Bible, he cannot deny that Jesus and his apostles taught that some did not just fall down, but that they verily *"fell away."* We cannot successfully deny that, without accusing Jesus and his apostles of being liars. At any rate, those five were virgins who had believed, but were not faithful and fell away and the Lord no longer knew them (*"I know ye not"*).

"Watch therefore, for ye know neither the day nor the hour wherein the Son of man cometh" [Matthew 25:13].

To show the connection between these three chapters, consider that the following verse sounds exactly the same, except that the word *"ready"* is used instead of *"watch."*

> *"Therefore be ye also **ready**, for in such an hour as ye think not the Son of man cometh"* [Matthew 24:44].

If they were ready, they were watchful, for both verses teach that both qualities were necessary to enter into the marriage. This verse is an almost exact duplication of Matthew 24:42, where Jesus was speaking to his apostles in both cases.

> *"**Watch** therefore, for ye know not what you're your Lord doth come."*

Jesus was **still** speaking of the *"day and hour"* of his coming (**not two different comings**). Therefore, since they *"knew"* that the *"day and hour"* would come in their generation [Matthew 24:34], but did **not** know the exact day and hour, they were to *"watch"* and be *"ready."* Matthew 25 is but an extension of Jesus' discourse in Matthew 24. It is very unfortunate that some man separated his continued discourse by a change of chapters.

By Jesus using the word *"ye"* in this verse, it is evident that he was still speaking to his apostles in that 1st century generation. He told them to watch and be ready. Of what purpose would that be to them if they had been dead for 2,000 years or more?

For our consideration, the ending expression *"wherein the Son of man cometh"* is **not** found in the Textus Receptus (from which the King James Version is translated) nor is it found in the Nestle Greek text.

However, the thought (from the other verses that we have already studied) is present, so the translators decided to **add** it to this verse. I have no problem with that thought, but it is not an exact translation, for the Greek was no corresponding words.

> *"For __the kingdom of heaven__ is as a man travelling into a far country, who called his own servants, and delivered unto them his goods"* [Matthew 25:14].

We have discussed the phrase that is highlighted above, but there is one thing of which we must make note. The *"kingdom of heaven"* is used many times but it only occurs in the book of Matthew, and has a separate meaning but it will take an entire book to explain all of the differences. With this verse, we begin another of the Lord's parables about the time of his return in that first century generation (the exact day and hour they did not know), although they did know that it was in their 1st century generation.

We have already discussed the *"kingdom of heaven"* in Matthew 25:1. Please review that verse for an extended explanation. Note that Jesus introduced the parable of the ten virgins by the same expression, i.e. *"the kingdom of heaven is likened ..."* It is in the same manner that he introduced this parable.

It seems that it is implied, but the expression *"the kingdom of heaven is"* has no corresponding Greek words and therefore is an **addition** to the two Greek texts from which we are working. There is a continuation of thought, and to translate from Greek to English, it probably would make more sense to *"add"* the expression, but we must remember to look very closely at what the translators add, for their opinion may be slipped in when it is wrong.

The parabolic form here is a man who went abroad, who traveled into a far country, meaning that Jesus left the earth and went to heaven (he traveled to the heavenly country). What did this man do before leaving on his journey to the far country is asking what did Jesus do before he ascended to heaven. The first thing was to call his own (not someone else's) servants together. In this case, it was Jesus who called his apostles together to give them some instructions.

The Greek word *"paradidomi,"* means not only to *"deliver,"* but to **entrust** the apostles with something. What was entrusted? The Greek word implies either *"property or possessions."* Such is the meaning of the parabolic use. Exactly what was it Jesus entrusted to his apostles? The servants in the parable received *"goods"* from their master. What *"goods"* did the Lord give to his apostles? How about letting the *"good news"* be the gospel? That is the definition of the word *"gospel."* Would the apostles be faithful with the entrusted good news of the death, burial and resurrection of their master? He also gave his goods according to the abilities and opportunities for doing good.

> *"And unto one he gave five talents, to another two, and to another one; to every man according to his several ability; and straightway took his journey"* [Matthew 25:15].

Jesus shifted his emphasis in this parable to **three** persons (instead of ten, as in the previous parable of the virgins). However, he did not change his subject. He was still dealing with the question that was asked by his apostles in Matthew 24:3. He introduced again, in parabolic form, that he was to *"go away"* and later he was to return to them (the same ones that he was leaving) in the 1st century A.D..

Again, this parable is only for our learning of past redemptive history, because its fulfillment happened in the 1st century A.D.. That can easily be seen in the application of the parable, for the master *"took his journey"* which, of course, was to go to heaven, and I am sure that all of us who are reading this know when Jesus ascended [Acts 1:11].

Lest the women who are reading this, think that they are being excluded, the two connected Greek words (*ho-men*) includes the feminine use of the word. It is made more emphatic by saying *"this one,"* rather than just *"one."* We know that God gives the gifts.

> *"Every good gift and every perfect gift is from above, and cometh down from the Father of lights, with whom is no variableness, neither shadow of turning"* [James 1:17].

In this verse, we begin to learn from this parable that what is given requires **accountability**. We will study more on that in the next verse. There may be more to learn in the *"five"* and *"two"* and *"one"* than what is herein noted, but at this time, I fail to comprehend it, if there is. In my studies, I have noticed that a deeper study of some subjects with numbers has indeed shown that the numbers mean something more than just numbers. What is interesting is that he gave to the most able person the five talents, to the next, but seemingly less able person, the two talents, and to the least able person the one talent. All three were his servants and all three were responsible, therefore all three were accountable to their master (but only as they were able – had the ability). If we were to put it in the language that most would use today, it would be, *"Jesus gave to all three Christians exactly what they were capable of handling and expected them to use what he had given to them to his glory. They would be held accountable for what they did or did not do."*

The Lord knew the *"ability"* of each one, and did not overload them, but gave to each of them exactly what they could do and for which they would be accountable in the way that they used what the master had *"given"* to them. Every one of us is different. God will require of each of us only what we are able to do. The word *"talents"* here does not mean some gift or ability any one of the three servants had, but rather it is a term that means *"money."* How much money was a talent? We really have not given this subject due diligence. We usually think of *"one talent"* as not being very much. How much is a talent of gold worth?

When I looked at the price of gold today as I rewrite this book, it was $1,351.00 a troy ounce. In order to know how to calculate the value, we must do some figuring. First, let us look at some information that is given to us by the scholars.

"The Attic talent (the one current in the New Testament period) had 100 drachmas, the drachma being = 7 ¾ d.; the mina was 3 British pounds, 4 shillings, 7 pence, and the talent 193 British pounds, 15 shillings. The talent was not a coin but a sum. The Hebrew = 3,000 shekels, or 375 British pounds (about the weight of the Aegina talent), for 603,550 persons paid 100 talents and 1,775 shekels of silver, i.e., as each paid a half shekel, 301,775 whole shekels; so that 100 talents contained 3000,000 shekels. The gold talent was 100 manehs or minae, and the gold muneh was 100 shekels of gold; **the gold talent weighed 1,290,000 grains**, *a computation agreeing with the shekels extant. The talent of copper had probably 1,500 copper shekels, copper being to silver as 1 to 72"* [Fausset's Bible Dictionary].

*"**Talent** = the heaviest unit of weight in the Hebrew system. The talent was used to weigh gold (2 Sam 12:39), silver (1 Kings 20:39), iron (I Chron 29:7), bronze (Ex 38:290), and many other commodities. The common talent weighed about 3,000 shekels* **or the full weight that a man could carry** *(2 Kings 5:23). In Rev 16:21 giant heavenly hailstones are described as heavy as a talent"* [Nelson's Illustrated Bible Dictionary].

It is calculated by the scholars as being 125 pounds in weight. That is why it was considered about what a man could carry for an extended period of time. Can you imagine hail stones that weigh 125 pounds falling on a man? What do you think that a man would do if such did fall? Well, the Bible tells us.

"And there fell upon men a great hail out of heaven, every stone **about the weight of a talent;** *and men blasphemed because of*

the plague of the hail; for the plaque thereof was exceedingly great" [Revelation 16:21].

Well, back to the troy weight and how much each servant received. There are 480 grains to a troy ounce of gold. The gold talent weighed 1,290,000 grains. When one does the math figures, he will determine that a talent of gold was the equivalent to 269 troy ounces.

When one multiplies the $1,351.00 (per troy ounce) by 269 troy ounces, the value of one talent was $363,419.00. That is the amount that the one talent man received (if it was gold) to work with it for forty years. And how much money did he make for that long period of time during the **long** journey that his master took? Now, as we would say, *"That is not something to sneeze at."* That is a lot of money, not some pittance that we usually think of when we think of one talent.

That means that the two talent person received (in today's value - $726,298.00 – almost one million dollars). Now that may not be much in the mind of some people, but the crowd that I have known, that is one hefty sum.

It also means that the five talent man received $1,817,095.00, almost two million dollars. After you have worked on your job for forty years, how much would you have besides the two million dollars?

The apostles **immediately** began their work as did the servants who received the five and two talents. They would be accountable to their master when Jesus returned in 70 A.D.. The two talent person **profited** $726,298.00 – not bad, huh? But the one talent man showed no profit at all. What did his master think of that? The next few verses tell us the answer.

Jesus said that the talents were given to each according to *"his several ability."* The Greek word *"idios"* is translated *"his several."* The word primarily means *"pertaining to self, i.e. one's own; by implication, private or separate.*" It should be recognized here that it is from this Greek word that we get the English word *"idiot."* While it is used by some to downgrade another person, that is not the meaning of the word. For a person to have a mind that is not developed as much as a *"normal"* person is no reflection on **how good** a person is. In fact, for those *"simple-minded"* people, they probably have a better attitude and a spirit of forgiveness than do most of us. They have their own world – it is not our world. It is *"their own"* world, their own *"private and separate"* world. So, next time that you are tempted to call someone an *"idiot,"* remember the definition and do not use the word in a derogatory sense.

Well, the world of the servant who received almost two million dollars was certainly not the same world as the person who only received a little more than ¾ of a million dollars. What application is that for us in the 21st century? Or better yet, what application did that have for the apostles to whom Jesus was directly speaking in the 1st century?

Do you believe that Peter, Andrew, James and John *"who seemed to be pillars"* of the believers in Jerusalem, had the same ability (therefore accountability) as did Bartholomew? Do you believe that all of the apostles had the same and equal ability? Were all of the apostles selected to have the *"keys of the kingdom"* or was Peter the only one to whom they were given? Interesting question, is it not? Did the apostle Paul have the same, less or more *"ability"* than the other apostles? I think that this verse in the parable teaches that Jesus was speaking directly to and about those eleven apostles and telling them that they had different abilities and would be given responsibilities that differed one from another, and that each of them would be accountable **only** for their own ability and **not slack it**, even though it differed from the other ten apostles.

In my seminars, I usually began with something like the following. *"If God wanted all of mankind to understand the Bible exactly alike, He made the biggest mistake that He has ever made, because no two people have ever understood it the same and no two people ever will."* Now, give some serious thought to that. Even those of you who are married do not have the exact same understanding as your spouse – never have – do not now – and never will. How can we expect a person who studies the Bible 15 minutes a week to understand exactly the same as a person who studies it 8 hours, 7 days a week? How can we expect a person who has only studied the Bible for one day to understand it exactly the same as one who has spent 60 years in studying it? And, does not each person have a different learning *"ability"* as to how fast or how much he or she can learn or absorb? Let us apply that to our fellow believers and quit being judgmental of them. Let us judge them based on the faithfulness and love of God and their fellow man, not on how much they understand about the Bible. Do we not, in our impatience and lack of kindness, sit in judgment on others or shun them or *"kick them out?"* How would (does) God treat them in their lack of understanding the Bible? Would (or does) He treat them according to their love, kindness and forgiveness of their fellow man? Of course, that depends on each person as to whether he/she will accept the truth when it is pointed out to them. It has been my experience that the majority does not want you to tell them the truth even if they say that they do. Those eighty or ninety percent just tell people that what they believe is the way it is and that they will believe what they want even if the real truth it pointed out to them. Very sad!

That is enough on that subject for the time being, **but this paragraph is probably the most important one that I have written so far.**

It is important to know that the Greek word *"dunamis"* is translated by the English word *"ability"* in this verse. It is the word from which the English word *"dynamite"* is derived. It primarily means *"power"* or *"force."* Here, it may even mean more than that. It is especially used in other places of the *"miraculous power"* that was given and/or manifested by the apostles. Maybe the real import of the meaning of this verse is that each apostle would be able to work *"miracles,"* but some would have more than others. For example, Paul raised a dead person.

*"And there sat in a window a certain young man named Eutychus, being fallen into a deep sleep; and as Paul was long preaching, he sunk down with sleep, and fell down from the third loft, and was taken up **dead**"* [Acts 20:9].

Did all twelve of the apostles raise the dead? Whatever response you made to that question, how would you prove it? Did all twelve apostles speak in tongues? I suppose that you would answer that with the word *"yes"* (in view of Acts 2:4). And, I think rightfully so. However, did they all have the *"ability"* or *"power"* to speak in the **same number** of languages? In other words, did Paul have the *"ability"* and *"power"* to speak in **more** and different languages than all of the other apostles? Did Andrew have the ability and power to speak in more than two languages that was not his native language? I think that the next passage will show that they differed (as the amount of talents differed in this parable). Paul said …

*"I thank my God, I speak with tongues **more than ye all**"* [1 Corinthians 14:18].

Would that not mean that the apostle Paul received more *"talents"* (power) than some of the other apostles? Would that not mean that he had more accountability for the *"ability"* that was *"given"* by God? It does say that each one had his *"several ability,"* which in itself implies that each was given different things (amounts).

Then the master of the parable took his journey. In making an application, we all understand the master to be Jesus. He gave to his apostles their jobs according to their abilities and told them that they would be accountable for the way that they carried out their responsibilities, was then murdered, buried, resurrected and then *"took his journey"* or *"ascended into heaven,"* to *"come again"* in 70 A.D..

*"And when he had spoken these things, while they beheld, he was taken up; and a cloud received him out of their sight. 10. And while they looked steadfastly toward heaven as he went up, behold, two men stood by them in white apparel; 11. Which also said, Ye men of Galilee, why stand ye gazing up into heaven? This same Jesus, **which is taken up from you into heaven**, shall so come in like manner as ye have seen him go into heaven"* [Acts 1:9-11].

"Then he that had received five talents went and traded with the same, and made them other five talents" [Matthew 25:16].

The Greek word *"eutheos"* is translated as **then** which means *"directly. i.e. at once or soon."* There was no delay in the actions of the apostles. Soon (note what the word *"soon"* means), they began (continued?) their work. Such is recorded in Acts 2.

There is one more thing that we will talk about in our study of the word *"talents."* The various Greek texts normally indicate the word to be *"five"* talents, but the Greek text called the <u>Textus Receptus</u> (from which we get the <u>King James Version</u>) has the word that indicates *"five times a thousand"* or *"five thousand,"* such as the feeding of the *"five thousand men"* with the five loaves. If indeed that is correct, then the man with the five talents actually (in today's money) would have received about how many **trillion dollars?** Even with a calculator, you probably cannot count that many dollars. There would have been very much accountability to that much.

The Greek word *"ergazomai"* is translated by the English word **traded**. Its primary meaning is *"to toil, as in a task or occupation; by implication, to be engaged in or with."* Variously, the <u>King James Version</u> translated the word with such words as *"commit, do, labor for, minister about, trade, work."* The apostles did not *"trade"* the gospel (as we normally use the word), but it seems that probably any of the other words would do quite well in reference to their work.

"And likewise he that had received two, he also gained other two" [Matthew 25:17].

The definition of the Greek word *"hosautos"* is *"in the same way."* His accountability was the same and he doubled his money, exactly for what he was responsible. His work was equally accepted by the master. Jesus showed his apostles that they had different abilities, and that they would be judged by their performance of their own abilities, not that of one of the other apostles. However, they must preach the gospel – they must perform to the best of their ability. **But** they could not stray from the exact truth of the good news.

"But he that had received one went and digged in the earth, and hid his lord's money" [Matthew 25:18].

There was the **possibility** that an apostle would not do his work. In this parable, Jesus told his apostles what would happen if one of them did not perform as he was directed. Of course, Judas did not do properly, but he is probably not included in the future work **after** the master *"took his journey."*

It is not improper to begin this verse with the word *"but,"* for it is contrasted or exactly the opposite of the previous two verses.

There is a deeper meaning to the word *"went"* than is usually used in our language. The proper use of the Greek word *"aperchomai"* means *"to go off, i.e. depart, to go aside or behind."* This servant *"went,"* of course, but he *"went off and departed"* from the master's instructions. By not following the proper instructions, he would not, and did not, double his money. What was going to happen to him?

The next thing to notice is that this unprofitable servant went and *"digged"* in the earth. I am not trying to show any expertise in the Greek language. Hopefully, I am saving you a lot of time by showing (at times) the Greek words and their meaning. The word rendered as *"digged"* here is *"orusso,"* which means *"to burrow"* in the ground, hence to dig.

The word from which the word *"earth"* is translated is the Greek word *"ge."* It is translated variously in the <u>King James Version</u> by such words as *"country, earth, earthly, ground, land and world."* I believe that in this parable the word is best translated as *"earth,"* but in other cases, it has a wide variety of issues which means more than the **soil** (the primary meaning of the word).

"Ge" (pronounced *"ghay"*) is defined as *"soil, and by extension, a region or the solid part or the whole of the terrene globe (including the occupants in each application)."*

The **probable** application to the apostles is that they could totally go back to the old Mosaic covenant and not preach the gospel. The *"earth"* (in that usage) would be the Judean system of worship. If they *"looked back"* (as did Lot's wife, a **type** of desiring to return totally to that old covenant system), they would not be using the things that Jesus entrusted to them, in order to *"deliver"* them through the fiery trials that were to soon come upon them and those who believed on Jesus through their preaching. For their own sake and the sake of their world, they could not afford to *"hide"* their entrusted *"talents."*

The Greek word *"apokropto"* means *"to conceal away (fully): figuratively, to keep secret."* It is translated as *"hid."* The apostles were being told not to *"hide"* the gospel. They were to shout it from the house tops. It was not something that was to be done on the *"sly,"* but preached openly, not secretly doing the work that the master gave them to do.

Now, in case that you had any doubts as to the meaning of the word *"talents,"* this verse should totally clear them up. The unprofitable servant had his lord's **money**. Return and study previous verses about the *"talents."*

> *"After a long time the lord of those servants cometh, and reckoneth with them"* [Matthew 25:19].

Depending upon which *"case"* it is, the Greek word that is translated as *"after,"* has various meanings. Here it is used as a *"sequential"* thing. The idea in this word is that the lord first went away and **then** he came again to them. However, it is connected to the next phrase, *"a long time."* It is properly translated. However, the time is man's time and forty years is a long time and to leave on a journey that lasted from age 33 to age 70 was a *"long journey/time."*

We must take a closer look at the Greek word *"chromos,"* which is defined as *"a space of time, in general, not specific, but properly distinguished from kairos,"* which signifies a set time or proper time, a fixed or special occasion. It is also different in meaning from *"aion,"* which is properly *"an age"* (the adjective is used elsewhere in this chapter). There was no specific *"day and hour"* that the servants knew when their lord would return and require an accounting of the way that they had used their lord's money. **They were to expect him while they were still alive.** We have already seen the application. The 1st century believers were to expect Jesus's return while they were still alive – in that 1st century generation. Let us be reminded of the passages. Let us notice carefully that the first one is in the middle of this very discourse by Jesus on the Mount of Olives.

> *"Verily I say unto you, **This generation** shall not pass, till **all these things** be fulfilled"* [Matthew 24:34].

> *"Whosoever therefore shall be ashamed of me and of my words in **this** adulterous and sinful generation; of him also shall the Son of man be ashamed, **when he cometh** in the glory of his Father with the holy angels. 9:1. And he said unto them, Verily I say unto you,*

*That there be **some of them that stand here**, which shall **not taste of death**, till they have seen the kingdom of come with power"* [Mark 8:38 – 9:1].

As we have seen throughout these three chapters of Matthew 23, 24 and 25, the *"long time"* from the time that their Messiah took his journey until his return was from 33 A.D. till 70 A.D.. It was about a forty year period.

When Jesus returned in 70 A.D., it was time for the *"judgment"* of those servants. Since the parable is speaking about talents (money), it is no surprise to find a term that refers to the accountability of the money with which they were entrusted.

The <u>King James Version</u> translates the Greek word *"sunairo"* as *"reckoneth."* However, this word is compounded with another Greek word, which is *"logos."* Together they are defined as *"something said, by extension, a computation,"* tied in with *"to make up together, i.e. to compute."* The application of this parable is that when Jesus returned in 70 A.D., his apostles (and those who believed in him because of the apostles' preaching) would give account of the work [talents – money] with which they had been entrusted. One would expect that the lord of the parable would use a calculator (of course, they did not have them at that time, but we need to show this parable in today's language) to determine how much, if any, profit was made by his servants. In other words, it was *"judgment day"* for those servants. The same could be said of the time in 70 A.D. of the return of Jesus. It was judgment day for those who were alive listening to him speak – shortly before his crucifixion. The closer to 70 A.D. that the writings of the Bible came, the closer to the judgment day that those people came. Notice what the apostle Peter said of the judgment day (he died before 70 A.D.. And while we are reading it, let us note that the judgment day of the Bible is not in our day or future time – it was for those of the 1st century generation.

*"For **the time is come that judgment must begin** at the house of God; and if it first begin at us, what shall the end be of them that obey not the gospel of God"* [1 Peter 4:17].

Is it not time that we recognize that Jesus was talking **to** the 1ˢᵗ century believers, **about** the 1ˢᵗ century believers and **for** the 1ˢᵗ century believers, not to, about or for us in the 21st century? That, of course, does not mean that there are not **principles** in the Bible that we can apply to all of mankind (before 30 A.D. and after 70 A.D., including our time in the 21ˢᵗ century.

"And so he that had received five talents came and brought other five talents, saying, Lord, thou deliveredst unto me five talents: behold, I have gained beside them five talents more" [Matthew 25:20].

Strong's still says that (in the Textus Receptus, from which the King James Version is translated) this person did not receive only five talents, but five times 1,000 talents. At any rate, either figure was a very large sum of **money** and much was required of him. He did what was required of him to do and that was to double his money.

I am really impressed with the Greek word *"proserchomai,"* which is translated by the word *"came."* It literally means to *"draw near."* When a person is faithful to his master, he has no reason to have any distance between him and his master. If the correct application is made here, this faithful servant could stand face to face with his master, Jesus and not be ashamed of anything that he did. **He drew near** – is that not a nice way of stating the relationship of a man with his master – even today?

Maybe I am going a little deeper in my studies than the reader would like, but I feel that I must take a closer look at the Greek word *"prosphero,"* which is translated by the word *"brought."* I can see the one talent man *"bringing"* the one talent back to his master, but I think that the Greek word has a more interesting tenor to it, namely, that one servant *"tendered"* five **other** talents to his master. For your further consideration, if you care to look up other places, the <u>King James Version</u> renders the Greek word by the following wording: *"bring, bring to, bring unto, deal with, do, offer, offer unto, offer up, present to, and put to."*

The word that is rendered *"other"* is the Greek word *"loipoy,"* which means *"the remaining ones,"* i.e. the ones *"other"* than the original five talents. I hope that I am helping you save time in looking up the original words. That is my intention. It will also more quickly present a good flow of the teaching of the parables.

If I can relate a happy experience here, when I was studying Greek in my beginning semester of college, and we came to the word *"lego,"* and studying its meaning, we would usually converse with each other as we met and passed each other on a walk somewhere and say, *"lego – I say,"* for the meaning of the Greek word *"lego"* fundamentally means *"I say."* That was the way that we associated some of the wording in trying to learn the basic meaning of words. In this verse, it is simply translated by the word *"saying."* Properly, the word has the meaning of *"to 'lay' forth, i.e. (figuratively) relate (in words). Usually they are words that are systematic or are a set discourse."* Note the **discourse** that followed the word *"saying."*

The remainder of the verse seems rather simple, the faithful servant stood close to his master and told him that he had been faithful and returned the master's five talents and that he had *"traded"* and *"profited"* five *"other"* talents (money) that also belonged to his master.

The words *"besides them"* have no Greek words. They are either correctly implied in the translation or an addition that should not be there. In places like this, we must study the whole verse and context carefully and see if there is any violence done to a text by inserting words that are not in the original text. No violence seems to have been done here, so it might help in understanding the verse in English. Jesus had said …

> *"For unto whosoever* **much is given, of him shall be much required***: and to whom men have committed much, of him they will ask the more"* [Luke 12:48].

Of the three servants who received talents, this man received five talents – **the most** of the three. Of him, much will be required, so he had to do his best and produce five more talents. He was faithful in accomplishing his responsibility.

Again, let me say that the application to this parable is that when Jesus returned in 70 A.D., his apostles (and those who believed in him because of the apostles preaching), would give account of the work (talents – money) with which they had been entrusted. The application was for the 1st century believers, not for us today in the 21st century (applications are fine for today).

> *"His lord said unto him, Well done, thou good and faithful servant: thou hast been faithful over a few things, I will make thee ruler over many things: enter thou into the joy of thy lord"* [Matthew 25:21].

Let us look at a few definitions before any application is made. The word *"said"* is from the Greek word *"phemi,"* which means *"to show or make known one's thoughts,"* hence to say or speak. The words *"well done,"* come from the Greek word *"eu,"* which primarily means *"good,"* but when used as an adverb, it means *"well,"* The <u>King James Version</u> translates it by *"good, well, well done,"* depending upon the context.

The Greek word *"agathos"* that is translated as *"good,"* primarily means "*good, in any sense,*" and is to be distinguished from the word *"eu"* that is previously used in this verse.

The word that is translated as *"faithful"* comes from the Greek word *"pistos,"* which is used both objectively (trustworthy) and subjectively (trustful). Depending upon which way it is used; it is so translated in the <u>King James Version</u> as *"believe, believer, believing and faithful, faithfully, sure, true."*

One of the very interesting things of this verse is the use of the Greek word *"oligos,"* which is translated as *"a few things"* in the <u>King James Version</u>. The meaning is primarily **puny**. What thoughts does that word conjure up in your mind? To what **extent** – to what **degree** – to what **duration** – to what **value**, had this servant been faithful and/or trustworthy? As an adverb, it would be translated by the word *"somewhat."* Well, as we use the word (not as the Bible uses it), *"no one is perfect."* But the servant was considered faithful by his lord and master. But, whether five talents or 5,000 talents, in that he doubled his lord's money, he was considered to be faithful. **He made progress**, not sit still or go backward.

The phrase *"I will make ruler"* comes from the one Greek word *"kathistemi,"* which primarily means *"to place down (permanently), i.e. to designate, constitute or convoy."* To what was this faithful servant **designated or constituted?**

Was this servant really faithful? Absolutely, because Jesus said that he was. Did he not sin for forty years? Surely. Jesus does **not** speak of anything in which he sinned during that forty year period, for in that forty year period, the servant kept on going strong and even with his ups and downs, he ultimately received his just reward in the doubling of his lord's money. A truly faithful slave.

It is here that we must stop and analyze the verse more closely. To whom was Jesus speaking? The answer is, of course, his apostles. Was he speaking to you or me? Obviously not. We were not to be born for about another 2,000 years. There are some questions that we need to ask.

- ❖ Were the apostles without sin for those forty years?
- ❖ Were they 100% faithful?
- ❖ Were they *"over"* everything while they lived and preached the gospel?
- ❖ If so, were they given *"more"* in 70 A.D. than they had in 30 A.D.?
- ❖ If so, what was given to them at that time that they did not already have?
- ❖ Did they exercise any *"rulership"* in 30 A.D.?
- ❖ Did they exercise any *"rulership"* in 70 A.D.?

Let us explore the questions and look for scriptural answers.

Were the apostles without sin for forty years? I need not answer that. Here is what one of the apostles said on the subject. Or, what did Jesus mean when he said to Peter, *"get behind me satan?"*

> *"If we say that we have no sin, we deceive ourselves, and the truth is not in us"* [1 John 1:8].

Were the apostles 100% faithful? Obviously not, as the above verse from one of the apostles testifies. It was probably a very good translation when it was made by the phrase *"a __few__ things,"* being that their faithfulness was only *"puny"* in comparison to what was to come for them.

Were the apostles *"over"* everything while they lived and preached the gospel? If this parable is true, it is obvious that they were *"over"* something, but not everything when they were given talents and began to execute their duties. They had the delegated authority by Jesus to *"go into all the world and preach the gospel to **every** creature."* Yes indeed. There was much over which they were entrusted from 33 A.D. to 70 A.D.. **Every** one of the Judeans, who were scattered throughout the entire earth, had to hear the gospel. God was not so unmerciful as to destroy the unbelievers without giving them the opportunity to repent. At least, that is what the apostle Peter said …

> *"The Lord is not slack concerning his promise, as some men count slackness; but is longsuffering to us-ward, not willing that **any** should perish, but that **all** should come to repentance"* [2 Peter 3:9].

If so, were the apostles given *"more"* in 70 A.D. than they had in 30 A.D.? Again, if this parable is true (and I believe that it is), then they were to be given **more authority** than they had in the beginning of their ministry.

It was during their anticipation of the coming of Jesus into his kingdom, that the apostles had a confrontation. James and John (and their mother) came to Jesus and requested that one be set on the right hand and the other on the left hand in Jesus's kingdom (i.e. possessions of authority). Here was that request.

> *"Then came to him the mother of Zebedee's children with her sons, worshipping him, and desiring a certain thing of him. 21. And he said unto her, What wilt thou? She saith unto him, Grant that these my two sons may sit, the one on thy right hand, and the other on thy left, in thy kingdom"* [Matthew 20:21-22].

If so, what was given to them at that time that they did not already have? According to this parable, they were to be given more authority. What *"more"* would the apostles have? They eventually, after preaching the gospel to every creature, would sit as judges.

> *"And Jesus said unto them, Verily I say unto you, That ye which have followed me, in the regeneration when the Son of man shall sit in the throne of his glory, ye also shall sit upon twelve thrones, **__judging the twelve tribes of Israel__**"* [Matthew 19:28].

This passage shows that the *"ye"* was the apostles. **We will not sit on twelve thrones**, nor will we judge the twelve tribes of Israel. Other passages indicate that the time element was in 70 A.D.. I will not side-tract to study *"the regeneration."* It would be wise for each of you to study the word and when the event happened.

Did the apostles exercise any *"rulership"* in 30 A.D.? If the application to this parable is primary to the apostles (and I believe that it is), then *"yes,"* they were rulers over the *"talents"* that Jesus gave to them. They were indeed shepherds or as close to the shepherd as they could be. They had a responsibility to preach to the lost and convert them (i.e. returning more believers for their work). They also had some rule or responsibility to the believers. Do you remember that Jesus told Peter to *"feed my sheep?"*

Did they exercise any *"rulership"* in 70 A.D.? As we have already seen, at the end of their work, they were to *sit on twelve thrones, judging the twelve tribes of Israel."* Was that more *"rule"* than they had at the beginning? It must be answered in the affirmative.

The other word that I found interesting is the Greek word *"chara,"* which is translated as *"joy."* It means *cheerfulness, meaning calm delight."* There are many things that are delightful to God. In context, using the application, it was delightful and joyful for God to see His servants doing that which He had instructed them to do. God was delighted and He invited His faithful servant to share (enter into) and participate in the *"joy"* that He was experiencing. Is that not nice to know that God will allow people to share with Him the joy, calmness and delight that He experiences when people do what is expected of them?

However, let us not overlook the obvious. Jesus was not speaking to us. He was especially speaking to his first century disciples and their work and the joy that they would share in 70 A.D. with him. Remember as you study Matthew 25, that it is an extension of Matthew 24.

Jesus ended this verse with *"enter thou into the joy of thy lord."* In parabolic form, the word *"lord"* would be small letters, as the servant's *"master"* would be their lord. It is interesting to note that the word *"thy"* is a very good translation, i.e. not just *"the"* lord, but *"thy"* lord. The application to us, of course, is that we who believe experience all of the *"joys"* of our Lord.

> *"He also that had received two talents came and said, Lord, thou deliveredst unto me two talents: behold, I have gained two other talents beside them"* [Matthew 25:22].

There really is not much to add to the comments concerning this verse. It seems that the only difference is that this servant received only two talents, whereas the previous servant received five talents. Both did their work according as they were assigned and according to their ability. In the parable, both servants doubled their money. Review the five talent servant's comments to explain this verse in detail.

It seems that if *"he that is given much, much is required,"* then *"he that is given less, less is required."* However, remember the barren fig tree and its cursing. You must produce something. This verse indicates that to be true.

> *"His lord said unto him, Well done, good and faithful servant; thou hast been faithful over a few things, I will make thee ruler over many things: enter thou into the joy of thy lord"* [Matthew 25:23].

This verse is an exact word for word statement as is v-21. Review the comments from that verse for the explanation.

> *"Then he which had received the one talent came and said, Lord, I knew thee that thou art an hard man, reaping where thou hast not sown, and gathering where thou hast not strawed"* [Matthew 25:24].

The word *"then"* is **not** a sequential thing. The Greek word *"de"* properly means **and** in this context. Judgment is the key interest, not the sequence of the judgment of the servants.

This verse is about the servant who only received one talent. That meant that his requirement was not as much as the previous two servants. But, according to his ability, he should have made another talent – he should have doubled his lord's money. But, he was not faithful.

The words *"I knew"* are translated from the Greek word *"ginosko,"* which is translated by various words in the other places in the <u>King James Version</u>. This one talent person *"knew – understood – was aware of – perceived – was sure of"* the mind of his master.

The Greek word *"anthropos"* is usually thought of simply as a *"human being,"* not necessarily of a male. However, the entire parable seems to indicate a male, so it may be proper to translate it by the word *"male"* rather than just saying *"I knew thee that thou art a hard **person**."*

The word *"skleros"* is translated as *"hard."* The word properly means *"dry."* Hence the figurative use of *"harsh or severe"* would be a good translation, comparing it to *"hard dry ground."* Extensively, it could be translated as *"tough."* If this servant knew that his master was harsh, severe and a hard man, of all people, he should have known what would happen to him if he did not produce the desired results that were expected of him by his lord – especially since the lord knew exactly what his ability was.

Does this parable, at this point, indicate that Jesus was not only a loving lord, but that he also was a person who would render vengeance and destroy the rebellious Judeans? Consider that he was still speaking to his apostles about the 70 A.D. destruction of Jerusalem from the **first four verses of Matthew 24**.

At this point of looking at the parable, would we not expect the master to render a very harsh verdict against the slothful servant? Of course, we must keep in mind that Jesus was still talking here about his response to the apostles' questions in Matthew 24:3, that concerned the *"end of the Mosaic age,"* which was to come in their generation, almost 2,000 years ago. He was going to judge the slothful *"Jewish"* nation at his return in 70 A.D..

The remainder of the verse is pretty well self-explanatory. The lord or master expected his servants to sow and reap, to scatter and harvest – to do the actual work. In that sense, the apostles were to go and preach and they would be accountable to Jesus to the extent that they followed his commands.

They did accomplish that in the first century!

*"Which is come unto you, **as in all the world**: and bringeth forth fruit, as it doth also in you, since the day ye heard of it, and knew the grace of God in truth"* [Colossians 1:6].

*"If ye continue in the flesh grounded and settled, and be not moved away from the hope of the gospel, which ye have heard, and **which was preached to every creature which is under heaven**; whereof I Paul was made a minister"* [Colossians 1:23].

Evidently, many have not read these two scriptures, for the preaching of the gospel *"to the whole world"* was the duty of the apostles in the first century A.D. and they did that very thing. It is not something that is commanded today in order for *"the end"* of the Mosaic age to come.

> *"And I was afraid, and went and hid thy talent in the earth; lo, there thou hast that is thine"* [Matthew 25:25].

The Greek word *"phobeo"* is translated by the phrase *"I was afraid."* It does mean to be *"frightened or alarmed,"* but it also means *"to be aware of, i.e. to revere or reverence someone."* It is difficult here to determine which wording should be used, but as far as the end result is concerned, it makes little difference.

If his action in hiding the talent was motivated by fear or reverence for his master, the end result of both would be that the fear of losing the talent was uppermost. In trading talents, it is always a possibility of losing them. He might have reasoned, *"Which would be better for the master in case that the talent was lost? Would it have been better to not trade and still have the talent that my lord gave to me, or revere him and not wanting to lose it, hide it instead of losing it?"* See, it makes no difference, but I wonder how we would have reacted? Would we **respect him** in that we would not want to lose his money, so we just hid it; or would we be **scared to death** of losing someone else's money, especially our master's money and do nothing with it to be profitable to our master?

What is continually interesting is that this servant considered the talent to belong to his lord. He did not consider that it was his. He knew that it had been entrusted to him and that he should be faithful in watching over it. He did watch over it. Not watching over it was not a problem. As the depression was over, my grandfather still did not trust banks. So he asked my dad to hide his money. So, dad went out into his one-half acre garden and hid it. Both of them watched over it. No other person knew of the hiding spot (kind of like this one talent man). It was kept there until grand-dad died and it was time to account for his money. So dad went out in broad daylight and dug it up where anyone could watch.

For the next week, dad watched as many people with flashlights, totally hand-plowed all of the garden but dad just hid it in one spot and he had recovered it all rather quickly. Wonder how many people were digging in the earth trying to uncover the talent that the slave had already delivered to his lord? The biblical slave was unprofitable. He did not make any money for his lord like the first two servants did.

The term *"thou hast"* probably denotes two qualities, i.e. the lord was *"holding his possessions"* but also in the same *"condition"* in which he had entrusted the talent to the servant. Essentially, the servant said to the master, *"Lord, here is your money, exactly in the same amount and the same condition in which you gave it to me. I kept it securely and safely for you."* He possibly thought that such faithful watching (while doing nothing) would provide a blessing for him from his lord – but he was frightfully mistaken.

Again, we must be reminded that Jesus was speaking of his servants, the apostles, about the work that they were to perform. They were not only to be faithful in watching after the work to make sure that it was not tainted, but they were to be active in the work of preaching the gospel. This was instruction to Jesus' apostles previous to 70 A.D., and is not **specific** instruction for us today. However, let us use the **principle** and be ever faithful in carrying out the work that we can do for God.

> *"His lord answered and said unto him, Thou wicked and slothful servant, thou knewest that I reap where I sowed not, and gather where I have not strawed"* [Matthew 25:26].

It is worthy to note again that this was HIS lord, not just THE lord.

The word that is translated as *"answered"* is the Greek word *"apokrinomai,"* which means *"to conclude for oneself, i.e. by implication, **to respond**, to begin to speak where an address is expected."* The unprofitable servant made his speech and his lord responded accordingly.

The Greek word *"poneros"* is translated as *"wicked."* Unless we use another acceptable translation, *"evil,"* the translation is accurate enough. The <u>King James Version</u> translates it otherwise by the following words – *"bad, evil, grievous, harm, lewd, malicious and wickedness."*

The Greek word *"okneros"* is translated here by the word *"slothful."* Additionally, in the <u>King James Version</u>, it is also translated by the word *"grievous."* Primarily, the word means *"tardy, i.e. indolent; and figuratively it is used as irksome."* For example …

> - You wicked, **lazy** servant – <u>NIV</u>.
> - You wicked and **lazy** servant – <u>NKJV</u>.
> - You wicked, **lazy** slave – <u>NASV</u>.
> - You wicked, **lazy** slave – <u>NAS</u>.
> - Wicked man! **Lazy** slave – <u>TLB</u>.
> - You bad and **lazy** servant – <u>TEV</u>.

Do we not get the idea that the word *"slothful"* is best described in today's language as *"lazy?"* Yes, for the apostles to have to go preach the gospel to the entire Israelite world would be much work. Would they do it or be lazy and not do it? Of course, looking back, we can see that they accomplished such in the 1st century A.D.. There are no specifics for us here, but we certainly need not be lazy in whatever work we do for God.

For the remainder of the verse about sowing and reaping, see the notes on 25:24.

> *"Therefore, my beloved brethren, be ye steadfast, unmoveable, **always abounding in the work of the Lord**, forasmuch as ye know that **your labour is not in vain in the Lord**"* [1 Corinthians 15:58].

"Thou oughtest therefore to have put my money to the exchangers, and then at my coming I should have received mine own with usury" [Matthew 25:27].

Yes, I know that you are thinking about what God said about interest in the *"old testament."* If you have studied it carefully, have you come to the conclusion that what He desired was the love of brother to brother, and that none of the biological children of Israel could charge *"interest"* of another Israelite? Have you also determined that it was acceptable if the Israelites charged interest for a debt to one who was not an Israelite?

> *"Unto a stranger thou mayest lend upon; but unto thy brother thou shalt not lend upon; that the LORD thy God may bless thee in all that thou settest thy hand to in the land whither thou goest to possess it"*
> [Deuteronomy 23:20].

The Israelite could **not** take usury on anything; be it money, food, or anything else, when such items were *"loaned to"* or *"borrowed by"* another brother who was an Israelite.

> *"Thou shalt not lend upon to thy brother; of money, of victuals, and any thing that is lent upon"* [Deuteronomy 23:19].

Would you say that such a principle should be true today, i.e. that a believer could not extract interest when another believer is the other party?

When the apostles preached to every one of the Israelites, it was the word of God that was going forth and it would produce a return for Him. If it failed, it was not God's fault – it would be the apostles' fault, for God had said …

> *"So shall my word be that goeth forth out of my mouth: **it shall not return unto me void**, but it shall accomplish that which I*

please, and it shall prosper in the thing whereto I sent it" [Isaiah 55:11].

So, while this verse is specifically speaking of Jesus' instructions to his twelve apostles in the 1st century A.D., we can still find an application to us in the 21st century – will require a return, He will not accept *"nothing"* – He will not accept a *"void."* We must ask ourselves right now, *"Are we working acceptably for God?*

The word *"oughtest"* is an interesting study. When a thing *"ought"* to be done, is it a necessity? The word can be translated as *"must,"* as well as *"necessary."* Yes, it was a sin for that lazy servant not to have traded the money that his master had entrusted to him. Remember that Jesus was speaking to his apostles. Whatever instructions he gave to his apostles, they were to diligently carry them out, not being indifferent, lazy or unfruitful. Indeed, it appears that they understood, for they did take the gospel to the entire Judean world in that 1st century generation.

I have been asked questions about the phrase *"all the world"* of Mark 16:15. It was in the Roman world that the apostles were instructed to go, for God would not destroy those rebellious Israelites in 70 A.D. by the Romans, until He had given them plenty of time to repent. Forty years up to that time was sufficient time for the Judeans to hear God's warning messages as well as the gospel of His saving power to those that would believe. Then *"the end"* would come to the old Mosaic system when the temple was destroyed in 70 A.D.. God had promised to destroy them and a complete end to their ritualistic worship and He was not *"slack concerning His promise."* He was not *"tardy"* – He was not one second late. The apostles did their job. They were neither slothful nor lazy. And God kept His promise of making sure that all of those things happened in the 1st century generation. Here is what He had earlier told His disciples.

It is here emphasized again that the money belonged to the lord or master – not the servant. That point has been emphasized at least four or five times in this parable. Therefore, it must be very important to keep that in mind.

The word *"therefore"* would have been better translated as *"accordingly."* Accordingly, the lazy servant could have at least done one small thing – lent the money to the exchangers and it would have received at least a little profit for his master. Now please do not forget that chapter 25 is an extension of the previous chapter which was being said to four of the eleven apostles. We must not forget that it must be interpreted in the context of the first century A.D..

As we continue to study this verse, we must look at the word *"exchanger,"* which comes from the Greek word *"trapezitais."* From the two sources at which I am looking, it appears that this is the only place in the Bible that the word occurs.

> *"A money-exchanger, broker, banker, one who exchanges money for a fee, and **pays interest on deposits**"* [A Greek-English Lexicon of the New Testament, J.H. Thayer, page 629].

This word is not to be confused with the *"moneychangers"* of Matthew 21:12; Mark 11:15 or John 2:15, which comes from an entirely different word.

Here, I would like to share with you a quote from my dear departed friend, Jim Rittenhouse. It should give you something good to think about for awhile.

> *"I think that the term exchangers, is a reference to "the ones that doubled by trading," is it not? I had thought about it maybe meaning the money changers in the temple but that does not seem to fit the context. So, it appears to me at first glance that Jesus was asking "why did you not at least give it to my 'hard working' servants" (exchangers) if you were not willing to risk it to make a profit with it," is simply making a profit using money*

which they did in this context (since they followed the ways of Jesus) by "giving and it shall be given back to you, pressed, shaken together, and flowing over shall men give unto your bosom." You don't plant a grain of corn and expect back only one grain of corn. It had to be a sure thing for to profit, even for the one that got only one talent but required trust in the Master's teaching which the wicked/lazy servant did not have, or some of what Jesus is referring to would be sophistry.

*"The only way prosperity was ever espoused by Jesus, was giving it away and letting God pay you back instead of the person you are giving it to. It says don't give to those that can pay you back. Two of the three did that, risking losing it by giving it away but simply **trusting** on the Master's instructions of how to increase. The wicked servant did not believe giving it away would come back with profit so **he distrusted** the Master and should have given it to those who did trust him.*

*"Was this not the full-time job of Judas – to go and give away money and to collect it from others? But Jesus, whose only employer at that time was God, seemed to have so much that they could buy anything they needed, keep Judas with a little extra embezzlement and had more left over to give away. Call it the paradox of trust, if you will. It doesn't have to be money, it merely is in this parable (easier for people to relate to I guess) but giving anything you have as a talent, but the principle is that you must get rid of it to increase it whatever your "coin or the realm" is. Whether it be your time, your food, your clothing, your time to visit the sick, your skills in the understanding of the word, etc. if you **give it away** in His name, it by definition must be increased or Jesus would be embarrassed by the things he instructed us **[his apostles]** to do,"*

The bold was supplied by me. The trust that the apostles had in Jesus was what made them successful. At any rate, this verse concludes that at the *"coming"* of Jesus in 70 A.D., he would hold his apostles accountable for their service. What application can we make of us doing the will of God today, almost 2,000 years later?

> *"Thou oughtest therefore to have put my money to the exchangers, and then at my coming I should have received mine own with usury"* [Matthew 25:27].

Yes, I know that you are thinking about what God said about *"usury"* in the *"old testament."* If you have studied it carefully, have you come to the conclusion that what He desired was the love of brother to brother, and that none of the biological children of Israel could charge *"interest"* of another Israelite? Have you also determined that it was acceptable if the Israelites charged interest for a debt to one who was not an Israelite?

> *"Unto a stranger thou mayest lend upon; but unto thy brother thou shalt not lend upon: that the LORD thy God may bless thee in all that thou settest thine hand to in the land whither thou goest to possess it"* [Deuteronomy 23:20].

The Israelite could **not** take *"usury"* on anything, be it money, food, or anything else, when such items were *"loaned to"* God or *"borrowed by"* another brother who was an Israelite.

> *"Thou shalt not lend upon to thy brother, of money, of victuals, of any thing that is lent upon ..."* [Deuteronomy 23:19].

Would you say that such principle should be true today, i.e. that one believer could not extract usury (interest) when another believer is the other party? Well?

The apostles to whom Jesus was speaking in the three chapters were to *go into all the world and preach the gospel* (good news of God) *to every creature"* [Mark 16:15]. When they did preach it, it was the word of God that was going forth and it would produce a return for Him. If it failed, it was not God's fault – it would be the apostles' fault, for God had said …

> *"So shall my word be that goeth forth out of my mouth:* **it shall not return unto me void***, but it shall accomplish that which I please, and it shall prosper in the thing whereto I sent it"* [Isaiah 55:11].

So, while this verse is specifically speaking of Jesus' instructions to his four apostles in the first century A.D., we still can find an application to us in the 21st century – will require a return, He will not accept *"nothing"* – He will not accept a *"void."* We must ask ourselves right now, *"Are we working acceptably for God?*

> *"Verily I say unto you, This generation shall not pass, till all these things be fulfilled"* [Matthew 24:34].

Ooooops! Here we go back to the Greek again. It is very interesting to see a word come up here that defines what the *"talents"* were that were entrusted to the servants. The Greek word is *"arguion"* and means *"silvery,"* which by implication, means *"cash,"* especially a *"silverling, i.e. a drachma or a shekel."* It is not an uncommon usage, for everyone surely remembers that Judas sold Jesus for thirty pieces of *"silver."* At least, the lord of that unprofitable servant would have had a little return (as silver was not as profitable as gold). And, I know that you will recall that in the early part of the book of Acts, Peter said, *"Silver and gold have I none."* Before we get away from those thoughts of v-27, let me again quote from brother Rittenhouse. Please re-read his preceding thoughts before reading this.

> *"Silver and gold have I none, but 'such as I have I give to you, rise up and walk.' Again, that confirms that a talent is a talent in the parable but it is both literal and metaphoric. Paul had no money but had something that was worth far more than money. So you could say that Paul would double his talent by sowing it. I*

think that the talent is a trust in God in whatever form. Peter had to trust God to heal the man. The rich man had to trust in God to have riches in heaven where they were not stolen or moth eaten. He could not do it. We do not need wealth in heaven, so a treasure in heaven would make heaven a sort of 'bank account' that requires trust in God but pays tremendous interest. The rich man blew one of the best deals that he had ever been offered to increase. He chose to walk by sight.

"Even though the talent is used apparently in a literal sense in the verse, all of the kingdom is governed by the same laws of sowing and reaping. The wicked servant had no trust in his Master, which led to the evil behavior. The other two trusted their Master – like the farmer who has to bury his seed and 'trust' that it will grow. If he has doubts that it will grow, he might dig it up and kill it.

"Silver and gold was not the lame man's problem. Peter considered his trust in God to heal that man, his talent. Peter considered his trust for healing the man to be a possession of his (representing the Master as a good servant) and gave it away. This walk by faith and not by sight, seems stupid to men following mammon, but it is our role in this 'paradox of trust.' The beatitudes are entirely on the 'paradox of trust.' The beatitudes (and events like them) were where his servants learned how to prosper 'the Master's way.'

"I saw that verse and the thing that Peter 'had,' come to mind as a talent. Had Peter have had a lot of silver and gold, which of the two, 'healing' or 'wealth,' if offered, would the lame man have chosen? Now imagine what it was like being lame in those days. Which would you prefer?"

"Take therefore the talent from him, and give it unto him which hath ten talents" [Matthew 25:28].

Behold, how quickly some questions arise!

> ➢ Who was to take the talent away from the last servant?
> ➢ Why was it given to the five talent man instead of the two talent servant?
> ➢ Why was it not given to another servant?
> ➢ Why was it *"given"* instead of having the servant do some more work for it?
> ➢ What was the application for the apostles who were being told this parable?
> ➢ And … what is the application for us today – if there is any?

It is stated in Luke 19:24, that there were those *"that stood by."* I do not know who they were in the parable, but I would venture an opinion, based on other verses in the Bible, that the application would be that Jesus was instructing the angels to take everything from the unprofitable apostle (if such be the case). Also, in v-27, he instructed the same ones that stood by to bring the unprofitable servants (who were his enemies) to him and slay them. Does it sound like God was going to destroy the wicked and lazy servants?

Maybe you have studied this verse more than I, and maybe you have some answers to all of these questions, but I frankly do not have many answers here. Maybe in time, with much more research on my part, I shall come to understand more (if there is any more concerning this aspect of the parable). I did something that I do not normally do. I went to different commentaries to see what the scholars of past generations had to say of this verse. I consulted Barnes' Notes, Jamieson, Fausset and Brown, Matthew Henry, Wycliffe Bible Commentary, Adam Clark's Commentary, and what do you think that I found? Absolutely nothing! Nada. However, we can know a few things from the next verse.

"For unto every one that hath shall be given, and he shall have abundance: but from him that hath not shall be taken away even that which he hath" [Matthew 25:29].

In his follow-up to the preceding verse, Jesus shows that there is *"no respect of persons"* with him. It did not matter whether a person had ten talents or four talents, each would be given more, and each would have abundance.

On the other hand, he makes it **explicitly clear** that not only would the unfaithful servant lose what was entrusted to him, but anything that he personally had, he would also lose.

What have we learned so far? First, the talent was probably of silver. Second, the talent and money were **used figuratively** of anything that was entrusted to servants (in this case, the apostles). The words *"that hath"* are taken from the Greek word *"echo,"* which **figuratively** means *"possessions, ability, continuity, relation and condition."* Do not all of these apply to what the apostles were given? Why did I bold and underline the word **figuratively**? I did so because Jesus had already used the exact phrase in chapter 13. Having already used it, the context should tell us the **figurative** use of it here in this chapter. Let us look at it (along with the context).

"And the disciples came, and said unto him, Why speakest thou unto them in parables? 11. He answered and said unto them, Because it is given unto you to know the mysteries of the kingdom of heaven, but to them it is not given. 12. ***For whosoever hath, to him shall be given, and he shall have more abundance: but whosoever hath not, from him shall be taken away even that he hath****. 13. Therefore speak I to them in parables: because they seeing see not; and hearing they hear not, neither do they understand. 14. And in them is fulfilled the prophecy of Esaias, which saith, By hearing ye shall hear, and shall not understand; and seeing ye shall see, and shall not perceive: 15. For this*

people's heart is waxed gross, and their ears are dull of hearing, and their eyes they have closed; lest at any time they should see with their eyes, and hear with their ears, and should understand with their heart, and should be converted, and I should heal them. 16. But blessed are your eyes, for they see: and your ears, for they hear. 17. For verily I say unto you, That many prophets and righteous men have desired to see those things which ye see, and have not seen them; and to hear those things which ye hear, and have not heard them" [Matthew 13:10-17].

Since Jesus had already very clearly used this phrase, I think that it is permissible to conclude that the talents or money in the context of this chapter refers to the **<u>understanding</u>** that was entrusted to the apostles.

Jesus told the apostles why he spoke to the people in parables – so that they **<u>could not understand</u>** the unseen, spiritual truths that were later explained to the apostles. The apostles were given answers to the understanding of past ages and they were to *"give them away"* so that the Lord would bless their efforts. If they did not **<u>trust</u>** their Lord that much, then they would indeed be his enemies and worthy of death.

This unprofitable servant was *"useless"* in understanding. That reminds me of about the only thing that I can remember from college days (if you really want to know how useless I am). I recall a poem that I learned. Now remember that I learned it 61 years ago.

> The more you study, the more you know.
> The more you know, the more you forget.
> The more you forget, the less you know.
> So why study?

> The less you study, the less you know.
> The less you know, the less you forget.
> The less you forget, the more you know.
> So why study?

Now that is useless, is it not? Was this lazy servant as useless?

"And cast ye the unprofitable servant into outer darkness: there shall be weeping and gnashing of teeth" [Matthew 25:30].

Maybe even more profound is to understand that the word *"unprofitable"* comes from the Greek word *"achreios,"* which means *"useless"* – and indeed the servant was useless.

Then there is the compound Greek word *"ekballo"* – *"ek"* means *"out"* and *"ballo"* means *"to throw."* When taking Greek, I associated *"ballo"* with throwing a ball. That helped me to remember what the word meant. So, technically, it means to *"throw out,"* and is translated in the <u>King James Version</u> as *"cast ye."* The <u>King James Version</u> otherwise translates the word by various words, such as *"bring forth, cast forth, cast out, drive, drive out, expel, leave, pluck, pull, take, thrust, put forth, put out, send away, and send out."*

To many reading this, a more focused attention will now be given to where the unprofitable servant was cast. It is said to be into *"outer darkness."* Just what are we to make of those words?

First of all, it will be helpful to note that the Greek word is *"exoteron,"* which is translated by the word *"outer"* meaning *"exterior."* Keep that in mind as it is connected to the next Greek word, which is *"skotos,"* which is translated by the word *"darkness"* which means *"obscurity."* To misunderstand that meaning, it will be necessary for us to go to the English dictionary and see what the word *"obscurity"* means (a lesson in English).

Among the definitions are found statements like *"indefinite for lack of adequate illumination"* and *"not well known."* Those English words should give us some clue as to what *"outer darkness"* means. What would **exterior obscurity** conjure up in your mind?

First of all, it should tell us that this lazy servant would no longer be in the presence of his lord, i.e. if one of the apostles did not use the knowledge and understanding that Jesus was giving to him, he would be banished from the presence of God, where all **light** dwells. Is such true of us today?

> *"This then is the message which we have heard of Him, and declare unto you, that God is light, and in him is no darkness at all"* [1 John 1:5].

> *"In him was life; and the light was the light of men. 5. And the light shineth in darkness; and the darkness comprehended it not"* [John 1:4-5].

Secondly, maybe it would remind us that John the baptizer went before Jesus, preparing his way, and first told of the *"casting out"* of the ones who did not produce good fruit.

> *"And now also the axe is laid unto the root of the trees: every tree therefore which bringeth not forth good fruit **is hewn down and cast into the fire**"* [Luke 3:9].

Now, look at all of the associated scriptures where Jesus told of that fulfillment.

> *"Every tree that bringeth not forth good fruit is **hewn down and cast into the fire"** [Matthew 7:19].

> *"The kingdom of God **shall be taken from you, and given to a nation** bringing forth the fruits thereof"* [Matthew 21:43].

> *"And I say unto you, That many shall come from the east and west, and shall sit down with Abraham, and Isaac, and Jacob, in the kingdom of heaven. 12. But the children of the kingdom **shall**

be cast out into outer darkness: there shall be weeping and gnashing of teeth" [Matthew 8:11-12].

*"As therefore the tares are gathered and burned in the fire; so shall it be in the end of **this** ~~world~~ (**age**). 41. The Son of man shall send forth his **angels**, and they shall **gather out** of his kingdom all things that offend, and them which do iniquity; 42. And **shall cast them into a furnace of fire**; there shall be wailing and gnashing of teeth"* [Matthew 13:40-42].

*"And he saith unto him, Friend, how camest thou in hither **not having a wedding garment**? And he was speechless. 13. Then said the king to the servants, **Bind him hand and foot, and take him away, and cast him into outer darkness**; there shall be weeping and gnashing of teeth"* [Matthew 22:12-13].

*"Ye are the salt of the earth: but if the salt have lost his savour, wherewith shall it be salted? It is thenceforth **good for nothing, but to be cast out**, and to be trodden under foot of men"* [Matthew 5:13].

Have we learned anything about the parable of the talents by comparing other verses? We should have. The time for the unprofitable servant to be cast out (exterior – gathered out) was at the end of the Mosaic **age** (**mis**-translated *"world"*) in 70 A.D.. It was the time of the wedding of Jesus to his ekklesia (called out people ~~church~~), which happened in 70 A.D.. It is not something that is to happen in our generation or future time. Reviewing …

"Outer darkness" is compared to *"a furnace of fire"* and *"trodden under foot of man."*

Those that *"stood by"* were the angels" [Matthew 13:40-42].

The unprofitable servant was to *"be bound hand and feet," – "cast into outer darkness" – "cast into the furnace of fire."*

Such lazy servants were to be *"hewn down" – "gathered together"* for burning, the *"kingdom taken from them" – "taken away."*

They were *"useless," – "good for nothing," – "not producers of fruit" – "not producers of **good** fruit" – "as no good salt"* and was at the wedding without the proper *"wedding garment."*

Due to the controversial nature of this next subject, it will be a little longer. I would like to pause here and go on with the remainder of the verse, but as yet, I think that I have not given enough information in the **exterior obscurity**, of which I have previously written.

Since we now know that Jesus was still answering questions of his apostles in Matthew24:3 about the *"end of the (~~world~~) age"* (the end of the Mosaic age), we know that the end of the age was in 70 A.D.. It was then that the wedding took place with Jesus and his bride. It was then the day for the lazy servant to give account (judgment day) for his slothfulness. It was then the time for the punishment of the evil doers (enemies) and the time for the righteous servants to be given more abundance. There is nothing in Matthew 24-25 for our day in the 21st century – although there are some **principles** that we must apply in our lives.

I will get a little more controversial now. Before I show you what I am going to show you, which interfaces with those two chapters, it is necessary to inform you that much study should convince the honest truth seeker that the book of Revelation was written **before** the destruction of Jerusalem and the Mosaic system in 70 A.D.. That being said, let us proceed. (If you have not seen that yet, just be patient when studying and thinking about it.)

Most people want to use the last two chapters of the book of Revelation to talk about what it will be like in heaven. But, we need to look closer at them.

> *"And I John saw the holy city, new Jerusalem, coming down from **out of heaven**, prepared as a bride adorned for her husband"* [Revelation 21:2].

Notice that the new Jerusalem, the bride of Jesus, was **coming down from, out of heaven,** no longer to be in heaven, but to be on the earth. Now what do we know of that city, the **new** Jerusalem? Among many other things, we note that …

> *"… the city had no need of the sun, neither the moon, to shine in it, for the glory of did lighten it, and the Lamb is the light thereof"* [Revelation 21:23].

From those two passages, we can ascertain that if one is *"ejected"* (a word that we have already discussed in this parable of the talents) from the city, that he will have no light, therefore he will be in *"exterior"* or *"outer"* darkness – away from the presence of God and Jesus. As far as any acknowledgement of God, he would be in *"obscurity."* Those two aspects can be seen in the expressions, *"I **never** knew you"* Matthew 7:23, and *"I know ye **not**"* Matthew 25:12. Now, we can see a little more of **when** the unprofitable servants would be *"cast out"* and **how** they would be in *"outer/exterior"* darkness. But, another point needs to be made.

> *"And **the gates of it shall not be shut** at all by day: for there shall be no night there"* [Revelation 21:25].

That means that people can get in or out. Why would one that was **in** the city want to get out of it, or why would he do anything to get **ejected** from the new Jerusalem?

It also means that a person who was on the outside of the new Jerusalem could still have an entrance into it. Was there anyone on the outside, or were all of those not in the city already sentenced to an eternal conscious life of punishment in what we call *"hell?"* I have a new book out now that is called <u>Satan, the Devil and the Adversary</u>. It is a very large book and has about 430 pages. Go to AMAZON.COM and type in my name, Ron McRay in the blank spot and it will come up with the rest of my books.

> *"And there shall in no wise enter into it any thing that defileth, neither whatsoever worketh abomination, or maketh a lie: but they which are written in the Lamb's book of life"* [Revelation 21:27].

If one of those bad, abominable, defilers or liars could not **<u>change</u>** and enter the city, why are they even mentioned? And if the gates were always open, does that not mean that God will continue to let them repent and go through the gates into the city? Does not the Bible teach the principle that *"He is not willing that any should perish"* 2 Peter 3:9? But let us look at another passage.

> *"Blessed are they that do his commandments, that they may have right to the tree of life, and **<u>may enter in through the gates into the city</u>**. 15. For **<u>without</u>** are dogs, and sorcerers, and whoremongers, and murderers, and idolaters, and whosoever loveth and maketh a lie"* [Revelations 22:14-15].

This verse shows who were on the *"exterior"* and in *"obscurity"* or darkness. But they could see the light and *"enter – the city"* because **<u>the gates were/are open</u>**! That is all that we will study about Revelation in our study of Matthew 24-25. An entire book of about 5,000 pages needs to be written. Anyone volunteer?

As we have seen in Luke 19, the lazy servant was slain. Knowing what would happen, do you suppose that the slothful servant would weep and gnash his teeth?

The Greek word for *"weeping"* is *"klauthmos"* and is best translated as *"lamentation."* It is here translated as *"weeping,"* but it is a more emphatic word and action. The English word is defined as *"to express sorrow, mourning, or regret, meaning regret strongly."* Can you just imagine how the lazy servant would like to have gone back and traded the talent and made some money for his master? I am sure that it was with very, very deep regret (weeping) that he was bound head and foot, taken away and was killed. He *"existed"* then in a state of death, no light, on the exterior of the city *"which hath foundations, whose builder and maker is God."*

Gnashing, grating or grinding of the teeth, probably would be connected with the *"figurative"* mental anguish that was associated with regret, being bound and being slain.

There can be no question but that the apostles were forewarned of their being rejected or ejected from the kingdom of God if they did not utilize properly the **understanding** that Jesus had given them for over three years. I doubt that there is anyone who understands that the primary instructions here were to the apostles, who would also doubt that the prophets and other believers of the 1st century A.D. would also fall into the same category, depending upon whether they were faithful or lazy. How does that apply to you and me today?

> *"When the Son of man shall come in his glory, and all the holy angels with him, then shall he sit upon the throne of his glory"* [Matthew 25:31].

There are two aspects to the Greek word *"hotan,"* which is here translated as *"when."* It carries the idea of whenever, that implies a hypothesis of more or less uncertainty, which certainly would be the case when the exact *"day and hour"* was not known to Jesus **at the time** that he was uttering those words.

It also carries the idea of being a conjunction. In that case, Jesus connected the punishment of the unfaithful servant with the exact time of his coming in 70 A.D.. In either case, the time element cannot be honestly misunderstood. It was in that current generation [Matthew 24:34]. He told his apostles …

> *"But when they persecute you in this city, flee ye into another: for verily I say unto you, Ye shall not have gone over the cities of Israel, **till the Son of man be come**"* [Matthew 10:23].

Therefore *"the coming of Jesus"* had to be in the 1st century A.D. while the apostles were still doing their work of preaching the gospel.

The expression *"son of man"* occurs 88 times in the *"new testament."* All but four of them are uttered by Jesus himself. (Hey, that took me a long time to count them and see if Jesus uttered each one!) Three of the four are referring to Jesus, while only one refers to an actual human being. Jesus always used the expression *"Son of man"* when referring to himself. Never did he initiate any conversation that would refer to himself as the *"son of God."* Only in John 10:36, in response to his accusers who wanted to stone him to death, did he admit that he said that *"I am the Son of God."* And, looking a little deeper, there probably needs some more study to even prove that to be a correct translation or interpretation. If any of you would like to do that, I would be more than happy to see what your research finds.

The Greek word *"doxa"* is translated as *"glory."* I have heard very few try to define the word *"glory,"* and the ones who have tried, have summed it up as only *"brightness,"* which to me really does not do justice to the Greek or English word. I found (out of twelve ways in which the word is used in the English language) the following four definitions that might probably fit in this context.

(1) Very great praise, honor, or distinction bestowed by common consent, renown, to win glory on the field of battle.
(2) Something that is a source of honor, fame or admiration, a distinguished ornament or an object of pride, a sonnet that is one of the glories of English poetry.
(3) Resplendent beauty or magnificence: the glory of autumn.
(4) A state of great splendor, magnificence, or prosperity.

Notice that there is a difference in the expression *"His glory"* i.e. *"the glory of Jesus"* and *"the glory of God,"* which is thusly translated fifteen times in the *"new testament."* There is one time that the translation is *"the glory of the Father"* and two times that we have the expression *'in the glory of His Father"* in the *"new testament."*

Jesus did **not** have all authority. That is correct. While the Bible stated at his ascension, that Jesus said *"All power is given unto me in heaven and in earth"* (Matthew 28:18), his Father did not allow himself to be put under his son. Neither did he know the day and hour, only the Father knew that.

> *"For he hath put all things under his feet. But when he saith, all things are put under him, it is manifest that he is excepted, which did put all things under him"* [1 Corinthians 15:27].

While the subject needs some good study, I am not going to let this study get side-tracked to a study of the *"trinity issue,"* but there seems to be a distinction made here between the glory of Jesus and the glory of his Father. It can hardly be disputed though, that when Jesus did anything, that he did it under the authority of his Father. Therefore, it seems most likely that to *"come in His glory"* and to *"come in the glory of his Father"* were actually the same coming. That seems especially true since Jesus had already stated to the apostles that …

*"... the Son of man shall **come in the glory of the Father** with his angels, and then he shall reward every man according to his works"* [Matthew 16:27].

And then, Jesus immediately followed it up in the next verse with his coming and the time of his coming.

*"Verily I say unto you, There be **some standing here, which shall not taste of death,** till they see the **Son of man coming** in his kingdom"* [Matthew 16:28].

In writing about the same event, Luke sums up all three as being the same event.

"For whosoever shall be ashamed of me and of my words, of him shall the Son of man be ashamed, when he shall come in his own glory, and in his Father's, and of the holy angels" [Luke 9:26].

The context of the three chapters has shown us that the **coming** (*erchomai)* under consideration is that which occurred in 66 A.D. to 70 A.D.. It is expressly stated two times that it was Jesus' current contemporary **generation** that would experience those things in these three chapters. It is not for us to question. It is not for us to dispute. It is only for us to accept and try to harmonize it with the remainder of the Bible. It is very hard to be consistent at times, is it not? If what I have written is not proper, maybe the Lord will be gracious and help me to understand more. I keep on trying.

I was asked: *"Are we studying Bible prophecies or are we being given lessons in the Greek language?"*

Our *"new testament"* was written in Greek. The only way for us to really know the truth is to know what the Greek words mean. I am trying to keep it to a minimum and then to make sure that what is stated is in simple form. I have had about one hundred emails that really like what little Greek I am putting in, and only two that question its use. Since the term *"moneychangers"* is used in different places in the Bible, without knowing that there were two Greek words, one with a bad meaning and the other with a good meaning, we might lump them both together, thereby arriving at wrong conclusions. That is the problem with the English translations. So, in some cases, the Greek is necessary in understanding truth. All of Matthew 24-25 are prophecies (originally in Greek). We are studying Greek and English in order to understand **prophecy**. No, not lessons in Greek, although there are many adverse arguments that are made based on the use of Greek words and their tenses, moods, voices etc. In a couple of places, it might even be necessary to go into a short lesson on Greek tenses, moods, voices, etc. to show why an interpretation is incorrect, but I have not given any Greek lessons yet. I have only given definitions of English words through the use of **definitions** of the Greek words from which the English translations came. I just have to do the best that I can. Sorry that I cannot do any better. I will warn you that I will be forced to dig deeper in one part of a *"coming"* verse to help all to see the **mis**understanding of the reign of Jesus. I think that you will even appreciate the deeper aspects when you study them. I will try to keep them simple for those of you who know no Greek.

Others of you may have similar thoughts, so, now if you want a quick introductory lesson to the Greek language in which the *"new testament"* was written – consider the following. Otherwise skip this next section. (If it is any help to you, copy it off and paste it on your wall.) Here is what an **introductory Greek lesson** looks like.

CONSONANTS – there are three classes – Labials, Gutturals and Dentals (along with pronunciations that are necessary). There are four punctuation marks – comma, semi-colon or colon, expressed by a point above the line, the full stop, as in English, the note of interrogation. This latter is the same form as the English semi-colon, but must be distinguished from it.

INFLECTION – signifies the change in form of words to express variation in meaning.

DECLENSION – is the system of change in the terminations of nouns, adjectives and pronouns to express different relations.

GENDERS – there are three – masculine, feminine and neuter. These are not determined as in English by conditions of sex. Even names of inanimate objects are of different genders. The terminations of the words are a considerable guide.

NUMBERS – there are two – singular and plural. There is a duel (two) in Greek.

CASES – there are five – **nominative** expresses the subject; **vocative**, used in direct address; **accusative**, expressing the object of a verb, and used after certain prepositions to express motion towards, etc.; **genitive**, which originally signified motion from and hence separation but afterwards came largely to denote possession; **dative**, signifying the remote object.

ARTICLE – of different forms (there is **no** indefinite article "a").

The **iota** under the vowels in the dative singular must be observed carefully, it is very important. It is called iota subscript.

The **nominative and accusative** are always the same in the neuter.

The **genitive** plural always ends in wv (omega/nu).

Masculine and neuter dative forms are always alike.

And then there is the learning of the declensions, demonstratives, personal pronouns, possessive pronouns, the regular verb, active and passive voices, contractions, participles in all forms, pronouns, moods of different verbs, syntaxes, optative mood (and other moods), aorist tenses (and other tenses), the middle voice, deponent verbs (and other verbs), irregular verbs, adverbs, prepositions, interrogatives, particles, numerals, dependent clauses, accents, the 24 letters of the alphabet (or 26) and many associated things.

Even in this outline, I have not given anyone a Greek lesson, only what to expect if one wants to take lessons in the Greek language. In this, you have only had an introduction to the Koine Greek, the one used when Jesus walked this planet. We will get back to the simple study of English in trying to determine what the Bible prophecies really meant to the 1st century believers and any application for us today.

> *"Who hath delivered us from the power of darkness, and hath translated us into the kingdom of his dear son"* [Colossians 1:13].

Some object to a study of the original Greek, but here it **becomes absolutely necessary** to try to figure out what is the truth. Various opinions even exist among Greek scholars. But first, let us notice that the Greek wording for both *"delivered"* and *"translated"* are in the aorist tense. **They are also in the indicative mood**. With both of those known elements of the wording, just what does that prove? Here are some comments from Greek scholars (each paragraph is from a different author).

> ***"The aorist*** *is somewhat to grasp, so don't be frustrated if you don't receive any glowing practical insights initially. If you continue to perform* Word Studies *(including verb tense, voice & mood) as an integral part of your Bible study, you will begin to appreciate the meaning of the aorist tense & you will begin to receive insights from this understanding.*

> *"The term "aorist"* (**no mood involved**) *comes from the Greek, meaning "undefined" or "not specified." It is the tense used when one wishes to express the type (aspect) of action as mere*

occurrence, without reference to completion (perfect) or to duration or repetition or attempt (imperfect).

*"In the indicative, the aorist usually indicates **past tense** with reference to the time of speaking.*

*"The aorist is the **simple past tense**.*

*"States that an action occurs without regard to its duration. It is analogous to a snapshot which captures an action at specific point in time. In indicative mood, aorist can indicate **punctiliar** action (happens at a specific point in time) **in past**.*

*"In my view, "punctiliar" is too restricted. The way that I like to think of it is as the **unmarked** past, when it's in a normal narrative setting. It's not emphasizing anything about the action – not its punctiliarity, not its extension, or anything else. **It's the simple, unremarkable past**. So in that sense, the aorist indicative is relatively "perfective" in its usual sense. But "punctiliar" is too specific for me."*

Webb Mealy –

*"**The Historical Aorist** – The Aorist Indicative is most frequently used to express a **past event** viewed in its entirety, simply as an event or a single fact. It has no reference to the progress of the event, or to any existing result of it."*

*"**The indicative aorist** – usually does refer to **the past**: it bears an augment regularly and that is generally said to be an indicator of **past time** on an indicative verb. Where there may be ambiguity is with an aorist in one on the non-finite moods: infinitive, participle, subjunctive, optative, imperative. And even there, one can learn to make appropriate distinctions in context."*

- Department of Classics – Washington University - Carl W. Conrad

Recently, I read in one of the Greek books that the aorist indicative **is always translated as past**. If all of those quotations are the truth, then indeed the words *"delivered"* and *"translated"* (past tense in English) are correct in Colossians 1:13 and all of those scholarly translators were correct. That would definitely mean that Jesus was already on his throne and in his kingdom (reign) when Paul wrote the Colossian letter. But, maybe there is more to the subject than we have studied.

Of necessity, the following comments will be somewhat lengthy; a Greek lesson that was necessary.

The gun has been fired. The flack is obviously forth coming. It may hit me or miss me, but this is the course and I will watch for the flack – I do not want to be shot down. We have had to get deeper into the Greek **because that is where we are led**. There are some who believe that Jesus was only a Prince and did not have all power that he said that he had until after 70 A.D.. I may be mistaken but it seems that their idea of truth is in what the aorist tense in the Greek means. And their definition means something different from the scholars that I have noted above. However, let us look at some more scholars' comments. I have many friends who are scholars – who translate the entire Bible. The following are specific comments regarding Colossians 1:13.

Here is the comment and question that I posed to Mr. Verner Uleich.

> *"In Colossians 1:13, the aorist tense is used twice, 'delivered' and 'translated,' if I have looked at it correctly. In both cases, both are translated as 'past tense.' Is it always true that when an **aorist** tense verb is in the **indicative mood**, that it must always be translated in the past? And, if*
> *so, is the fact a reality that the two events had already occurred?"*

The Sign Of The End Revealed

Here was his response:

*"First Aorist **always** deals with **past time** – and with **punctiliar action** – that is a **point in time** – so, **yes it must be translated that way** – and that is the reason for choosing it instead of **Perfect tense** – which talks of something completed in the past with results continuing into the present (or imperfect which focuses on **continuous** action in past time)?"*

My response to him was the following:

*"If that is true, had indeed the 1ˢᵗ century believers **already been delivered and translated into the basileia (kingdom)** (not ekklesia, for I do not see them being the same) of their Messiah?"*

Mr. Ulrich's response was as follows:

*"Yes, that would be my way of seeing it – finished action in past time. That would be harmonious with Ephesians 2:6 where we **now** sit, by faith, with Jesus in the heavenly realms."*

I asked Mr. Remington Mandel to comment:

"What (very little) information I have found is that the aorist can only be translated in the past when it is in the indicative mood or past. Do you have more or different information?"

His response was as follows:

"The very first thing I learned about the aorist tense is that a-orist means without horizon (definition). Most aorist verbs are easily recognized by the sign of the future affixed and the sign of the past prefixed.

"I thought I had a fairly easy definition but didn't find the book. **_I've never met a scholar who would concede that the aorist was anything but past tense._** *"Aorist: a past tense of Greek verbs denoting an action without indicating whether completed, continued, or repeated ..." Sounds like a cop out. So if you say, "God loved the world and so he gave His only Son ..." you are saying in essence, "He loved those bitten by the fiery serpents, He loves the 1st century Israelites, and He will continue loving ..."*

"In A Grammar of the Greek New Testament in the Light of Historical Research, *Prof. A.T. Robertson has this to say regarding the translation of the aorist into English: "The Greek* **_Aorist ind., as can be readily seen, is not the exact equivalent of any tense in any other language_**. *It has nuances all its own, many of them difficult, or well nigh impossible to reproduce in English. We merely do the best we can in English to translate in one way or another the total result of a word, context and tense. Certainly one cannot say that the English translations have been successful with the Greek aorist ...(Page 847). The English past will translate the Greek aorist in many cases where we prefer 'have' ...(Page 848). The Greek aorist and the English past do not exactly correspond. The Greek aorist covers much more ground than the English past. The aorist in Greek is so rich in meaning that the English labors and groans to express it. As a matter of fact the Greek aorist is translatable into almost every English tense except the imperfect ..." Again, "The aorist is, strictly speaking, timeless."*

And so, I asked him how he would translate Colossians 1:13. His response was:

"Who draws us (to himself) out of the authority of darkness and removes us into the kingdom of His dear Son of His love."

One other literal translation is interesting. It is by the same author as Young's Analytical Concordance.

> "... who **_did rescue_** us out of the authority of the darkness, and **_did translate_** us into the reign of the Son of His love ..." Young's Literal Concordance.

I find that it does **not** in any sense, in any way, indicate that the verse is to be translated or to have the meaning of only the future, such as ...

> "... who ~~will rescue~~ us out of the authority of the darkness, and ~~will transport~~ us into the kingdom of the Son of His love ~~at a future time~~."

If you were alive in 63 A.D. and the apostle Paul had written the above to you, would you consider that you **had been** drawn/rescued out of the power of darkness and **had been removed** (transported) **into the kingdom** of Jesus? Or, would you have considered that you were awaiting the rescue and waiting to be transported into the kingdom of Jesus?

Now, with everyone confused, what is the difference? If Paul, writing the Colossian letter in the mid 60's A.D., said that those believers **before 70 A.D.** were **being drawn** (rescued) and **were being removed (transported) into the kingdom** of Jesus, does it not indicate that he already had a kingdom and was sitting on his throne? And there is obviously more that connects with this, but this addresses this particular point.

Well, maybe I do not see the entire picture or missed it entirely – or maybe an entire book needs to be printed that deals adequately with the subject.

But, is it still not true that in the verse here in Matthew 25:31, that Jesus was going to **continue** to sit on his throne in 70 A.D. to judge between the *"sheep and goats?"* But that there is no indication in the verse that such time was the **beginning** of his throne or reign? I know that there are differences of understanding on these verses, so I will be expecting some responses. If you write to me, please do not tell me that you differ, please tell me why and give to me some solid argumentation. Now let us return to our normal study without (hopefully) any more in-depth Greek studies.

The study of the word *"glory"* (doxa) is a very difficult one. Not very many people or scholars even touch the subject, so there is not much available for a person to obtain to even get a primary glimpse into the real meaning. I do not want this to go very deeply into a study of the word, as it is used in many, many verses in the *"new testament."*

It appears that it probably is better expressed in different passages by different other English words. Using Jesus for an example, it appears that the Bible speaks of him having *"glory"* at the foundation of the world, having *"glory"* during the forty apostolic years of 30 A.D. to 70 A.D. and a *"glory"* that continued without end. That being the case, it becomes more of a problem to translate the Greek word *"doxa"* correctly, according to the text and context in which it is used.

In this verse, it seems that for Jesus to sit on the throne of his glory, and that he was to come in his glory, that he had to already have the glory in order for him to come in his glory. I see nothing in the passage to indicate that 70 A.D. was the time when his glory **began** – do you?

If Jesus was to come in his glory (which he was), then he was to come in *"very great **praise, honor or distinction** that was bestowed upon him by his Father."* Does that imply that he did **not** have praise, honor or distinction while he was here on the planet? Maybe I am wrong, but I think to ask that question is but to answer it.

There was praise, honor and distinction that were attributed to Jesus, to his Father and to all of the holy angels. It is interesting that the word *"holy"* has no corresponding Greek word, which implies that it should not be in the text. That means that we do not have to consider what might have been *"__un__holy angels."* Earlier in Matthew 24, I said …

> *"The Greek word is "angelos," hence a transliteration of the word would be "angel," but that is not the definition of the original word. It means __a messenger__ and is translated in the <u>King James Version</u> as a "messenger" and practically transliterated as "angel."*

It seems that we might have an understanding problem. This verse says that he will bring __all__ of his angels with him. Just how many angels (messengers) was he going to bring with him? If both Jesus and his Father and all of the angels came at the same time – who was left in heaven?

I think that Jesus had already given to the apostles the clue to understand who the angels (messengers) were – previous to this statement. For example …

> *"The Son of man shall send forth his angels, and they shall gather out of his kingdom all things that offend, and them which do iniquity"* [Matthew 13:41].

> *"So shall it be at the end of the world (age): the angels shall come forth, and sever the wicked from among the just"* [Matthew 13:49].

Have we not recently ascertained that it was the apostles to whom he had promised to sit on twelve thrones, judging the twelve tribes of Israel? It would be reasonable then to interpret the <u>all</u> here as *all of the apostles (messengers).*

I do not think that it would be quite understandable here that in 70 A.D., in judging the Judeans, that he would bring __all__ of the *"angels in heaven."* When Jesus was taken captive to be sentenced to death, he asked …

> *"Thinkest thou that I cannot now pray to my Father, and he shall presently give me **more than twelve legions of angels**"* [Matthew 26:53].

A legion was a division of the Roman army amounting to more than 6,000 men. Does that mean that Jesus had at his disposal 75,000, maybe 100,000 (heavenly) angels that could protect him and his apostles from the men that wanted to murder him? Can you imagine Jesus bringing all of those with him in 70 A.D. when he returned? Would he bring all of them at that time? I think that we either have to consider what I first said or something that I have overlooked. The 75,000 (heavenly) angels would not be necessary; in fact, who would doubt but that only one heavenly angel could have protected him from the consequences of Judas' betrayal? And just a thought to leave with you, how many heavenly angels does God have? Does He have a million (but only allowed 75,000 to Jesus)? Does He have 100 million? – 100 trillion? – more than the sands of the seashore or more than the stars of heaven for multitude?

We continue our study of v-31 that says *"then shall he sit upon the throne of his glory."* This becomes a verse that is very *"touchy"* with many people. I do not claim to have all of the answers and I am still studying the responses that I have previously received (and those that I, no doubt, will receive after writing this). Right now, this is what I understand.

First, the word *"then"* (Greek = tote) is used as something that happens in consecutive order from what is before, so at the time of the coming of Jesus in 70 A.D., he would sit on his throne.

Secondly, I do not see anything in this verse that says that this is the time of the **beginning** of his sitting on his throne.

Thirdly, it seems to me that the purpose overrides his sitting on his throne, i.e. that the purpose of sitting on his throne was to judge the sheep and the goats.

Does that mean that he did not occupy his throne (reign) before 70 A.D.? I see nothing in this passage to indicate such. That, of course, would cause other questions to arise as to when Jesus actually began his reign.

Was he a king while he was biologically on the planet? Was he a king after Acts 1? Was he a king from 33 A.D. till 70 A.D.? Or did he begin his reign after 70 A.D.? Many various ideas are set forth by different people regarding those time periods.

Had believers already been "***translated*** (past tense **in English**) *into the kingdom*" of Jesus when Paul wrote the following in Colossians 1:13 that …

> "… hath ***delivered*** us from the power of darkness, and hath ***translated*** us into the kingdom of his dear Son."

Not only did the King James Version translate those two words in the **past tense**, but so did the New King James Version, the American Standard Version, the New American Standard Version, the Revised Standard Version, The Living Bible, Today's English Version, the New International Version, and the New American Standard – Updated Edition.

Now, who wants to say that all of the scholars of those translations were wrong? Between the King James Version and the American Standard Version, there were 101 scholars who translated just those two translations. I do not believe that anyone really believes that any translation of the Greek scriptures always have translated every word correctly. If they do, they need to return and study the original scriptures. If they do not know and study the original texts, then it only becomes their opinion without any vital research.

> *"And before him shall be gathered all nations: and he shall separate them one from another, as a shepherd divideth his sheep from the goats"* [Matthew 25:32].

"In front" of Jesus in 70 A.D. would collect all the *"ethnos."* The word *"ethnos"* is most generally translated in the <u>King James Version</u> as either *"nations"* or *"gentiles."* The form of the word here is *"ethne."* The word *"gentiles"* should not be in our English translations. The word properly means *"nations,"* like *"goyim"* of the *"old testament."*

The indication here is that Jesus was speaking of all *"nations"* of the then world-wide peoples. The Bible does not give much information about any travels that the eleven apostles might have made, but it does teach us that Paul was in Asia, then the European area, and later in Italy. So, he did much preaching to the *"nations" (ethnos)*. There were some outside of this area of *gospel preaching,"* for Paul notes in Romans 2:14-15 …

> *"For when the Gentiles* **[nations]**, ***which have not the law****, do by nature the things contained in the law, these, having not the law, are a law unto themselves: 15. Which show the work of the law written in their hearts, their conscience also bearing witness, and their thoughts the mean while accusing or else excusing one another."*

To whom was the law given on Mount Sinai? Was it given to the *"nation"* of Israel? Was it given to any other nation? Would the word *"gentile"* fit in where I have put the word *"nation?"* Well, let us try it. Was the Law of Moses given to the nation of Israel or to the gentiles of Israel? See, such a word really is not a good biblical word at all. An entire book needs to be written on the subject, and if I live long enough, maybe I will do that (if someone does not beat me to it – you are welcome to do it soon), but in this study, there is only room for this small discussion. Study further for yourself.

Again, it will be profitable for us to look in the Greek text at the word *"ethnos."* The first definition of the word is *"a race (as of the same habit), i.e. a tribe."* In view of that definition, it behooves us to consider that each **tribe** of Israel was considered to be a *"nation."* As we study the **context**, it appears most likely that the twelve tribes (nations) of Israel are the *"all nations"* that Jesus (and his apostles) were to judge. We have already touched on the area of the twelve apostles sitting on twelve thrones, judging the twelve tribes (ethnos or nations) of Israel. Recall what you have previously read and what shall be said later on as to the **context**, and I believe that you will at least give consideration to the twelve **tribes** being referred to as the twelve **nations**. Recall what Jesus had already stated about the time of the happenings of Matthew 24-25, in Matthew 24:34. If necessary, read it again.

At that time in the first century A.D., at the end of the *"world = age,"* i.e. the Mosaic age, Jesus was to divide, sever (separate) the *"ethnos"* one from another. How was he going to separate the *"nations?"* According to the context, it was on an individual, personal basis, as either a sheep or a goat, not the whole *"flock"* (nation collectively). He was to sever the wicked from among the just. Since Matthew had already recorded that Jesus had already told of that event previously, it is only right that we interpret it as being the same, and that he was repeating it now, only in a different wording.

> *"So shall it be at the end of the* ~~world~~ (age)*: the angels shall come forth, and sever the wicked* (goats?) *from among the just* (sheep?)*"* [Matthew 13:49].

In 70 A.D., at the end of the *"age,"* he was to draw a boundary that separated them *"away"* from each other. It was to be *"exactly alike"* (hoper) a shepherd who would make a division.

The next part is where I believe that people begin to stray from truth. Were the sheep the good ones and the goats the bad ones? Well, consider that in the *"old testament,"* the sheep and the goats were acceptable sacrifices to the Lord. Both the sheep and the goats were His, and both were clean animals, otherwise they would not have been acceptable sacrifices. Was it not the blood of a goat that the high priest carried into the Most Holy Place one time a year to make the blood of a goat the atoning sacrifice for the ignorant sins of the Israelites – the people of God?

> *"Then shall he kill the **goat** of the sin offering, that is for the people, and bring **his blood** within the vail, and do with that blood as he did with the blood of the bullock, and sprinkle it upon the mercy seat, and before the mercy seat"* [Leviticus 16:15].

Do not all of those things prove to us that both the sheep and the goats belonged to God and both were acceptable to Him?

It will be noted that the separation of the people of the *"nations"* was **as** a shepherd who divides the sheep from the goats. The word *"his"* is **not** in the original Greek – **the** sheep and **the** goats. But, who would want to deny that the application was that both the sheep and the goats were His, and that He could do with them as He pleased (according as He had purposed, elected and foreordained)?

Would not a better explanation of the **enemies** to the sheep be enfolded in the word **wolves**, especially *"wolves in sheep's clothing?"* As Gormer Pyle used to say, *"Surprise! Surprise! Surprise!"*

While Moses and Aaron were in Egypt, the Lord was introducing the Passover to them. Here is the way that He introduced it to them.

> *"Now the Lord said to Moses and Aaron in the land of Egypt, 2 "This month shall be the beginning of months for you; it is to be the first month of the year to you. 3 "Speak to all the*

congregation of Israel, saying, 'On the tenth of this month they are each one to take a lamb for themselves, according to their fathers' households, a lamb for each household. 4 'Now if the household is too small for a lamb, then he and his neighbor nearest to his house are to take one according to the number of persons in them; according to what each man should eat, you are to divide the lamb. 5 'Your lamb shall be an unblemished male a year old; you may take it from the sheep or from the goats. 6 'You shall keep it until the fourteenth day of the same month, then the whole assembly of the congregation of Israel is to kill it at twilight. 7 'Moreover, they shall take some of the blood and put it on the two doorposts and on the lintel of the houses in which they eat it. 8 'They shall eat the flesh that same night, roasted with fire, and they shall eat it with unleavened bread and bitter herbs. 9 'Do not eat any of it raw or boiled at all with water, but rather roasted with fire, both its head and its legs along with its entrails. 10 'And you shall not leave any of it over until morning, but whatever is left of it until morning, you shall burn with fire. 11 'Now you shall eat it in this manner: with your loins girded, your sandals on your feet, and your staff in your hand; and you shall eat it in haste — it is the Lord's Passover. 12 'For I will go through the land of Egypt on that night, and will strike down all the firstborn in the land of Egypt, both man and beast; and against all the Gods of Egypt I will execute judgments — I am the Lord. 13 'The blood shall be a sign for you on the houses where you live; and when I see the blood I will pass over you, and no plague will befall you to destroy you when I strike the land of Egypt. 14 'Now this day will be a memorial to you, and you shall celebrate it as a feast to the Lord; throughout your generations you are to celebrate it as a permanent ordinance." [Exodus 12:1-14].

I did not emphasize anything in quotation marks or highlight anything. Did you see what I saw? Well, here it is again (with emphasis).

*"Your **lamb** shall be without blemish, a male of the first year: ye shall take it out **from the sheep, or from the goats**."*

Did I hear someone say, ***Lord, have mercy**!?* Today, we only think of a lamb as coming only from a sheep, but in approximately 1500 B.C., a lamb was considered the offspring of either a sheep or a goat. And there is a good reason for such.

Jesus was the **lamb** of God that took away the sins of the world. Was that antitype a sheep or a goat?

Jesus was **led** as a **sheep** to the slaughter. Was that antitype a sheep or goat?

Jesus was like a **lamb**, dumb before his shearers, so he opened not his mouth. Was that a sheep or a goat? Well, did it get a little easier here? Do people shear goats (watch this answer)?

Jesus was the antitype of the **scapegoat** that carried the sins of the people off into the wilderness, never to return. Was that a sheep or a goat? So, Jesus is pictured here as a goat (not a sheep).

Jesus was the antitype of the *"blood of the goat"* that was carried by the high priest into the Most Holy Place to offer the blood for the sins of the people. Was that a sheep or goat? Well, obviously it was a goat (not a sheep). To nail down this section, the following is stated …

*"Purge out therefore the old leaven, that ye may be a new lump, as ye are unleavened. For even **Christ our Passover** is sacrificed for us"* [1 Corinthians 5:7].

Since Jesus was the real Passover, he was to take on the roll of either or both a sheep and/or a goat. That he did. He was a sheep that was led to the slaughter. He was a goat whose blood was shed and carried into heaven, and he was the scapegoat, who carried away the sins of the people never to return. He was both a sheep and a goat. That fits the type/antitype of the Passover from Exodus 12.

> *"And he shall set the sheep on the right hand, but the goats on the left"* [Matthew 25:33].

It does not appear from my studies of my Bible that to sit on either side of the throne of an earthly king makes one side right and the other side wrong. Neither does it appear to me to be a bad thing to sit on either the right or left side of Jesus. However, the place of the most respect and honor was always on the right side.

It appears that sitting on the right hand was the highly honorable place by the throne. **Standing** on the right did not seem to give more honor than on the left.

> *"And he said, Hear thou therefore the word of the Lord: I saw the Lord sitting on His throne, and all the host of Heaven **standing** by him on his right hand and on his left"* [I Kings 22:19 – 2 Chronicles 18:18].

Jesus was always seen as either sitting or standing on the right hand of God. One could receive no higher honor except maybe occupying the throne **with** his Father, which Jesus eventually did, according to the book of Revelations.

> *"And he showed me a pure river of water of life, clear as crystal, proceeding out of the **throne of God and of the Lamb"*** [Revelation 22:1].

However, in Matthew 25:33, Jesus used the shepherd's illustration of dividing people from people (**as** a shepherd divides sheep from goats) to differentiate between good and bad people. The things that made the two classes different are covered in the remainder of the verses in this chapter.

"Then shall the king say unto them of the right hand, Come, ye blessed of my Father, inherit the kingdom prepared for you from the foundation of the world" [Matthew 25:34].

Again, the word *"then"* shows consecutive order. There was to be no time delay between the time that Jesus separated the good from the bad until the time that he began to say these things to those (first) on his right hand. It was the *"good ones"* that were set on His right hand.

The word that is translated as *"king"* more appropriately means *"a sovereign,"* but most do not understand that word, so just understand that Jesus was a king at that point, and ready to judge the twelve tribes of Israel.

The phrase *"ye blessed of my Father"* probably entails more than to *"be well spoken of"* by the Father, but even more so *"to be blessed, to be thanked."*

The next Greek word is *"kleronomeo,"* which is translated by the word *"inherit"* in the <u>King James Version</u>. It properly means *"an heir,"* so it is correctly translated. However, behind this one word, is a Bible full of very interesting things. I will try to keep my comments as brief as possible.

In *"old testament"* times, the righteous were to *"inherit the **land**"* [Psalms 37:29]; they were to *"inherit the **earth**"* [Psalms 37:9]; they would *"inherit **Zion**"* [Psalms 69:35-36]; they would *"inherit **glory**"* [Proverbs 3:35]; they would *"inherit **substance – treasures**"* [Proverbs 8:21]; and they would *"inherit ('s) **holy mountain**"* [Isaiah 57:13].

It is written in the *(new testament)* that the *"the meek shall inherit the earth"* [Matthew 5:5], (the quotation is from Psalms 37:11); they would *"inherit **everlasting life**"* [Matthew 19:29]; and here they were to *"inherit **the kingdom**;"* they were to *"inherit the **promises**"* [Hebrews

6:12]; they were to *"inherit **a blessing**"* [1 Peter 3:9]; in fact, they were to *"inherit **all things**"* [Revelations 21:7].

The faithful servants who were on the right hand of Jesus in his judgment of the *"nations"* that we have studied previously, were the heirs of **all** of the promises and blessings that Jesus had promised to the righteous saints.

If I have counted correctly, the word *"heir"* only occurs eighteen times in the <u>King James Version</u>. One passage in the *"old testament"* should give to us a very good understanding as to how the word is used. After Abraham fathered both Ishmael (the oldest) and Isaac, Sarah, the mother of Isaac, said of the bondwoman (the woman who bore Ishmael) and of Ishmael himself …

> *"Wherefore she said to Abraham, Cast out this bondwoman and her son, for the son of this bondwoman **shall not be heir with my son**, even with Isaac"* [Genesis 21:10].

This entire story is dealt with by the apostle Paul in Galatians 4, in reference to the old covenant and the children of the old covenant, as being contrasted to the new covenant and the children of the new covenant. Consider this reading very carefully.

> *"Tell me, you who want to be under law, do you not listen to the law? 22 For it is written that Abraham had two sons, one by the bondwoman and one by the free woman. 23 But the son by the bondwoman was born according to the flesh, and the son by the free woman through the promise. 24 This is allegorically speaking, **for these women are two covenants**: one proceeding from Mount Sinai bearing children who are to be slaves; she is Hagar. 25 Now this Hagar is Mount Sinai in Arabia and corresponds to the present Jerusalem, for she is in slavery with her children. 26 But the Jerusalem above is free; she is our mother. 27 For it is written,"REJOICE, BARREN WOMAN WHO*

*DOES NOT BEAR; BREAK FORTH AND SHOUT, YOU WHO ARE NOT IN LABOR; FOR MORE NUMEROUS ARE THE CHILDREN OF THE DESOLATE THAN OF THE ONE WHO HAS A HUSBAND." 28 And you brethren, like Isaac, are children of promise. 29 But as at that time he who was born according to the flesh persecuted him who was born according to the Spirit, so it is now also. 30 But what does the Scripture say? "CAST OUT THE BONDWOMAN AND HER SON, **FOR THE SON OF THE BONDWOMAN SHALL NOT BE AN HEIR WITH THE SON OF THE FREE WOMAN**." 31 So then, brethren, we are not children of a bondwoman, but of the free woman. 5:1 It was for freedom that Christ set us free; therefore keep standing firm and do not be subject again to a yoke of slavery"* [Galatians 4:21-5:1].

The free children of the new covenant were to be the *"heirs"* of the blessings, not the slave children of the old covenant. Are you *"free"* or in *"bondage"* or *"both or neither?"*

When the book of Hebrews was written, the old covenant was still in existence and being practiced, but was about to *"vanish away."*

> *"In that he saith, A new covenant, he hath made the first old. Now that which decayeth and waxeth old is **ready to vanish away**"* [Hebrews 8:13].

That transformation was completed in 70 A.D.

The expression *"prepared for you from the foundation of the world"* has been a real *"toughy"* for me in my research. I believe that there is more to understanding it than just a simple *"when God created the planet."*

Maybe we should examine the clause backwards. What does the word *"world"* mean? The word comes from the Greek word *"kosmos."* Strong's gives us the following definition.

*"Probably from the base of NT 2865; **orderly arrangement**, i.e. decoration; by implication, the world (in a wide or narrow sense, including its inhabitants, literally or figuratively [morally])."*

Notice that the basic definition is – orderly arrangement. Only from that is it *"implied"* as the *"world."* Notice also that the *"orderly arrangement"* **includes** its inhabitants, not just the planet (if the planet is the subject at all).

Thus, our question should be: What does the expression *"prepared for you* [when humans did not exist] *from the foundation or conception of the orderly arrangement"* of God mean? What world?

We have noticed previously that the King and his twelve apostles were to sit on thrones and judge the twelve tribes of Israel – the twelve *"ethnos,"* i.e. the twelve *"nations"* of Israel. If that group of people was anyway connected to the *"orderly arrangements,"* then the question would be *"when?"*

That would be when the *"foundation"* (or conception) of that *"orderly arrangement"* happened. If it did refer to the Israelites, then when did the *"foundation"* of the Israelite nation(s) begin?

It would have been in God's plan since Adam and Eve's day, but developed over the centuries, very involved with the promises that God made to Abraham and his seed, culminating in the birth and growth of Jacob (whose name was changed to *"Israel."*)

I think that we can find the *"foundation"* in the promise that God made to Abraham that *"in thee and thy seed shall all the nations of the earth be blessed."* We then see all of the events that led to the increase of the nation(s) in Egypt. At that time, God made a covenant with Israel and delivered them from their bondage in Egypt. Shortly after they were delivered from Egypt and traveling to their promised land, they were given the written law on Mount Sinai.

I understand that this is talking about the *"orderly arrangement"* in the making of the covenant with Israel and adding in the written law at Mount Sinai. That *"orderly arrangement"* lasted until the *"vanishing away"* of the old covenant in 70 A.D. and the *"new" (kainos)* covenant became the **spiritual** *"orderly arrangement"* that God had in mind for His people. Now, I am sure that you have ten thousand questions and that is good. Begin to think for yourselves, if you are not already doing that. If you have a different idea that has some merit, I would be happy to hear from you.

To be a part of that old world, one would find it absolutely necessary to be associated with Moses, the law, the prophets and the fleshly sacrificial ordinances to which they were required. If one thinks that he is in that world, he needs to consider that the old world vanished (without the globe [world?] vanishing) in 70 A.D. [Hebrews 8:13]. The *"Jews"* of today favor the idea that the foundation of the world was when Sarah gave birth to Isaac. That was the world of *"Judaism"* - the orderly arrangement of the system that almost exclusively became known as *"Moses and the prophets."*

In 70 A.D., the *"old world (orderly arrangement)"* vanished, and in its place God gave to mankind the *"new world (orderly arrangement)."* Maybe we can study it better if we ask ourselves what *"old world"* was replaced by the *"new world?"* Was not the new world that the believers inherited in 70 A.D. the unseen, eternal kingdom of God? Is that not what this verse is teaching?

> *"For I was an hungered, and ye gave me meat: I was thirsty, and ye gave me drink: I was a stranger, and ye took me in"* [Matthew 25:35].

As used in many passages of which all of us are fond, the Greek word *"gar"* means to introduce a reason. The reason that Jesus was here explaining the giving to the faithful servants their *"inheritance"* in the kingdom of his Father is laid out in physical terms. As we shall see in later verses, there is much more involved than giving Jesus something to eat and drink.

It was interesting to me to find out that the Greek word *"peinao"* means more than just that someone was hungry. It is far more **intensive** than that. It means that one is so hungry that he *"craves"* something to eat or drink, that he is *"famished."* Find someone who has not eaten for a week and you will probably find one who is hungry.

The word *"meat"* is not a good translation of the Greek word *"phago"* in our language. Jesus was not speaking of fish or venison or sheep *"meat."* The Greek word is a word that expresses the general thought of *"to eat."* So, this part of the verse would best be translated as *"ye gave me (something) to eat."*

The same can be said of being *"thirsty."* The faithful servant provided the water to quench his thirst. Notice in both cases that the translators used the word *"gave"* rather than *"sold"* him some food and water.

The Greek word *"xenos"* can be translated by the words *"guest, alien, guest or entertainer."* If you were the one to translate it in this verse, which word would you select?

In view of the remaining part of the verse that says *"and ye took me in,"* the word *"alien"* would best fit the context, would it not? So, the word that the <u>King James Version</u> translators selected, *"stranger"* is a very good word.

The bottom line is that the faithful servants were given an inheritance from Jesus' Father, which was the *"kingdom"* that had been *"prepared for them"* precisely because they were faithful. Faithful in and to what? Jesus will further explain.

> *"Naked, and ye clothed me: I was sick, and ye visited me: I was in prison, and ye came unto me"* [Matthew 25:36].

Just in case there is any doubt, the word *"naked"* means *"nude."* And it did not mean that Jesus got that way on purpose. The idea is that outward circumstances caused him not to have any clothes. Whether from being poor or not able to purchase any, or of being robbed of his clothes, or they were just plain worn out, or whatever the cause, he had no clothes.

The first part of the next compound Greek word is *"peri"* from which we get words in the English language like *"peri-scope,"* which also is a compound word. The ending part is *"scope"* which means *"to see"* and the first part, *"peri"* means *"all around."*

The second part of the Greek word is *"ballo,"* which means *"to throw,"* like throwing a ball. So the whole word means *"to throw (something) all around,"* like throwing a blanket all around a person who is cold, wet, hungry, shivering etc. It does not necessarily mean what we would consider *"clothing"* in the 21st century. The faithful servant did something to cure the problem of being nude.

Another thing that he said was that *"he was sick."* I had never even considered the Jesus ever got sick for thirty-three years – did you? Or maybe he did not – or maybe he got the flu. However, the original word for sick is *"astheneo,"* which means *"to be feeble (in any sense)."* It is translated variously in the King James Version as to *"be diseased, impotent, sick and weak.'*

I have no idea why the King James Version translators used the word *"visited."* It is so far off the tract. While it does carry the idea of *"to inspect,"* the idea, by extension, is to *"relieve"* one of whatever problem that the person had. It could have very easily and correctly been translated as *"I was diseased, with no strength and you inspected to find out what the problem was and after making the diagnosis, you relieved me to where I no longer suffered from the problem."*

"I was in prison" (caged in, guarded) is a good translation. Was the condition reversed? It is not so stated. But the idea is that the faithful servant was **not ashamed** and went *"near"* to the Master while he was in prison and gave as much help and encouragement as possible. Compare what Paul said of Philemon and his slave, Onesimus, while Paul was in prison.

> "I appeal to you for my child Onesimus, whom I have begotten in my imprisonment, 11 who formerly was useless to you, but now is useful both to you and to me. 12 I have sent him back to you in person, that is, sending my very heart, 13 whom I wished to keep with me, so that on your behalf he might minister to me in my imprisonment for the gospel; 14 but without your consent I did not want to do anything, so that your goodness would not be, in effect, by compulsion but of your own free will. 15 For perhaps he was for this reason separated from you for a while, that you would have him back forever, 16 no longer as a slave, but more than a slave, a beloved brother, especially to me, but how much more to you, both in the flesh and in the Lord. 17 If then you regard me a partner, accept him as you would me. 18 But if he has wronged you in any way or owes you anything, charge that to my account; 19 I, Paul, am writing this with my own hand, I will repay it (not to mention to you that you owe to me even your own self as well). 20 Yes, brother, let me benefit from you in the Lord; refresh my heart in Christ. 21 Having confidence in your obedience, I write to you, since I know that you will do even more than what I say" [Philemon 1:10-21 <u>NASU</u>].

When Jesus was actually *"caged and guarded,"* was Peter ashamed of him? Did Peter come *"near"* to him? Did Peter do anything to help him under that condition? There seems to be quite a difference in what Peter did under that circumstance and what Onesimus did for the apostle Paul. We know which action was pleasing to God.

> *"Then shall the righteous answer him, saying, Lord, **when** saw we thee an hungered, and fed thee? Or thirsty, and gave not drink? 38. **When** saw we thee a stranger, and took thee in? or naked, and clothed thee? 39. Or **when** saw we thee sick, or in prison, and came unto thee?* [Matthew 25:37-39].

I put these three verses together because all three of them are questions that relate to the previous verses. See the comments there.

There are only a couple of things that need to be observed. First, there is no gap between the time that Jesus made his remarks to the righteous people in the previous verses and the questions that were asked by the same righteous people.

Secondly, as you will notice, the overriding question was **when** did they see Jesus, their master in such conditions? His answer is in the next verse.

> *"And the King shall answer and say unto them, Verily I say unto you, Inasmuch as ye have done it unto one of the least of these my brethren, ye have done it unto me"* [Matthew 25:40].

The king immediately began to speak where an answer to respond was needed. That is the meaning of the original words that are translated as *"shall answer."*

There is something here that most should come to understand. When the Greek word *"amen"* is used at the beginning of a sentence, it is most always translated by the word *"verily,"* and such is the case here.

The Greek word *"heis"* is used here properly as *"one."* It was not necessary to do something good to everyone, but only doing something good to one of the believers was very pleasing to the king and the faithful servant would be rewarded.

It is interesting here that the analogy that Jesus used was *"his brethren."* His brethren were the sheep. His brethren were not only his biological brothers, but all of those who were later to be called believers. He was the elder brother. He was not ashamed to call them brothers.

> *"For both he that sanctifieth and they who are sanctified are all of one: for which cause he is not ashamed to call them **brethren**. 12. Saying, I will declare thy name unto my **brethren**, in the midst of the church will I sing praise unto thee"* [Hebrews 2:11-12].

Like the parable of the *"good Samaritan,"* who essentially told the inn-keeper, *whatever the cost is, put it on my bill, I will take care of it,"* is that Jesus would take care of the person who treated his fellow human being well, especially, *"those who are of the household of faith."*

> *"As we have therefore opportunity, let us do good unto all men, especially unto them who are of the household of faith"* [Galatians 6:10].

Essentially he said that if you treat one of my brethren well, I will count it the same as if you actually treated me well.

Notice that Jesus preached to *"the world."* It certainly was not the planet.

> *"Jesus answered him, **I spake openly to the world**; I ever taught in the synagogue, and in the temple, whither the Jews always resort; and in secret have I said nothing."*

"Then shall he say also unto them on the left hand, Depart from me, ye cursed, into everlasting fire, prepared for the devil and his angels" [Matthew 25:41].

We have already covered this scenario, except that it was those on his right hand. It is exactly the opposite here.

"Ye cursed" is an interesting wording. Thayer says that the word means *"to curse, doom, imprecate evil on."* They were doomed. They were to have all sort of evil pronounced upon them because they had not produced the proper fruit. Was it all simply a matter of **neglect**, or was it more of a willful act of rebellion and unbelief. Well, neither action was proper.

As we have previously discussed the sheep and the goats, as both belonged to the chief shepherd, how could those *"neglectful and unlearned"* servants depart from him if they were not in his presence?

Nevertheless, they were told to remove themselves from the presence of the King. Of course, they thought themselves worthy to stay in his presence and asked why they were being *"driven out."*

Strong's defines the word *"everlasting,"* which comes from the Greek word *"aionios"* as …

> *"**Aionios** (ahee-o'-nee-os); from NT:165; perpetual (**also used of past time, or past and future as well).***

So, we can see that a good clear definition is not that easy to obtain. **Thayer**, who has the Greek Lexicon, says, numerous things about the word, including …

> *"The adj. achronos independent of time, above and beyond all time, is synon, with aionios; where time (with its subdivisions and limitations) ends eternity begins."*

While most of his comments point to *"perpetuity,"* he even said that …

> *"Habitations of the blessed in heaven are referred to …* **_similarly Hades is called aionios topos_** *(place)."*

Yet we find in the Bible that *"hades"* was destroyed, it did not last forever nor was it *"eternal or everlasting."*

> *"And death and hell **[hades]** were cast into the lake of fire. This is the second death"* [Revelation 20:14].

It seems that full acceptance of the scholars' comments cannot be depended on. I will deal with this more in detail when I get to v-46, although I still have problems in understanding some verses. At least, at this point, you have something about which to give some very serious thought.

Notice that the word *"everlasting" (aionios)* is connected with fire, denoting destruction. For whom was this certain fire prepared? The *"everlasting fire"* was prepared for the devil and his angels. Who are the devil's angels and who is the devil? You might want to order from AMAZON.COM my **large** book on Satan, the Devil and the Adversary.

The word *"devil"* comes from a word with which we are familiar. It is *"diabolos"* from which we derived our English word *"diabolical."* Do you remember the use of the word in the Batman series? It is translated in the King James Version as *"false accuser, devil and slanderer."* The context must determine who the diabolical one was/is. Technically, anyone who is a *"false accuser – slanderer"* can be called a devil. Even a **system** can be a false accuser or devil. Of what *"devil"* (diabolos) was Jesus speaking in this series of chapters? In the context of chapters 23-24-25, the *"false accuser/slanderer"* was the **Judaic system**. It must have been destroyed and God's spiritual people recognized as the true *"Israel of God."*

We have previously discussed the word *"angel."* It comes from the Greek word *"angelos,"* which simply means *"a messenger."* There were many messengers of *"Judaism."* Those messengers also must have been stopped. They were stopped in 70 A.D. and the **new spiritual** system of God put completely into place.

In this context, the *"everlasting fire"* was **prepared** for the Judaic system and the messengers of their unGodly way of life. While used in different senses in the Bible, in this context, it is **figuratively** speaking of the thing that **destroyed** the devil and his messengers. Compare the following verses that speak of the *"lake that burns."*

> *"The same shall drink of the wine of the wrath of God, which is poured out without mixture into the cup of his indignation; and he shall be tormented **with fire and brimstone** in the presence of the holy angels, and in the presence of the Lamb: And the smoke of their torment ascendeth up for ever and ever: and they have no rest day nor night, who worship the beast and his image, and whosoever receiveth the mark of his name"* [Revelation 14:10-11].

> *"And the **devil** that deceived them **was cast into the lake of fire** and brimstone, where the beast and the false prophet are, and shall be tormented day and night for ever and ever"* [Revelation 20:10].

"Everlasting fire" would be essentially the same as *"everlasting destruction."* Note the following verses …

> *"And to you who are troubled rest with us, when the Lord Jesus shall be revealed from heaven with his mighty angels, 8 **In flaming fire** taking vengeance on them that know not God, and that obey not the gospel of our Lord Jesus Christ: 9 Who shall be*

*punished with **everlasting destruction** from the presence of the Lord, and from the glory of his power"* [2 Thessalonians 1:7-9].

"For I was an hungered, and ye gave me **no** meat: I was thirsty, and ye gave me **no** drink: 43 I was a stranger, and ye took me **not** in: naked, and ye clothed me **not**: sick, and in prison, and ye visited me **not**. 44 Then shall they also answer him, saying, Lord, when saw we thee an hungered, or athirst, or a stranger, or naked, or sick, or in prison, and did **not** minister unto thee? 45 Then shall he answer them, saying, Verily I say unto you, Inasmuch as ye did it not to one of the least of these, ye did it not to me" [Matthew 25:42-45].

As you can see, I have grouped these four verses together. The only difference in these verses is that they are exactly opposite from the other four. You can see that from the underlined words above, e.g. *"no"* and *"not."* If you desire more detailed information, please return and read the comments in verses 35-40.

"And these shall go away into everlasting punishment: but the righteous into life eternal" [Matthew 25:46].

We have a long study on this verse that **will take much time to study.** First of all, it should be noted that the (adjectives) words *"everlasting and eternal"* come from the same Greek word, *"aionios,"* which is also an adjective. There is no reason not to translate them by the same word. As far as the English is concerned, there probably is no difference in their meaning to most of us. Most of us have been taught that the meaning of both words is *"without end."* There seems to be major differences among the scholars as to what the real meaning of *"aionios"* is. Some desire that the meaning is *"perpetual,"* while others want to have the meaning as an *"age,"* from whence the noun occurs.

An *"age"* has both **a beginning and an ending**. If such be true, then we could not translate the noun by either of the words *"eternal/everlasting."* In such cases, we would have to determine the meaning each time that the noun is used as to what *"age"* (from when to when) the passage refers. The word *"aion"* is used in the following verses accordingly.

> *"And whosoever speaketh a word against the Son of man, it shall be forgiven him: but whosoever speaketh against the Holy Ghost, it shall not be forgiven him, neither in this **world**, neither in the **world** to come"* [Matthew 12:32].

It is easy to see that the first *"aion"* (age/~~world~~) had an end because there was a world *"to come."* If the first *"aion"* had an end, then why is not the second one also seen as having no end?

> *"He also that received seed among the thorns is he that heareth the word; and the care of this **world**, and the deceitfulness of riches, choke the word, and he becometh unfruitful"* [Matthew 13:22; cf Mark 4:19].

In explaining the parable, Jesus said that things, cares and worries of *"this age"* would make a person unfruitful. He was speaking of the age that preceded 70 A.D.. It was to end when the *"new age"* (new ~~world~~) came in its completeness in 70 A.D.. He was still speaking of the same *"this ~~world~~"* (this age) in the following passage.

> *"The enemy that sowed them is the devil; the harvest is the end of the **~~world~~** (age); and the reapers are the angels"* [Matthew 13:39].

The harvest was the end of *"this age,"* which was the end of the Mosaic age. What is usually referred to as the *"Christian Age"* would follow in 70 A.D.

> *"As therefore the tares are gathered and burned **in the fire**: so shall it be in the **end of this ~~world~~ age**"* [Matthew 13:40].

We can see the **figurative** use of the word *"fire"* in this verse. It is the same **figurative** use that is used in previous verses in this chapter, and that *"world"* had an *"end"* to it, so this verse teaches. But there was the *"eternal"* age that was just around the corner in 70 A.D.. I like the way that the New American Standard Version renders the following verse.

> *"But grow in grace and knowledge of our Lord and Savior Jesus Christ. To Him be the glory **both now and to the day of eternity.** Amen"* [2 Peter 3:18].

> *"So shall it be at the **end of the ~~world~~ (age):** the angels shall come forth, and sever the wicked from, among the just, 50. And shall cast them into the furnace of fire: there shall be wailing and gnashing of teeth"* [Matthew 13:49-50].

The apostles had asked about the end of the world, that is, *"the end of the age"* in Matthew 24:3. Jesus had continued in explaining the answer to their question. The end of *"the age"* (~~world~~ – aion) would come in their lifetimes. You can go back to those two verses and find the comments that might answer your questions (if you still have any). It can be easily seen that the noun is used as having an *"end"* for such is stated in this verse. I will quote again what started all of this discourse of Jesus that covered two entire chapters.

> *"And as he sat upon the mount of Olives, the disciples came unto him privately, saying, Tell us, when shall these things be? and what shall be the sign of thy coming, and of **the end of the world**"* [Matthew 24:3]?

Again, it can be plainly seen that the word carries with it the idea of an *"end"* for such was asked by the apostles of Jesus. The *"end of the (Jewish) age"* came in 70 A.D.. If you have not grasped that yet, I would suggest that you return and read the comments on the entire two chapters of Matthew 24-25.

*"Teaching them to observe all things whatsoever I have commanded you: and, lo, I am with you alway, even unto **the end of the world**. Amen"* [Matthew 28:20].

This was spoken to the apostles, yet it could not be correct if Jesus was speaking of the end of the globe. I think that you can see two things by now.

1. The "aion" (age – not ~~world~~) was the old Mosaic system.
2. That *"age"* had an end to it.

*"But he shall receive an hundredfold now **in this time**, houses, and brethren, and sisters, and mothers, and children, and lands, with persecutions; **and in the world to come eternal life**"* [Mark 10:30].

The *"age to come"* is referring to the succceding age of the Mosaic age. In the other passage that is almost identical to this one, *"this time"* was called *"this world."* In the world (age) to come in 70 A.D., there was eternal life. Do you have it? Is it for you only when you die biologically? Watch your answer!

*"In that he saith, a new covenant, **he hath made the first old**. Now that which decayeth and waxeth old **is ready to vanish away**"* [Hebrews 8:13].

The old covenant was still in existence and being practiced when the Hebrews letter was written after the middle of the first century A.D.. But, it was becoming obsolete very quickly and was *"ready to vanish away."*

"Blessed be the Lord God of Israel; for he hath visited and redeemed his people. 69. And hath raised up an horn of salvation for us in the house of his servant David: 70. As he spake by the

*mouth of his holy prophets, which have been **since the world began**"* [Luke 1:68-70].

The *"beginning"* of the world (age) is seen today by the supposed Jewish people as with Isaac. So, if that be the case, God's prophets told of the Christ from that point on.

*"And the lord commended the unjust steward, because he had done wisely: for the children of **this world** (what world and time?) are in their generation wiser than the children of light"* [Luke 16:8].

This was somewhat of condemnation to the believers for not completely fulfilling their duty to the Almighty One. **This world** was the world of those living under the Mosaic law at the time that Jesus was speaking.

*"Who shall not receive manifold more in **this present time** and **in the world to come life everlasting**"* [Luke 18:30].

"This present time" is the same as *"this world."* It was ending and there was a *"world to come"* shortly in 70 A.D..

*"And Jesus answering said unto them, The children of **this world** marry, and are given in marriage: 35. But they which shall be accounted worthy to **obtain that world** and the resurrection from the dead, neither marry, nor are given in marriage"* [Luke 20:34-35].

*"Since **the world** began was it not heard that any man opened the eyes of one that was born blind"* [John 9:32].

Again, *"the world"* is the *"old covenant age."* The remainder of the verse is self explanatory. Not just a blind person is under consideration, but a person who was **born** blind.

*"Repent ye therefore, and be converted, that your sins may be blotted out, when the times of refreshing shall come from the presence of the Lord; 20 And he shall send Jesus Christ, which before was preached unto you: 21 Whom the heaven must receive until the times of restitution of all things, which hath spoken by the mouth of all his holy prophets **since the world began**"* [Acts 3:19-21].

This is not speaking of the creation of the planet on which we live.

*"And be not conformed to **this world**: but be ye transformed by the renewing of your mind, that ye may prove what is that good, and acceptable, and perfect, will of God"* [Romans 12:2].

Again, *"this world"* was the world of the *"Jews,"* not planet earth. The believers were told not to *"form with"* that world, but to be *"formed across"* to the **world to come**. That was done by the renewing of their minds.

*"Where is the wise? Where is the scribe? Where is the disputer of **this world**? Hath not God made foolish the wisdom of **this world**"* [1 Corinthians 1:20].

In this verse, we have two different words that are translated as *"this world."* It is only the first one that is speaking of the **age**, called the Mosaic dispensation. That ended in 70 A.D.. The first one is *"aion"* and the second one is *"kosmos."* As we have seen, the word *"kosmos"* means *"an orderly arrangement,"* which of course was the Mosaic age.

*"Howbeit we speak wisdom among them that are perfect: yet not the wisdom of **this world**, nor of the princes of **this world**, that come to nought: 7 But we speak the wisdom of God in a mystery, even the hidden wisdom, which ordained before **the world** unto our glory: 8 Which none of the princes of **this world** knew: for*

had they known it, they would not have crucified the Lord of glory" [1 Corinthians 2:6-8].

In these three verses, we have the word *"aion"* (age) translated by the word *"world"* four times. The meaning is the *"age"* that began with Isaac and culminated in 70 A.D. in all four verses.

> *"Let no man deceive himself. If any man among seemeth to be wise in **this world** let him become a fool, that he may be wise"* [1 Corinthians 8:13].

The eternal wisdom of God was not to be found in its complete state in *"this world,"* i.e. the age that we refer to as the Mosaic dispensation. But it would be found in *"the world (age) to come."*

> *"Wherefore, if meat make my brother to offend, I will eat no flesh **while the world standeth**, lest I make my brother to offend"* [1 Corinthians 8:13].

Again, there is no reason to change the meaning of the word as it has occurred in all of the other verses. *"While the world standeth"* indicates that it was to **end**. And end it did in 70 A.D., being replaced by *"the world to come."* We are still seeing that *"aions"* have a beginning and an ending.

> *"Now all these things happened unto them for ensamples; and they are written for our admonition, upon whom the **ends of the world** are come"* [1 Corinthians 10:11].

The Greek word *"telos"* is defined as *"the point aimed at as a limit, i.e. (by implication) the conclusion of an act or state (termination [literally, figuratively or indefinitely], result [immediate, ultimate or prophetic], purpose)."* The *"consummation of the ages"* **had come upon that first century generation**. A new age was about to arrive.

*"But if our gospel be hid, it is hid to them that are lost: 4 In whom the God **of this world** hath blinded the minds of them which believe not, lest the light of the glorious gospel of Christ, who is the image of God, should shine unto them"* [2 Corinthians 4:3-4].

"This world" was still the law system under Moses. The laws and rituals that were written blinded the eyes of man, and the light of the good news of Jesus could not enter.

*"Who gave himself for our sins, that he might deliver us **from this present evil world**, according to the will of God and our Father"* [Galatians 1:4].

It is easier to see in this verse that *"this world"* was not the planet, for the planet itself is neither good nor evil in itself. The insertion of the words *"present evil"* between *"this"* and *"world"* shows conclusively that reference was being made to the law system under Moses to which the unbelievers were holding and being lost. This passage is giving the reason why God was going to destroy the natural *"Jewish"* system in 70 A.D., because it was *"evil."* It was then *"present,"* but about to end.

*"Which he wrought in Christ, when he raised him from the dead, and set him at his own right hand in the heavenly places, 21 Far above all principality, and power, and might, and dominion, and every name that is named, **not only in this world, but also in that (world) which is to come**"* [Ephesians 1:20-21].

Jesus had been elevated by God to be above all (except Himself), in *"this world"* (the Mosaic dispensation) but also in the *"age"* that was about to come in 70 A.D..

*"And to make all men see what is the fellowship of the mystery, which from the **beginning of the world** hath been hid in who created all things by Jesus Christ"* [Ephesians 3:9]

We have covered many times what time it was when it was *"the beginning of the age."*

> *"Now unto him that is able to do exceeding abundantly above all that we ask or think, according to the power that worketh in us, 21 Unto him be glory in the church by Christ Jesus throughout **all ages**, **world without end**. Amen"* [Ephesians 3:20-21].

In this verse, we need a definition of the word *"ages."* In this verse, it is translated from the Greek word *"genea,"* which is defined as *"a generation"* and sometimes *"by implication, an age."* Since the primary word is *"generation,"* it seems better to be translated as *throughout all generations."*

There is a very strange thing in this verse; it has a double negative in it. The phrase *"world without end"* in the Greek, looks like this: **aionon ton aionos**. The first and last words are the same. So, should it be translated the same, such as *"age without age?"* How could it be translated *"perpetuity without perpetuity"* or *"eternal without eternal?"* Do any of those make any sense?

> *"It means, in the strongest sense, **forever**. It is one of "the apostle's self-invented phrases" (Bloomfield), and Blackwall says that no version can fully express the meaning. It is literally, "Unto all generations of the age of ages," or "unto all the generations of the eternity of eternities, or the eternity of ages." It is the language of a heart **full** of the love of God, and desiring that he might be praised without ceasing forever and ever"* [Barnes' Notes].

> *"To all the generations of eternal ages' – literally, 'of the age of the ages.' Eternity, as one grand 'age,' is conceived as consisting of "ages" (these again consisting of 'generations') endlessly*

succeeding one another" [Jamieson, Fausset, and Brown Commentary].

That comment does not sound like heaven, does it? Generations endlessly succeeding one another – forever? What happened to the previous generation? Is it not possible that Paul was speaking of the one, great, eternal age that began in 70 A.D. that would never end?

*"... should and will be praised **thus throughout all ages, world without end**; for he will ever have a church to praise him, and he will ever have his tribute of praise from his church"* [Matthew Henry's Commentary on the Whole Bible].

"Throughout all ages, world without end. Literally, to all the courses of the age of the ages. A very strong expression for eternity" [The Wycliffe Bible Commentary].

"Through all succeeding generations – while the race of human beings continues *to exist on the face of the earth ... Throughout eternity ... in the coming world as well as; in this"* [Adam Clarke's Commentary]. *[He probably missed the change of the ages in 70 A.D., as "this age" being the Mosaic age and the "coming world" being that age that began in 70 A.D. – rm].*

Let us look at some more translations of Ephesus 3:21.

*"Unto him (be) the glory in the church and in Christ Jesus unto **all generations for ever and ever**. Amen"* [ASV].

"To God be the glory in the church and in Christ Jesus for all time, forever and ever" [TEV].

That *"ton"* that is between the two words *"aionon"* and *"aionos"* is simply the word that is usually translated as *"the,"* the simple article, maybe looking something like this: *"age (of) the ages."*

*"For we wrestle not against flesh and blood, but against principalities, against powers, against the rulers of the darkness of **this world**, against spiritual wickedness in high places"* [Ephesians 6:12]

Again Paul was speaking of the world of *"Judaism,"* which was the *"present evil age"* that the believers were wrestling against. The natural system had to go – the new *"age"* had to begin shortly after Paul wrote this.

*"Charge them that are rich **in this world**, that they be not highminded, nor trust in uncertain riches, but in the living God, who giveth us richly all things to enjoy"* [1 Timothy 6:17].

Paul was not speaking literally. He was **figuratively** using the word *"rich"* as those that thought that they had everything in the world of *"Judaism,"* but in reality they had nothing. The things under the Mosaic system were not certain, but those things of the *"new world – age"* would be eternally certain.

*"For Demas hath forsaken me, having loved **this present world**, and is departed unto Thessalonica: Crescens to Galatia, Titus unto Dalmatia"* [2 Timothy 4:10].

Demas forsook Paul on his missionary journey and returned to the world of *"Judaism."*

*"Teaching us that, denying unGodly and worldly lusts, we should live soberly, righteously, and Godly, in **this present world**; 13. Looking for that blessed hope, and the glorious appearing of the great God and our savior Jesus Christ"* [Titus 2:12-13].

As long as they had to live in that temporary, present world that would soon end in 70 A.D. with the arrival of the *"age to come,"* they were to deny the bad things and live properly before God, looking for that glorious appearance of Jesus in 70 A.D.. Yes, they, the first century believers were *"looking"* for it.

> *"And have tasted the good word of God, and the powers of the* **world to come**" [Hebrews 6:5].

Before 70 A.D., they could not partake of the full meal of eternal powers, so the only thing that they could do was to begin to *"taste"* of those things that were coming to them in that *"age (about) to come."*

> *"For then must he often have suffered since the foundation of the world; but now once in* **the end of the world** *hath he appeared to put away sin by the sacrifice of himself"* [Hebrews 9:26].

Here again, we have two different Greek words that have been translated by the same word *"world,"* which we have learned means *"age,"* not the planet. Only the one highlighted means *"age."* The other, as we have seen, (kosmos) means *"orderly arrangement,"* which was the beginning of the Mosaic dispensation. The kosmos began with Isaac and as we have seen above, it had an *"end"* when the *"age"* had come to the end in 70 A.D. and replaced by the new age or the new world or earth.

When was it that Jesus, *"once"* and for all time, appeared to put away sin by his sacrifice? The writer of Hebrews says that it was in *"the end of the world,"* i.e. it was at the *"end of the (Jewish) age."* It is usually regarded as happening in 33 A.D. that he was murdered. That age *"ended,"* so this verse says. It finally ended in 70 A.D. with the arrival of the *"age to come."*

Unless I have miscalculated, I have covered every verse in the *"new testament"* that has the word *"aion,"* which is a noun that should have always been translated as *"age"* rather than *"world"* or thought of as

Planet Earth. When the word *"world"* was chosen, it made the passages obscure and misleading.

This verse and these words should be carefully studied to see if Jesus was talking about the **quality** of life, rather than the **length** of life. **THINK FOR YOURSELF!**

I shall appreciate your feedback (if it is presented in a format of a good attitude with an *"honest and good heart."*) God's blessings be on each of you.

Chapter Four

MATTHEW 26

"And it came to pass, when Jesus had finished all these sayings, he said unto his disciples" [Matthew 26:1].

As we have previously studied, chapters and verses never came along until the sixteenth century. This verse really belongs as well to chapter 25 as it does to the connecting thoughts after it.

When the disciples came to Jesus and asked him two questions concerning the *"when"* and *"what"* (a two-part question) in Matthew 24:3, the remainder of Matthew 24 and all of Matthew 25 was his answer to those questions.

It is emphasized here in 26:1, and the entire discourse of Jesus would not be complete without it.

The clause, *"When Jesus had finished all these sayings,"* shows conclusively that all of Matthew 24 and all of Matthew 25 belong together. There is never a verse anywhere in those two chapters that shows that he interrupted his response and started on a different subject.

Since Mark 13 and Luke 21 are parallel to this study by Matthew, and there are a few things in each of them that help explain some things that are not explicitly set forth by Matthew, I believe that it will be well for us to study the highlights and get that additional information in those two books.

As two translations render 0ne verse:

"Be not bondmen of men."
"Be not slaves of men."

Thank you for ordering this book. Thank you for reading it. It is my prayer of thanksgiving to Almighty God for your open-mindedness to carefully consider the contents and being honest with yourself, and, regardless of others, bless each of you!

Bonus:

Want to learn more about Matthew 24-25? Sign up for my weekly Bible study. www.EschatologyReview.com/Matt24-signup
This study will go into more depth and will be verse by verse study.
This free study will be emailed to you once per week. Join here now!

BOOKS BY RON MCRAY

- THE LAST DAYS
- THROUGH THE WATER, THROUGH THE FIRE
- BEHOLD, I AM MAKING ALL THINGS NEW
- BEHOLD, I AM COMING QUICKLY
- PEARLS OF GREAT PRICE
- WHAT IN THE "WORLD" HAPPENED BETWEEN 30 A.D. AND 70 A.D?
- THE LAZARUS AFFAIR: A novel
- DID JESUS HAVE LONG HAIR?: THE BIBLICAL VERDICT!
- THE WRITINGS OF YAHSHUA REVEALED
- THE HEAVENS DECLARE THE GLORY OF GOD: A LOST UNDERSTANDING OF THE ANCIENT ZODIAC
- WAS JESUS 3 DAYS & 3 NIGHTS IN THE HEART OF THE EARTH?
- SATAN, THE DEVIL AND THE ADVERSARY
- 666 AND THE ANTICHRIST OF REVELATION
- GOD CAME RIDING ON A CLOUD
- THE GOOD LIFE: A BIBLICAL UNDERSTANDING OF BEING SPIRIT FILLED

14 Book Series:
Things That Your Preacher Forgot To Tell You!

1. RIGHTEOUSNESS APART FROM SALVATION: IN THE FIRST CENTURY
2. THE CHURCH IS NOT THE EKKLESIA OF THE BIBLE
3. WHO SAW JESUS AND WHEN DID THEY SEE HIM FROM HIS CRUCIFIXION TO HIS ASCENSION – AND WHY IS THIS SO IMPORTANT?
4. ARE THERE THREE HEAVENS – OR MORE?
5. IS IT APPOINTED UNTO MAN ONCE TO DIE?
6. THE RELATIONSHIP OF THE CHURCH, THE KINGDOM AND HOUSE TO ESCHATOLOGY
7. A STUDY OF OLD TESTAMENT PROPHECIES AND THEIR FULFILLMENT
8. HOW TO INTERPRET THE BOOK OF REVELATION CONSISTENTLY

9. THE SIGN OF THE END REVEALED
10. THINGS THAT WERE "ABOUT TO HAPPEN" IN THE DAYS OF JESUS AND HIS APOSTLES
11. SOMEONE CHANGED MY BIBLE
12. EPHESIANS: NOT THE BOOK THAT YOU THOUGHT THAT IT WAS
13. THE LORD'S SUPPER
14. FIRST-BORN and SECOND-BORN: A STUDY OF TYPES AND ANTI-TYPES

DVD'S BY DR. RON MCRAY

- INTRODUCTION TO ESCHATOLOGY
- WHY AM I HERE – WHAT IS MY PURPOSE?

Use this link to access the web-site for all information concerning books
www.NewBibleConcepts.com
Toll-free ordering 1-888-393-5933

Be sure to get your free audio book here:

http://goo.gl/YqvUFA